MAX WEBER
AND SOCIOLOGY TODAY

EXPLORATIONS IN
INTERPRETATIVE SOCIOLOGY

GENERAL EDITORS

PHILIP RIEFF
Benjamin Franklin Professor of Sociology
University of Pennsylvania

BRYAN R. WILSON
Reader in Sociology, University of Oxford
Fellow of All Souls College

Also in this series

THE SOCIAL FRAMEWORKS OF KNOWLEDGE
Georges Gurvitch
Translated by M.A. and K.A. Thompson

Forthcoming

LUCIEN LÉVY–BRUHL
Jean Cazeneuve
Translated by Peter Rivière

THE CARNETS OF LÉVY–BRUHL
Translated by Peter Rivière

FALSE CONSCIOUSNESS
Joseph Gabel
Translated by M.A. and K.A. Thompson

MAX WEBER
AND SOCIOLOGY TODAY

Edited by
OTTO STAMMER

Translated by
KATHLEEN MORRIS

OXFORD
BASIL BLACKWELL
1971

ISBN 0 631 12290 7

First Published in German as
Max Weber und die Soziologie heute,
© 1965 by J. C. B. Mohr (Paul Siebeck),
Tübingen, and translated by arrangement.

Printed in Great Britain
by Alden & Mowbray Ltd, Oxford
and bound at the Kemp Hall Bindery

Publisher's Note

With the consent of Professor Stammer and of J. C. B. Mohr (Paul Siebeck), Tübingen, certain passages have been omitted from this English version of the transactions of the 15th German Sociological Congress held in Heidelberg to commemorate the centenary of Max Weber's birth. In particular the speeches of welcome to the delegates and Professor Adorno's tribute to the late President Theodor Heuss are excluded, and the summaries of the discussions at the end of the book have been curtailed.

The English of the papers and other contributions by Professors Talcott Parsons and Benjamin Nelson is their own, not the translator's. Professor Raymond Aron's paper is translated from his original French.

Contents

PART IV

Summaries of group discussions

Introduction[1]

OTTO STAMMER

Max Weber was one of the most important scholars of the turn of the century, the initiator of scientific sociology in Germany and co-founder of the German association for sociology, an analytical philosopher and open-minded political adviser and critic. As we know from the biography by Marianne Weber, and from biographical notes by his colleagues, friends and pupils—such men as Karl Jaspers, etc.—he was closely connected with the intellectual and cultural climate of Heidelberg. Despite the cruel illness, which attacked him shortly after his appointment to the chair of economics (formerly that of his teacher Knies) and forced him to retire from lecturing, he spent twenty fruitful years here, with certain longer or shorter interruptions by his numerous journeys in Germany and abroad. After a period of marked political 'engagement'—for example his famous inaugural speech at Freiburg, his appeal for a progressive social policy at evangelical–social congresses, his efforts in the Union for social politics, his close connection with Friedrich Naumann and the National–Social Union—the idea of retirement from vigorous political activity seems to have been connected for him with the acceptance of the chair at Heidelberg. Yet he remained involved in the conflict between scientific duty and political activity and this conflict was the occasion of his reflections on the objectivity of socio-scientific knowledge.

From his years in Heidelberg emerged his most important essays in methodology and theory, and here he developed his conception of the value-freedom of scientific knowledge in relation to the value-relatedness of all objects of cultural and social research. Here he published his well-known work *The Protestant Ethic and the Spirit of Capitalism,* and worked at his further sociological studies of religion. Here he founded together with

[1] This section is abridged from Professor Stammer's opening speech at the conference.

I

Edgar Jaffé and Werner Sombart the 'Archives for Social Science and Social Politics'. Here he decided to collaborate in the enquiry by the Society for Social Politics into the conditions of workers in heavy industry: here he sketched the outline of this research project, which was to prove methodologically so important for later research. And here finally he worked on his great sociological essay for the outline of social economics, which unfortunately because of his early death has come to us only as a fragment.

Max Weber did indeed try to keep out of political activity during these years in Heidelberg. Nevertheless the importance of this outstanding personality for the intellectual atmosphere of this town at that time seems to lie predominantly in the personal influence which he had not only on older and younger scholars belonging to his circle, but also on politicians and progressive intellectuals, on artists and students. In our memory of Weber we connect with Heidelberg the picture of the Max Weber Circle which for many years gathered regularly on Sunday afternoons around him and his wife. As we know from Marianne Weber, it consisted in the first place of younger scholars and his own pupils, but also of many colleagues who were older or his contemporaries, such as Troeltsch, Jellinek, Gothein and Vossler, and of his disciples at that time, Jaspers, Gundolf, Lukács and Lask. In 1926 Paul Honigsheim tried from his own memory to reconstruct the 'sociology of this Max Weber Circle', as he expressed it, whose advantage he saw to be that it did not become consolidated into a philosophical–sociological school, but remained open to—I quote —'the momentum, unteachable and untransferable, which proceeded from Weber's intellectual "obsession" '. The Academic Society, called into being by Marianne Weber four years after his death, has, we have been told, continued the tradition of the Max Weber afternoons, though in altered form, until the present day. In the forty years of its existence the meetings of this circle have been attended by many eminent social scientists of Heidelberg, such as Karl Mannheim, Emil Lederer and Karl Jaspers, Alfred Weber, Gustav Radbruch, Alexander Rüstow and Arnold Bergstraesser.

With regard to Max Weber and those who came under his intellectual influence, I should not speak of a Heidelberg School of Sociology, although when teaching I often do so. The thinking and the methods of representatives of the social sciences at the University of Heidelberg in past decades have been too disparate for that. The intellectual atmosphere of these circles of friends and scholars, and their interest in methodological questions of scientific theory, in the fundamental relationships and comparative analysis of the socio-cultural universe, and in specific historico-empirical research, were without doubt—both in Heidelberg and beyond— very much inspired by Max Weber.

It would be wrong to claim Max Weber exclusively for the Heidelberg tradition. Those who are familiar with his biography know that he was aware of his links with the intellectual and political climate of other universities in which he taught, other towns in which he lived for short or long periods; links that were qualitatively different, but no less intense. Besides this, the political fate of Germany and the cultural future of industrial society made such strong claims on him that it is difficult to ascribe local or regional characteristics to his image.

Although Weber's intellectual and scientific development is not fully understandable without both the breadth and the limitations of Heidelberg, he belongs as much to Berlin, to Freiburg, to Vienna (despite the shortness of his stay there) and to Munich. We know and respect the fact that our colleagues in Munich consider Max Weber's connection with their university in the politically agitated year before his death as particularly important, and we congratulate the Ludwig–Maximilian University on the progress made by the Max Weber Archives, established in Munich in his memory.

Max Weber belongs, not to one particular university, one town, one country: he belongs today, even more than in his lifetime, to the whole scientific world. As he was in Heidelberg, in Munich, and in Berlin, today he is at home also in many American universities, in Paris, Turin and Warsaw. In this respect it is not without symbolic significance that this sociological conference organized by German social scientists in Heidelberg is taking place with the participation of so many visitors from so many countries: we regret only that, even today, these are almost exclusively from the West.

One can hardly speak about Weber, the sociologist, without devoting at least a few words to the complex scientific personality of this scholar and politician, and to the almost incomparable breadth and depth of his knowledge. As a lawyer, Weber concerned himself even at the beginning of his scientific development with such varied questions as the trading companies of the Middle Ages, Roman agrarian history, the situation of agricultural labourers in eastern Elbe, and the reform of the Stock Exchange. As an economist, Weber turned his attention to problems of scientific logic and the premises for the objectivity of social scientific knowledge. Everyone who knows his work will recognize Weber as an established historian, a scholar who made a penetrating study of the historical and social realities of many cultures and countries. He was not however satisfied, as his well-known formulations show, with the analysis and identification of individual actions, structures and personalities of cultural significance; as a sociologist he sought at the same time to grasp the general rules underlying historical events, to understand social events clearly, and thereby to explain them causally with their aims and effects. Weber was as we know an opponent of all historical and social metaphysics: his 'comprehensive sociology' strives after a synthesis of historico-empirical and systematic methods of observation.

Finally, Weber was an extraordinarily acute and knowledgeable political thinker, and was not afraid to adopt a position, for the most part very critical, on contemporary political events at home and abroad. His typology of the forms of authority, his analytical essays on the sociology of bureaucracy, of parliamentarianism, of political parties and élites are one of the bases of political sociology. Weber also put forward substantial proposals—witness his famous articles in the *Frankfurter Zeitung*—which are still discussed today in public law, in political science and practice, for the reform and transformation of the constitution.

All this helps us to understand how difficult it is to fit the intellectual figure of this universal thinker into the traditional scheme of the arts and sciences, or indeed to ascribe it to any definite branch of the newer social science. His personality, like his work, does not fit into a rigid frame. His biographers have pointed out the greatness, the contemporary character, the ethical rigorism and the intellectual boundlessness as well as the internal contradictions in this unique man. The 'contradictory nature' of Weber, the contradictions in his thoughts and actions, which have been revealed by the later analysis of some parts of his work and his political activity, are still worth consideration today. Honigsheim has substantially withdrawn the warning he gave in the

1920s about an 'artificial integration and thereby dogmatisation of Weber's ideas' in his attitude to Wolfgang Mommsen's work, by asking whether in Weber it is not merely a matter of apparent contradictions, behind which there lies an ultimate unity. In the recent controversy between Henrich and Tenbruch on the question of the unity of the scientific doctrine and the ethics of Max Weber, the old dispute about the contradictions in Weber's whole work and about the correct interpretation of his teaching and his political activity is continued today. This goes to show that research on Weber is still in its infancy.

How great an interest Weber took in the theoretical foundation of the social sciences and in empirical sociological research was shown by his active participation in the founding of the German Association for Sociology in the year 1909. Disgusted by the internal squabbles about socio-political problems in the old 'Society for Social Politics', he had in common with Troeltsch, Simmel, Tönnies, Sombart and many other well-known scholars, heartily welcomed the founding of this association, and participated as an officer in the preparatory work in the modest but influential role of 'teller'. Now that our association can look back on more than fifty years of dynamic development, it is particularly interesting, and of significance not only to the history of the society, to read what Marianne Weber tells us about Weber's part in the founding of this association. This information has been amplified from another viewpoint and somewhat amended by, for instance, Leopold von Wiese and Honigsheim. In any case Weber put to the officials, and then to the assembly at the first Sociological Congress, held in 1910 in Frankfurt, a comprehensive programme of work, in the form of a business statement, in which he outlined not only a scientific theoretical treatment of the premises of value-free sociological thought, but also three great projects of empirical research—the Press, societies, and the connection between technology and culture.

Weber placed great hopes in the 'Sociological Association' which he imagined not as an esoteric club for scholars, but as a working society. Unfortunately, as a consequence of the attitude of many of his colleagues at that time, he did not succeed in creating the predispositions for undertaking these empirical studies. Perhaps he also made demands that were too great for the young association, demands which were not to be realized, because sociology in Germany was still in its infancy. Arguments soon arose in the new association, and to them Weber himself contributed by his inflexible attitude on the question of value-freedom, which led him finally to retire from the committee, in connection with the second Sociological Congress in 1912 in Berlin. From then on he was estranged from the Association. Marianne Weber consoled him about this division in her own typical way. According to her own records, she wrote in a birthday letter '. . . the devil take the Sociological Association, for which you spent yourself to the last ounce, for apart from its pretty conference, it will remain a hollow piece of apparatus'.

Our Association is meeting for the third time in Heidelberg; our members were here under the chairmanship of Ferdinand Tönnies for the fourth Congress in 1924, and under Leopold von Wiese for the twelfth in 1954. We decided in the preparatory committee and among the officers of the Association to give this fifteenth Congress the main theme of 'Max Weber and Sociology Today'. We pay all honour to the man and the scholar, an honour which will be plainly expressed on this occasion. However, we do not wish to pay tribute to Weber simply as a historical figure with a socio-scientific mind, as a hero dominating his times, whom we must follow uncritically as an expert, or as a great man, whose achievement has long been absorbed into the main stream of progressive teaching and research. A Weber cult is made impossible by the personality and work of the man himself.

At this congress we want to discover the significance of Weber's life-work for present-day sociology, for the social sciences in the broader sense of the term, and for the relationship between science and political and social practice, as they appear to us today. To this end we must analyse the historical–social situation which makes Weber's work and influence comprehensible. Weber lived in the transition from the nineteenth to the twentieth century—a time of spiritual upsurge, under social and ideological conditions which imposed themselves on his thought and work. We must ask clearly how far Weber, with all his genius, was a 'child of his time'; we must ask which parts and aspects of his teaching and socio-political aims must be seen as having since then been attained and surpassed, and which need to be critically re-assessed in the light of our own times and progress in research. Only in this connection can we try to determine what aspects of his attitudes to problems, his methods and the results of his research are of lasting scientific value, and what part of his total work can be made fruitful as a basis for the further development of social research.

An estimation of Max Weber must, therefore, proceed critically in two respects: on the one hand, it must size up critically, and from a sober distance, the intellectual figure of Weber as the Max Weber image outlined by the generation which was influenced by him in their thinking and experience. On the other hand, it must analyse his work in its comprehensive conception, decide what directions it has indicated to specialized research, and make critical judgment of Weber's reception in Germany and abroad. Although such a discussion of Weber's personality and work from the standpoint of present-day problems of social research is bound to be a task of lengthy investigation, recent years have seen the beginnings of critical research on Weber, which is apparent in the papers and contributions of the conference.

Max Weber and Sociology Today

ERNST TOPITSCH

I first met Weber in the Vienna of the years immediately after the last war, a town that had been particularly stricken in the previous decades by the vicissitudes of Central European history and now lay right on the line where new world-embracing conflicts were being mapped out. Hitler's Reich was militarily annihilated and his ideology morally despised, but the new situation concealed new problems and unresolved issues at every level. While power politics were being condemned and declared dead in a flood of books and articles, the foundations of the town still trembled at the slightest fluctuation of the stock-market and of the equilibrium of global power-blocks, and while the Age of the Proletariat was being loudly proclaimed, even the simplest labourer very soon realized how indifferent to his fate were the proclaimers of this doctrine. Meanwhile cultural development was coming more and more under the influence of pressures which claimed to have conquered modern thought by restoring an awareness of the eternal order of existence and values, but which in fact could scarcely produce one argument which could stand up against the critical rationality of modern thought. In this twilight atmosphere of furtive intellectual dishonesty contact with Max Weber's work had the effect of lightning: the blurred outlines suddenly stood out hard and clear, and whoever had once seen them now saw the world in an entirely different way.

But the most profoundly exciting aspect of his work was not the up-to-dateness of its discussion of the perennial questions of power-politics, nor its critique of Marxism, but the uncompromising quest for truth, with which the attack was here directed against all wishful thinking. The 'disenchantment of the world' by scientific knowledge, which naturally includes a disenchantment of science, is by no means confined to what is obvious and in the

8

foreground; it penetrates to the basic concepts with whose help the cosmos, society and the individual can be understood and interpreted. Here for the first time the much-discussed principle of value-freedom is seen in its whole convincing range and power: in expounding it, Weber not merely questioned the methods of empirical branches of science but touched on a cardinal problem of man's view of the world and self-interpretation.

This has as a rule been overlooked, and yet it is precisely this range of questions which up till now, covertly but nonetheless decisively, has determined any discussion of Max Weber that is not limited to single specific problems. Therefore it seems appropriate to deal with it in this paper in some detail, even if the great sociologist himself did not have time to think it through in every possible direction or to set it down in systematic form. The points at which the irrevocable contradiction between scientific knowledge and an evaluative interpretation of nature and society is pursued into the realm of categorical basic concepts are few in number, yet they constitute the most advanced positions and the most extreme conclusions that Weber reached from his methodological and historical hypotheses. These hypotheses lie in the process of rationalization of the world to which the great scholar deliberately directed his thought and his work, and to the clarification of which he devoted a substantial part of his research. In the course of this process, which can also be styled a scientific–industrial revolution, scientific research and economic development in constant alternation have broken through and thrust aside far older forms of thinking and social reality. The significance of these processes for the history of mankind—Karl Jaspers justifiably calls them the rise of the 'absolutely new'[1]—can no longer be doubted.

The importance of Max Weber's contribution to research into the scientific–industrial revolution and its pre-history must be at least indicated. Above all he made clear the two main directions in which the 'ratio' unfolded its revolutionary power: on the one hand, new branches of knowledge have by their practical application profoundly re-shaped both the social conditions of life and, indirectly, human consciousness; on the other, they have accomplished an immediate intellectualization of our view of the world and our self-interpretation. With admirable historical expertise Weber showed how, ever since the Middle Ages, Church and State,

[1] K. Jaspers, *Vom Ursprung und Ziel der Geschichte* (Zürich, 1949), pp. 107 ff.

B

economy and society, science and technology turn and turn about
have collaborated in this process or have been affected by it. This,
too, is the place for his much-contested thesis that links the rise of
modern capitalism with the rationalization of life by the ethos of
this-worldly asceticism, which was peculiar to the Calvinist puri-
tanical sects. However correct these assumptions might be, Weber
himself emphasizes that the spirit of ascetic Protestantism has
long since fled from the steel-hard shrine of a modern economic
order that was tied to the technical and economic prerequisites of
mechanical production, and that today decides the way of life for
us all. 'The Puritan *wanted* to have a calling: we *have* to have one.'[1]
These and other factors have combined to bring about the radical
materialization of human relationships in the modern world.
Traditional ties and those based on feeling retreat behind thought
and behaviour which are consciously purposeful, and which
mercilessly, though not arbitrarily, establish and apply the means
necessary for economic and political self-assertion. The groups
struggling for leadership or survival must protect free research, out
of economic or military interest in technical progress, and thus
further the emancipation of modern science from the traditional
view of life, determined by clerical authority and theological
metaphysical speculation. Thus value-free knowledge of the facts
of experience and their causal connections prevails against value-
orientated forms of interpretation of the world and the self which,
until now, had dominated human thinking, almost unchallenged,
for thousands of years.

Max Weber also saw his own work as a product of this development, and consciously set it within this framework. Admittedly he
was not the first nor the only one to focus his scientific efforts on
this question. Of his friends and contemporaries, Ernst Troeltsch
and Werner Sombart in particular devoted themselves to similar
and scarcely less comprehensive research, and already long before
his time the substance and consequences of modern science,
industrial society and capitalist economy had become the fundamental theme of the works of Auguste Comte and Karl Marx, who
in their turn had had their predecessors. Comte and Marx had
indeed taken seriously the problems which were bound up with the
rise of an industrialized society, and despite other differences, they

[1] Max Weber, *Gesammelte Aufsätze zur Religionssoziologie*, I (Tübingen, 1920),
203 (cited hereafter as R.S.).

were united in their conviction that the progress that was guaranteed by science would of necessity overcome these problems and
bring about a reign of happiness on earth. For Weber, on the
contrary, the belief that a historical law—whether in linear or
dialectical form—could guarantee the achievement of an objectively or absolutely valuable final position, did not belong fundamentally to the realm of what can be scientifically substantiated.

It is precisely the concept of progress which Weber made the
subject of a subtle and radical analysis in his work, *The meaning
of the 'value-freedom' of sociological and economic sciences*, in
which he extended substantially the well-known theses put forward in his discussion of value-judgments in 1909. Here it is no
longer a matter of single value-judgments, but of the fact that the
apparatus of sociological concepts in use at that time, and still
partially so today, is, like our everyday language, no vehicle for
value-free statements, but often contains by implication quite
massive evaluations. Thus it very frequently exercises a dual
normative–description function,[1] thereby concealing the problem of
values in a systematically misleading way. How to see through this
disguise and separate the cognitive from the evaluative elements in
a patient and perceptive analysis, Weber demonstrated in a
masterly way, precisely by means of the example of the concept
of 'progress'. He showed that such concepts are indeed sometimes
used in a value-free way, but that more often they are so permeated
by various value-elements that it is difficult to distinguish the
cognitive from the evaluative. Nor is this least the case when one
thinks there is an obligation or a possibility of drawing absolutely
valid conclusions for practical assessment from ostensible or real
'development tendencies'. To this claim Weber rightly makes the
following objection: no matter how unequivocal the developmental
tendencies may be, only such imperatives of action should be
derived from them as are relevant to the most appropriate means of
reaching a given position, not to the position itself.[2] In a similar
way the concept of adjustment (*Anpassung*) oscillates widely
between the realm of statements of fact and that of value-judgments. The danger of being misled by such questionable lines of

[1] Cf. H. Albert, *Oekonomische Ideologie und politische Theorie* (Göttingen, 1954)
p. 34.
[2] M. Weber, *Gesammelte Aufsätze zur Wissenschaftslehre*, 2nd ed. (Tübingen,
1951), p. 498 (cited hereafter as W.L.).

thought appeared so great to Weber that he considers their use
even in the sphere of empirically unquestionable applicability to
be very inopportune, and indeed would rather have them excluded
completely from sociological discussion. A similar role can be
played by the 'pure theory' of classical national economy, indispensable as a methodological aid when it is interpreted as a justification of the radical free-trade school, i.e. 'as an exhaustive image
of "natural" reality, "natural" here meaning one not falsified by
human folly. This is even more so when it is interpreted on this
basis as a desideratum [*Sollen*]—as an ideal valid in the sphere of
values, instead of as an ideal type useful in the empirical investigation of the existential [*Seiend*].'[1] Here indeed, according to Weber's
conviction, pure economic theory has proved so effective as a
methodological tool for research into the actual, that despite the
danger of misinterpretation as *Sollen* or ideal—or we might prefer
to call it a misapplication as an ideology of economic liberalism—it
deserves a place in the behavioural theory of the economic sciences.

These and related concepts with normative–descriptive double
meaning arise from very widespread forms of man's interpretation
of the world and the self which Weber came upon particularly
during his research into the sociology of religion. These are mainly
lines of thought which claim that it is possible to conceive of the
universe in its entirety as a meaningfully ordered cosmos. This
view of the world as a problem of meaning, a view related particularly to the rationalism of bourgeois and priestly groups of intellectuals,[2] is not concerned, or, at least, not primarily concerned, with
the recognition of actual invariables of empirical occurrence but
with the significance of the course of the world according to specific requirements of value- and sense-fulfilment; in short, with its
significance as a value-rational order of things.

Thus the claim is raised 'that the course of the world, at least in
so far as it touches the interests of men, is somehow a meaningful
process'.[3] Such a claim arises, as Weber points out, first of all as the
problem of unjust suffering, thus as postulating just compensation

[1] W.L., pp. 522 ff. Further observations on the use of evaluative, especially
'emanatistic', concepts and models in social economics are to be found in the
essay 'Roscher und Knies und die logischen Probleme der historischen
Nationalökonomie', in W.L., pp. 1 ff.
[2] R.S., vol. I, note 2, pp. 251 ff.; *Wirtschaft und Gesellschaft*, 4th ed. (Tübingen, 1956), pp. 304 ff., 711 (cited hereafter as W.G.).
[3] R.S., vol. I, note 2, p. 567.

for the unjust distribution of individual happiness within the world. Yet these lines of thought appear also in more general and more basic form: from the just 'world-order' absolute norms are to be derived, and in its framework nothing but good can follow from good, only evil from evil, the victory of the just cause is guaranteed, etc., etc.

The attempt to prove by intellectual means the existence of such a world-order finally brings about its own collapse; 'Rational knowledge, to which ethical religiosity itself had appealed, followed its own norms autonomously within this world and thus formed a cosmos of truths. These not only had nothing whatever to do with the systematic postulates of rational ethics, i.e. that the world as cosmos should satisfy their demands or exhibit some kind of meaning, but had, on principle, to reject these demands. The cosmos of natural causality and the postulated cosmos of the ethical causality of compromise were irreconcilably opposed to each other' (R.S. p. 569). The insolubility of the contradiction between the meaning of the universe as a value-rational order and the view of the world held by the modern empirical sciences is brought out by Weber time and time again with deliberate sharpness: 'Wherever rationally empirical knowledge has consistently achieved the disenchantment of the world and its transformation into a piece of causal mechanism, there is conclusive estrangement from the claims of the ethical postulate, that the world is ordained by a god, and therefore is somehow an ethically meaningful cosmos. For the empirical and, even more, the mathematically orientated view of the world rejects in principle the view that seeks above all the "meaning" of this-worldly events' (R.S. p. 564).

Thus men had become disenchanted with the world and, in particular, with society; at least for those who claimed to understand it according to traditional religio-metaphysical thinking as a value-rational cosmos, it had become meaningless. Yet even modern science, which had brought about this disillusionment. is itself affected by it. With uncompromising consistency Weber questioned what could now be the meaning of science as a vocation, since the dreams formerly connected with it, 'The Way to True Being', 'The Way to True Art', 'The Way to True Nature', 'The Way to the True God', 'The Way to True Happiness', have been lost. This question, and the way in which Weber dealt with it, caused consternation and even offence not only among the young men who had just returned from the war, but also among the notables of the humanities in Germany.[1]

All this shows clearly enough that Weber considered the rationalization process of the scientific–industrial revolution as inevitable, and affirmed that it was the fate of the modern world, while at the same time feeling it as a deeply disquieting and problematic development. Of 'scientific credulity' in the sense of naïve optimism, as was frequent in connection with the results of research particularly in the second half of the previous century, there is no further mention. The practical effects of capitalist industrialization are viewed with the same illusion-free examination of harsh reality, without extenuation and without palliatives. Yet Weber did not on that account oppose socialist lines of thought any less critically. He could not find any certainty in Marxist pronouncements about the society of the future, and considered the abolition of the so-called separation of the worker from his means of production as being out of the question under the conditions of modern technical production: above all he was firmly convinced that socialism would necessarily lead to further bureaucratization, thus not to a lessening, but to an increase, of men's domination of other men: 'It is the dictatorship of the official, not of the worker, which—at any rate for the present—is being advanced'.[2]

It is hardly surprising that there was bitter opposition to all these views. In particular, the shattering events which haunted Germany and Europe after the First World War so greatly impaired our readiness to accept and develop Weber's doctrines that for a very long time his work received more honour and exerted more considerable influence abroad—especially in the U.S.—than at home. As the tensions of the period between the wars became more acute, so the more urgent became the need of conflicting groups for a social theory to legitimize their respective interests, and such a theory could only be an evaluative doctrine of society. So there was a general return to ways of thinking which had been directly or indirectly the object of Weber's deeply incisive criticism, in particular to the conviction that from an ethically meaningful

[1] Cf. E. Wittenberg, 'Die Wissenschaftskrisis in Deutschland im Jahre 1919', in *Theorie*, IV (1938), pp. 235 ff.

[2] M. Weber, *Gesammelte Aufsätze zue Soziologie und Sozialpolitik* (Tübingen, 1924), p. 508.

order of things in the cosmos or in history one could derive absolute norms for human behaviour and, wherever possible, guarantees of success for behaviour corresponding to these norms. To defend this regression from obvious objections, Weber's concept of science in general and the principle of value-freedom in particular were attacked as the expressions of a narrow-minded rationalism and positivism or as an inadmissible transfer of methods proper to the natural sciences into the realm of the arts. Such tendencies were already plainly recognizable in the immediate reactions to the speech 'Science as a Vocation'.

If, especially in Germany, the revival of social metaphysics asserted itself relatively quickly against the principles defended by Weber, this was not only due to the rising need for an ideology on the part of the rival groups, who were ready and often in a position to lend powerful emphasis to the social theories in their service by extra-theoretical means. The balance was also tipped by the fact that Weber did not live long enough to pursue more precisely his research into the basic forms of the interpretation of the world as an ethically meaningful cosmos in all its presuppositions, consequences and implications right down to the concepts of the evaluative or normative–descriptive 'theories of society'.

That alone would have provided an adequate basis for a critique of these theories from their basic principles right through to their smallest details. The fact that Max Weber's work remained incomplete has had particularly fateful results in this connection.

It meant, for example, that it came to appear as if not only the power of the current social and political tendencies, but also the weight of better arguments lay on the side of his opponents, and those who clung to Weber's basic conceptions of scientific theory found themselves very much isolated, especially after 1933. Today, more than a generation later, we are indeed in a better position to judge whether the numerous attempts, often undertaken with passionate partiality, to 'defeat Max Weber' in fact reached their target, or whether, on the contrary, they led involuntarily to a confirmation of his views and those of thinkers like him. Many of these efforts are of only historical interest to us. But even today, mostly under the aegis of influential social groups, the reproach is levelled against Weber that because of his agnosticism he could not rise to any insight into the true order of nature and creation, or that, being trapped in formalistic abstract interpretation of science, he

Put in Introduction

has not penetrated the depths of dialectic–concrete thinking.

A critical discussion of these assertions is at this point only possible in the briefest form. First it must be pointed out that the ideas current in natural law and dialectic proceeded from the attempt—which Weber considered as scientifically untenable—to ascribe an ethically meaningful structure to the world and to history. They arise from the notion of a 'just world-order', which ever since the mythology of archaic high cultures has played a significant role in men's intellectual development, and also from the interpretation (which goes back to Judaic and gnostic origins) of history as the realization of a divine plan of salvation or of the great drama of the fall and redemption of the creation.[1] These historic genetic points of view have been subjected to logical–systematic criticism—in the case of natural law particularly by Pareto and Kelsen, in dialectic particularly by English-speaking and Polish writers.[2] In both cases we find tautologies, decisions about the usage of a certain vocabulary or other formulations with total or at least very wide logical scope, which are consistent with practically every kind of matter- or norm-content, and so can be put to the service of any and every moral or political conviction. At the same time each of the rival groups affirms that its own employment of those mock-arguments which yet command respect is the really correct and legitimate one, while every dissenting usage is represented as a misunderstanding, a misuse or a perversion of natural law or dialectic.[3]

The last few decades have produced an abundance of empirical examples of this free manipulability of the ideas that have been

[1] J. Taubes, *Abendländische Eschatologie* (Berne, 1947); K. Lowith, *Weltgeschichte und Heilsgeschehen* (Stuttgart, 1953).

[2] K. R. Popper, 'What is Dialectic?', in K. R. Popper, *Conjectures and Refutations* (London, 1963), pp. 312 ff.; T. D. Wheldon, *The Vocabulary of Politics* (Pelican Books, 1953), pp. 109 ff.; T. D. Acton, *The Illusion of the Epoch, Marxism–Leninism as a Philosophical Creed*, 2nd ed. (London, 1962); A. J. Ayer, Filosofijanauka (Philosophy and Science) in *Voprosy filosofi* (1962), vol. I; in German (Logische Analyse der Dialektik) in *Ost-Probleme*, XIV/19 (1962), 579 ff.; Z. A. Jordan, *Philosophy and Ideology—The Development of Philosophy and Marxism–Leninism in Poland since the Second World War* (Dordrecht, 1963). There is a striking lack of a corresponding literature of criticism in German, although here the political manipulability of dialectics, its function as 'derivations' in Pareto's sense, has emerged with extreme clarity during the last decade.

[3] Cf. E. Topitsch, 'Ueber Leerformeln', in *Probleme der Wissenschaftstheorie, Festschrift für V. Kraft*, edited by E. Topitsch (Vienna, 1960) esp. pp. 250 ff. We cannot speak of a misuse of dialectics, since no rules that are in any way clear have been drawn up for its correct use.

mentioned. It was indeed agreed that Max Weber's point of view had been disposed of with the help of those higher principles, but when it came to the question of what practical political inferences might be drawn from either the law of nature or dialectics, opinions were widely divergent, according to respectively held values, aims and interests.

Thus, in 1933, the scholastic law of nature was invoked in Austria to legitimize its transformation into a Christian authoritarian class-state (*Ständestaat*) whereas in Germany it was used at times to glorify National Socialism as a 're-assertion of the organic view of community and culture' and as 'the return to the order of nature and creation', or to justify the contention that it had restored the validity of 'order and reality derived from nature' as against 'the unnaturalness of liberalism and Bolshevism'.[1] Meanwhile Marxism also contains a doctrine of natural law, only in this case natural law is no mere ideal (*Sollen*) that may or may not be realized, but is deeply buried in and guaranteed by the course of history interpreted as an ethically meaningful order of things: the assertion of true justice and freedom is considered as the aim of history realizing itself with dialectic necessity.[2]

However, Marxism did not possess a monopoly for the application of dialectics. In the period between the wars influential philosophers justified the authoritarian class-state with the help of a dialectically evaluative doctrine of society.[3] While other theoreticians, scarcely less well esteemed, attributed to dialectics the view that the Hitler regime, but not the Weimar Republic, corresponded to the concept of the state and was legitimized by this idea, the same line of thought was used to prove that the Third Reich represented the reality of the intellect, of freedom, and true morality.[4] A corresponding justification was found for the diminution of the legal rights of so-called racial aliens: only in an abstract–individualistic interpretation of law can all men be considered as

[1] E. W. Bockenforde, 'Der deutsche Katholizismus im Jahre 1933', in *Hochland*, Year 53, Part 3 (1961), esp. pp. 226 ff.

[2] For Marxism as an implicit theory of natural law, cf. *inter alia* S. Marck, *Hegelianismus und Marxismus* (Berlin, 1922), pp. 24 ff.; W. Theimer, *Der Marxismus* (Berne, 1950), pp. 24 ff., 161; H. Kelsen, *The Communist Theory of Law* (London, 1955), pp. 20 ff.

[3] Esp. O. Spann and many of his pupils.

[4] J. Binder, 'Der Autoritäre Staat', in *Logos*, XXII (1933), 126 ff., esp. 129; 'Der Idealismus als Grundlage der Staatsphilosophie', in *Zeitschrift für Deutsch Kulturphilosophie*, I (1935), 142 ff., esp. 155 ff.

equally competent whereas for those who think of order dialectically and concretely in terms of the whole, it makes an essential
difference whether one be of the same race or alien.[1] Finally after
the outbreak of war came the glorification of the military policy
of expansion, acclaimed as the realization of the dialectics of the
concrete-general, the overcoming of the abstract ideology of
humanity and of the abstract concept of freedom, which are the
products of Western enlightenment.[2] These modes of thought
were similarly applied in the Soviet Union as a basis for the objec-
tives at that time of the political leadership, and in order to explain
away the contradictions between the doctrine of Karl Marx and
social conditions. Even the fact that the children of party officials
received bigger rations of foodstuffs than other children was
justified dialectically.[3]

The modes of thought mentioned above have, however, particularly since 1945, been used and interpreted also in the interests of
Western democracy. The scholastic law of nature, which had
legitimized not only authoritarian endeavours of the period between the wars, but also throughout the centuries the most diverse
forms of denial of liberty, including slavery and slave traffic[4]
now appeared as the only metaphysical guarantee of freedom and
human dignity, and ignoring the role it had played in the preparation and service of totalitarian systems both of the left and right,
dialectics claimed to be the shield of true democracy.

It has unfortunately been necessary to go into these facts,
which are not all of a pleasant nature, for they confirm almost with
the exactness of a carefully planned experiment the correctness of
Max Weber's basic positions. The philosophical tenets with which
it was intended to confound Weber, turned out, when confronted
not only with historical and scientific–theoretical criticism, but

[1] K. Larenz, *Ueber Gegenstand und Methode des völkischen Rechtsdenkens* (Berlin, 1938), p. 52; 'Zur Logik des konkreten Begriffs', in *Deutsche Rechts-wissenschaft*, V (1940) 279 ff., 289.

[2] K. Larenz, 'Der deutsche Rechtsgedanke und seine Bedeutung für ein neues Europa', in *Kieler Blätter* (1941), pp. 39 ff., esp. pp. 47 ff.; W. Schmidt, *Hegel und die Idee der Volksordnung* (Leipzig, 1944), pp. 154 ff., esp. pp. 158 ff.

[3] H. Kelsen, *The Communist Theory of Law* (New York, 1955), pp. 49 ff.; S. Ossowski, *Die Klassenstruktur im sozialen Bewusstsein* (Neuwied, 1962), p. 231.

[4] A. M. Knoll, *Katholische Kirche und scholastisches Naturrecht* (Vienna, 1962). A corresponding monographic survey of the application of dialectics to justify and champion political systems and individual measures is still lacking, although such a survey promises rich results. Important material and bibliographic references are to be found in W. R. Beyer, *Hegel-Bilder* (Berlin, 1964).

above all in historical–social reality, to be empty formulae, flexibly fitting every political impulse, and indiscriminately serving everyone who so desired: their success is due to their almost unlimited manipulability.[1] Thus attempts to defeat Max Weber brought about the most brilliant justification of Max Weber—a justification indeed which was bought dearly enough with human suffering. Those who became sociologists as a result of surviving such a period must regard it as their duty to see that understanding so bitterly paid for should not again fall victim to an unconscious process of repression or indeed to a consciously directed oblivion.

Even today, we must not overlook the strong tendency to sustain the persuasive psychological appeal of theories like natural law and dialectics by just such processes of repression, concealment and forgetfulness. With this in mind, certain features of the present-day discussion of Max Weber become more understandable when for instance, it is asserted or indicated that by his critique of evaluative social doctrine Weber, at least indirectly, countenanced the nihilism of the total state.[2] This is to ignore the fact that the totalitarian powers without exception considered Weber's thought hostile and destructive, because a value-free science would basically have had to deny them that higher legitimization and glorification which they so earnestly desired and for which modes of thought such as natural law offered themselves so willingly.[3] If we expect

[1] Cf. H. Kelsen, *The Political Theory of Bolshevism* (Berkeley and Los Angeles, 1948), p. 19; *Was ist Gerechtigkeit?* (Vienna, 1953).

[2] As in W. Mommsen, *Max Weber und die deutsche Politik 1890–1920* (Tübingen, 1959). The questionable attempt to ascribe to Max Weber, via the decisionism of Carl Schmitt, co-responsibility for National Socialism, is particularly interesting in view of the fact that the latter author, after turning to National Socialism, became clearly estranged from decisionism and with a direct appeal to Hegel represented a 'concrete idea of order', cf. C. Schmitt, *Ueber die drei Arten rechtswissenschaftlichen Denkens* (Hamburg, 1934), esp. p. 45: 'All these currents and directions of German resistance [against the liberal "ideas of 1789"—E.T.] found their systematic résumé, their "summa" in Hegel's philosophy of law and state. In it concrete notions of order come to life with an immediate power.' To those who used the empty-sounding formulae of 'dialectic and concrete thought' to serve Hitler, the Hegelian conversion of Schmitt did not appear satisfactory, cf. the review of the quoted book by K. Larenz (*Zeitschrift für Deutsche Kulturphilosophie*, I, 1935 112 ff).

[3] Cf. S. D. Stirk, *German Universities through English Eyes* (London, 1946). This clear, factual book, quite free from wartime emotion, gives good reasons for the view that a value-free concept of science in Max Weber's sense would have been the German university's best support against National Socialism; the author was Lektor at the University of Breslau during the National Socialist regime and so knew the conditions from his own observation. Assertions about

support from science against autocracy, this cannot consist of
the production of questionable 'evaluative social doctrines', but of
expert advice and logical practice of democratic forms of behaviour, and the construction and completion of appropriate institutional protection.

However necessary it is to counteract these and other influential
currents which are trying today to close, or rather to wall up the
door opened by Weber, it would be just as unsatisfactory to stand
still in this doorway, and indeed research has not done this. This is
wholly in accordance with the intention of the master who saw his
own work and influence as connected with a development pointing
far beyond them into the future—as connected, indeed, with the
scientific–industrial revolution.

What Weber in fact introduced, with this investigation into the
implicit value-significance of single terms, the dual normative–
descriptive function of, say classical economic theory and finally
all the interpretations of the world as an ethically meaningful
'cosmos', is a new phase of the rational analysis of sociological
concept-formation, in fact of the whole consideration of the
peculiarity of man's interpretation of the world and the self.
But we must confine ourselves here to the sphere which is relevant
to sociology.

In making the distinction between statements of fact and value-
judgments, which was only dealt with in a very late phase of
development of philosophical thought and was represented among
Max Weber's contemporaries particularly by Georg Simmel, the
neo-Kantian from Baden, and Werner Sombart,[1] the fact comes to
light that men's orientation of the world, as it appears in daily life
but also in mythical, religious and metaphysical thought-structures,
exercises several simultaneous functions which, from a scientifically
logical point of view, differ radically from each other. As later
research has shown, the unity of these functions, so questionable
from the standpoint of pure knowledge, is a phylogenetically
ancient inheritance of extraordinary significance for practical
living.

the alleged connection between Weber and National Socialism are intended to
distract attention from the actual connections linking the restoration of social
metaphysics between the wars with the authoritarian and totalitarian movements
of the time.

[1] A. Brecht, *Politische Theorie* (Tübingen, 1961), pp. 252 ff., but the distinction had already been clearly made by David Hume.

This unity is clearly observable especially in the higher animals: here we find not only the familiar forms of orientation and direction of behaviour by means of inherited selective release-mechanisms, but we can also recognize that the appropriate release stimuli provoke not only a motor reaction but also a corresponding upsurge of emotion. Thus these guiding mechanisms exercise a three-fold function in one: they inform us about the presence of environmental data significant for life, they instigate appropriate behaviour and at the same time produce an emotional excitement connected with this behaviour. Such a multi-functional orientation is also very marked in social life, and here the link is particularly obvious with man, whose instincts lose their selectivity and their significance for the stabilization of behaviour to a considerable degree and are complemented or indeed replaced by the cultivation of traditions and institutions. A decisive part in this social guidance of behaviour is played by speech, which bears this same multi-functional character: it offers man to a certain extent a ready-to-use philosophy, in which a certain emphasis and a corresponding direction of action are almost always linked. Speech however has substantially contributed to the fact that man has interpreted nature as a social creation on the analogy of his social relationships and has fused it together with society into a 'socio-cosmic universe'. These socio-cosmic notions not only play a great part in the thinking of primitive peoples, but an impressive mythology has evolved from them in the archaic cultures of the Near and Far East. This mythology formed the initial stages of those theological and metaphysical speculations, which claimed to understand the cosmos as an ethically meaningful order.[1]

In the framework of such speculations the themes of 'the omnipotent law of nature or reason' and of 'cosmic justice' or the conception of the course of the world and of history as a drama of decline and redemption and related forms of interpretation of the universe as a value-rational order have been handed down over the centuries. Their influence on the philosophy of contemporary Europe and in particular on social philosophy is far-reaching. For most thinkers in the Age of Enlightenment, physical and moral

---

[1] Cf. E. Topitsch, *Vom Ursprung und Ende der Metaphysik* (Vienna, 1958); *Sozialphilosophie zwischen Ideologie und Wissenschaft* (Neuwied, 1961); *Phylogenetische und emotionale Grundlagen menschlicher Weltauffassung* (Turin, 1962), and the literature quoted in these works.

order, 'natural law' and 'moral law' together formed a kind of cosmic constitution, a well-defined stock of rules of the divine exercise of power, and such ideas also entered into the classic national economy: its belief in the harmony of the liberal economic order is only understandable in the framework of the belief in a world-order whose harmony is guaranteed by a superhuman providence. In such lines of thought recognition, evaluation and direction of action are just as inseparable as in the ancient myths, and the same is true for the Marxist doctrine of the alienation of man and the removal of his alienation through dialectics—a doctrine which could be designated as a theodicy without a god.

The scientific–industrial revolution of the present era was the first to reveal the diversity of the components of such multi-functional theories and at the same time to defeat the suppression by means of which influential institutions had for thousands of years blocked any fundamental criticism of such theories. The exact natural sciences did away with the sociomorphic and techno-morphic analogies with the help of which previous projections of ethico-political meanings onto the cosmos and thence reflexively on to human society, had claimed absolute validity. Thus meta-physical legitimizations of existing or desired social orders by the alleged 'cosmic order' became impossible, and society could hence-forth much more easily be made an object of the same empiric–rational mode of observation which had proved so reliable in the exploration of nature. In the disenchanted world stands disen-chanted society in which the politically active person no longer has a 'national order', 'entelechial tendencies', a 'divine plan of salva-tion', or 'historical dialectics' with which to convince himself that he represents the absolutely correct and essentially victorious cause, while his opponents are deluded and doomed to failure.

At the same time the need of industrial society for scientifically trained forces eliminated the ascendancy of the established expo-nents of the pattern of thought we have been dealing with, an ascendancy they had possessed, both in number and institutional-ized influence, during earlier phases of intellectual development. As a consequence of the coincidence of all these conditions that older thought-pattern was itself finally made the object of a scientific–logical and ideologically critical analysis, which revealed its theoretical inadequacy and its predominantly practical and emotional character.

The development of sociology into a progressive autonomous science by way of a division of labour goes hand in hand with the out-distancing of evaluative social metaphysics. Particularly in Anglo-Saxon countries since the First World War sociology has developed quickly as an empirical science, and in a way which has been an example for other countries. These researches were frequently stimulated by quite concrete problems, e.g. in the U.S. by grievances and conflicts in connection with the growth of large settlements, the urbanization of rural populations, immigration, unemployment, integration of racial minorities, etc. They frequently offered a factual basis for practical social work such as slum-clearance, town-planning or other socio-political measures.[1] A close contact with practice is evident also in commercial and industrial sociology, market and opinion research, in the service of production and market planning or party politics, as well as research into the means of mass communication. For these purposes new methods and techniques were and are being developed, often drawing considerably on formal aids and following the pattern of the mathematical natural sciences. They have become internationally accepted and are substantially the same throughout the world. Finally the encroachment by the scientific industrial revolution upon the so-called developing countries has posed new problems for sociology, which possess a great practical range and importance beyond their purely scientific interest. In all these cases empirical research has in no way suffered in political relevance by renouncing thought-modes of evaluative doctrines of society.[2]

The rejection of the conceptions of the old multi-functional model simply meant the release of social theory from outmoded illusory problems and thereby a freeing of visions for genuine empirical and scientific logical questions newly presented for research—questions which at least in part have been hardly systematically treated, let alone solved. These problems arise mainly from the fact that in the social sciences we are not concerned with a solid body of theories, which describe a condition fixed once and for all, but with relationships which are thoroughly

[1] H. Maus, 'Geschichte der Soziologie', in *Handbuch der Soziologie*, ed. W. Ziegenfuss (Stuttgart, 1956), pp. 66 ff.

[2] H. Albert, 'Wissenschaft und Politik', in *Probleme der Wissenschaftstheorie. Festschrift für V. Kraft*, ed. Topitsch (Vienna, 1960), pp. 201 ff., esp. pp. 227 ff.; 'Die Idee der kritischen Vernunft', in *Club Voltaire*, I (1963), 17 ff.

dynamic and constantly shifting: a group of theories in a state of change (the word theory is used here in a very wide sense) relates to a society in a state of change, and these theories are themselves a part of the social scene they represent, and react on it in many different ways. The state of affairs is further complicated by the fact that the social position of sociologists changes in the process of the development of their subject and within the framework of general social change, whereby their scientific attitudes can also be influenced. These conditions which are difficult to survey, and which are constantly shifting, offer a considerable resistance to the formation of theories. In this connection the so-called autonomous dynamics of social theories deserve particular consideration. Sociological pronouncements can (as has been previously indicated) influence very substantially the social reality to which they refer. This distinguishes them from the theories of the natural sciences which do not alter their object. There are—to use R. K. Merton's terms—'self-fulfilling' and 'self-destroying predictions', i.e. predictions which bring about or impede their own realization. These, and similar processes of 'back-coupling', have until now, despite their importance, hardly been subjected to a systematic analysis.[1] The application of a model for harmony or for conflict in society can have practical repercussions. While the former can under certain circumstances lead to a moderating or a concealment of social tensions which are present the latter often leads to their sharpening and dramatization. The harmonizing and stabilizing tendencies of the so-called structural and functional theories should also be recognized.[2]

The necessarily brief comments are intended to illustrate what rich possibilities of empirical research, what far-reaching problems of scientific–theoretical self-determination and what fundamental insights into the structure and function of men's interpretations of the world and the self were opened up by Max Weber and since he wrote.

His pioneering scientific achievement was only possible against

---

[1] For the particular dynamics of sociological affirmations cf. H. Albert, 'Probleme der Wissenschaftslehre in der Sozialforschung', in *Handbuch der empirischen Sozialforschung*, ed. R. König, I (1961), pp. 38 ff., 56 and the literature quoted therein.

[2] R. Dahrendorf, *Soziale Klassen und Klassenkonflikt in der industrieller Gesellschaft* (Stuttgart, 1957); *Gesellschaft und Freiheit* (Munich, 1961), esp. pp. 128 ff.

the background of particular personal preconceptions. It demanded not only an extraordinary measure of perception and industry,
but above all the ability to look the hard facts of life straight in the
face, and an intellectual intrepidity which does not shrink from the
conflicts encountered in the world around and in one's own inner
life. Thanks to these qualities Weber could free himself from
traditions which for thousands of years have presented the world to
men as a value-rational order of things, and have thereby offered
them, not only political ideology, but also personal consolation.
He was able to break up these thought patterns without replacing
them by other forms of evaluative interpretations of the universe.[1]
The completion of the 'disenchantment of the world', and the need
for man to keep abreast of this process seemed to Weber to be the
task and fate of the scholar of his day. What he developed in this
connection is an ethos and a pathos of bitter disillusionment, and
his attitude has not unfittingly been characterized as one of
'heroic positivism', whose greatness and force have wrested
admiration even from those who think quite differently.[2] Perhaps
Weber's intellectual compaign was not free from traits which we
might feel as harsh and sombre, indeed the vengeful anger which
he displayed in many an argument might appear frightening to
more delicate natures. But what remains typical in this man is the
researcher's passion, elemental and yet held in incorruptible
control, the passion of the researcher striving for new truths
against external and internal opposition—well aware that that
which today has to be fought for with Promethean strength, will
tomorrow be taken for granted or indeed be out of date. As long as
there are men who live by science, they will experience in this way
both the limits and the fulfilment of their existence.

[1] Cf. E. Baumgarten, *Max Weber, Werk und Person* (Tübingen, 1964), who
rightly places Weber on the same plane as Marx, Nietzsche and Freud. We must
add that Weber dispensed with any substitute for destroyed illusions—the
Utopian dream of the 'non-alienated man', 'superman', and 'man without
repression'. Cf. also K. Lowith, 'Die Entzauberung der Welt durch Wissenschaft. Zu Max Webers 100. Geburtstag', in *Merkur*, 18th year (1964), Part 6
(196), pp. 501 ff.

[2] E. Troeltsch, *Der Historismus und seine Probleme*, I (Tübingen, 1922), 161.

PART I
Value-freedom and Objectivity

TALCOTT PARSONS

It is indeed both an honour and a challenge to be invited to partici-
pate in this most significant occasion, the observance of the one
hundredth anniversary of the birth of Max Weber. It is also a
great pleasure to revisit the University of Heidelberg though not
quite for the first time, just short of forty years after my enrolment
here as a student in 1925. This was too late to know Max Weber in
person, but of course his intellectual influence was all-pervasive
in the Heidelberg of that time, constituting the one primary
point of reference about which all theoretical and much empirical
discussion in the social and cultural fields revolved. I was also
privileged to know his gracious and highly intelligent widow,
Marianne Weber, in particular to attend a number of her famous
'sociological teas' on Sunday afternoons. It was an extraordinarily
stimulating intellectual environment, participation in which was
one of the few most important factors in determining my whole
intellectual and professional career.

I hope it is agreeable to Professor Stammer, and the other members of the Committee which planned this programme, if I
interpret my topic broadly rather than narrowly. In the sense in
which this is true of Professor Henrich, and Winckelmann and
many others, I am not a Max Weber scholar, in particular a
scholar of the intricate details of his methodology of science and its
relations to the currents of German philosophy of his time. It
seems much more appropriate for me to address myself to the
broad questions of Max Weber's place in and contribution to the
principal trends of development of thought in the Western world
on the theoretical understanding of the problems of man in society
and culture, which were both the problems of his own time, seen in
his perspective as a German scholar, and universal problems of all
time. As an American, deeply influenced by Weber, it is doubly

appropriate for me to consider his significance in this wider perspective. Moreover, I wish to see Weber's problem not only in the purely intellectual frame of reference, but also in terms of some of the social and political developments of the time, to which Weber himself was so sensitive. It is my conviction that the two aspects have been very intimately connected and that a certain approach in terms of the sociology of knowledge will prove to be fruitful in understanding them.

This of course is not at all to say that the problems of the relation of values to objectivity in the social and cultural sciences, as treated by Weber, were of secondary importance. On the contrary I would impute the greatest importance to them, perhaps, in the general intellectual development, at least as great as to that of his substantive contributions in social science. I am therefore by no means unhappy to be dealing in the first instance with the former rather than the latter, and I think it quite proper that they should be considered first in the present symposium.

To come to my central theme, I would first like to suggest that Weber's peak of intellectual maturity coincided remarkably with the outbreak of the greatest crisis of this century in the social and political order of the Western world both internally and in its relations to the rest of the world of our time, namely the beginning of the First World War in 1914. Fifty years of retrospect make it possible to be quite sure that this truly marked the end of an era. Politically it was the beginning of the end of the nineteenth-century system of European national states, which on the one hand has ultimately made their traditional 'sovereignty' *vis-à-vis* each other untenable, on the other hand has destroyed their hegemony over the rest of the world. In the first context the Common Market and the European Unification movement are sufficient indices that the old order has changed internally, the present position in the world power system of the United States and the Soviet Union, and the ending of colonialism, that the old Europe no longer plays its nineteenth-century role in relation to the rest of the world.

It is less well known but I think equally definite and important, that the generation spanning the turn to the twentieth century saw the decisive initial steps taken in a profound intellectual and cultural transformation, the full consequences of which are even now only beginning to emerge. I would like first to discuss Weber in the context of the latter set of problems and then relate the structure of these problems and of thought about them to the trends of evolution of the social and political system.

Max Weber's intellectual home, of course, lay in the 'historistic' aftermath of German Idealism as this worked out in the historical schools of jurisprudence, economics, and more generally of culture, e.g. in the work of Dilthey, and of religion as in the work of Troeltsch. The trend was, of course, to stress the internal integration and the historical individuality and uniqueness of the particular cultural system, such as Roman Law, or Renaissance Culture, or indeed 'rational bourgeois capitalism'. The way in which this was done tended to accentuate the dualism already present in the Kantian position between the world of Nature and the world of *Kultur* or *Geist*, involving Kant's 'practical reason', human values and problems of meaning. The cultural and social sciences, dealing with the latter realms, were thereby sharply set off against the natural, not only in terms of empirical subject-matter but also of basic method and mode of conceptualization.

This position not only accentuated a distinction between the two groups of sciences. It went further to structure the relation in favour of protecting the historical–cultural sphere against the encroachments of natural science perspectives and methods. The implication that these were dangerous to human values was certainly present. Closely related to this problem in turn was that of the relation between the individual observer and his subject-matter. As became perhaps particularly clear in the philosophy of Dilthey, the relativity inherent in the conception of the socio-cultural historical individual came to involve the individual because of his involvement in it. There was, then, the threat of a socio-cultural solipsism which in some respects was more profound than the individual version propounded by Bishop Berkeley.

The crucial problem from one point of view was that of the source of leverage whereby the individual scholar or scientist, and the scholarly community of which he was a part, could avoid involvement in a closed system from which there was no escape. From some perspectives the difficulty seemed to be insuperable because the understanding of motives and meanings (*Verstehen*), which were shared between observer and object, seemed to be the

essence of the cultural disciplines which separated them from the
natural. This was, of course, perhaps the most central point at
which Weber made his proposals for reformation.

The citing of these difficulties in German historicism—which
incidentally have tended to be repeated a half century later in
American cultural anthropology—is by no means meant to belittle
the major substantive contributions made under the aegis of the
'historical schools' in various disciplines during the relevant period.
They did, however, create tensions which were the starting points
for Weber's special contribution.

Before attempting to characterize this, I think it will be helpful
to sketch briefly the two principal alternatives to historicism which
seemed to be most readily available in the intellectual situation of
Weber's time. The first of these was relatively foreign to the main
German tradition, though constantly close to its centre of awareness. Indeed there was a strong tendency to define the main axis of
the differences between German and 'Western' culture in terms of
the contrast between the complex just sketched and Western
'rationalism', atomism and various other terms.

In intellectual history this contrast presents too many complexi-
ties to enter into here. The most salient elements for present
purposes, however, were those centring in British social thought—
and American, though the United States was not at the time a very
prominent focus of major intellectual movements to a central
European. Here the main focus, I think, lies in the broad Utilitarian
movement, which had two particularly important characteristics
for purposes of the present analysis. The first of these is that it
tended to assimilate the natural and the socio-cultural fields to each
other rather than, in the German tradition, separating them. The
most prominent movement in this direction centred about the
development of economics as a theoretical discipline, which had
become firmly established in Britain. The same general intellectual
framework had much to do with the beginnings of psychology as a
science. The level of economics was clearly one of the *Verstehen* of
human motives, of the relations of the 'wants' of individuals to the
measures taken to secure their satisfaction. In theoretical terms,
however, this was a sharply limited range of motives and utilitarianism also remained 'atomistic'—which is to say that it had no
theoretical way of establishing relations among individuals other
than at the level of means and the situation of action. As such it was

unstable and subject to pressures to 'reductionism', the purport of which was that the relevance of the theoretical model of 'natural science' tended to cover over the reduction of man to what was in fact a biological organism or even a physical particle. Considerations such as these seem to be related to the common German tendency to derogate the intellectual merits of utilitarian thought by treating it as merely an ideological expression of the 'materialistic' interest of its proponents. There were, however, profoundly important intellectual problems underlying the difference between German historicism and English utilitarianism.

French social and cultural thought of the time is much more difficult to characterize. On the one hand both positivism and rationalism of important sorts flourished in France. This circumstance is related to the German tendency at that time to treat French *Civilization* as somehow inferior to German *Kultur*. At the same time, as developments of special interest to the sociologist have made clear, there were more readily available openings for a sociological type of development in France than in England, in the more 'collectivistic' strain of French radical rather than conservative thought, i.e. from Roeussau, through St. Simon and Comte to Durkheim and other contemporaries of Weber. It seems fair to say that on the whole the French situation was intermediate between the German and the British and subsequently, though not in Weber's lifetime, came to be an essential intellectual bridge between them.

The second major movement toward which Weber had to assume a position was socialist thought. As by far the most philosophical version and over the long run the most influential, it seems justified to confine attention here to Marxism. Moreover, it was the version dominant in the German intellectual situation of Weber's time, though it should not be forgotten that the split between the Communist and the Social Democratic wings did not occur in time to affect Weber's basic orientation.

In the present frame of reference, Marx presented a peculiar synthesis between the German and British patterns of thinking just outlined, which he could achieve by, in his famous phrase, 'standing Hegel on his head'. I understand this to mean that Marx remained basically within the main frame of reference of German philosophy in this respect, above all in that he accepted a dichotomy which was not identical to that between the cultural and the natural science, but obviously very closely related to it, namely between the two categories of factors operating in the field of human behaviour, the *Idealfaktoren* and the *Realfaktoren*. Hegel, as idealist, clearly thought the former to be paramount whereas standing him on his head asserted the primacy of the other set, of the 'material' interests. This could even bring Marx closer to the natural sciences as in a sense the concept 'scientific socialism' suggested, but it still remained within the idealist–historicist frame of reference. It could also make possible a positive use of utilitarian economics, as a scheme for analysing the internal dynamics of the capitalistic system in modified Ricardian terms—though remaining true to historicism, by insisting that economic theory in anything like that sense applied *only* to capitalism. To be sure, finally, Marx stopped short of pure historicism in that he shared with Hegel a teleologically orientated scheme of the evolution of human society and culture as a whole.

My thesis is that these three intellectual movements, with reference in all cases to the problem of the sciences of human social and cultural affairs, defined the co-ordinates of Weber's problem. In fact he achieved a synthesis which, though refusing to accept any one of them on its own terms, ended by incorporating essential elements from all of them into a single frame of reference, and leaning on this, the beginnings of a theory, which was clearly on a level much higher than could be offered by any of these antecedents. Weber's innovations—in which he was not alone, but certainly in most respects pre-eminent, can I think best be put in terms of his 'methodological' conceptions on the one hand, his substantive contribution to social science on the other. This distinction, it seems to me, is roughly equivalent to that between frame of reference and theory in the broad scientific sense.

WEBER'S METHODOLOGY OF SOCIAL SCIENCE

1. *Wertfreiheit*

The concept of *value-freedom* may be said to be the foundation of his position. It stands in sharp contrast to all three of the above views from which Weber differed. From the historicist perspective the investigator was so firmly ascribed to his cultural position that capacity to transcend it in favour of a new level of objectivity was certainly problematical. From the Marxist point of view this embeddedness in a socio-cultural system, here the class-system, remained, but this time was compounded by the movement's commitment to political action in the name of the implementation of the doctrine's views of the iniquity of capitalism and the prospective glories of socialism. The case of utilitarianism is a bit more complex, for here no clear line was drawn between the grounds of objectivity in empirical judgment on the one hand, and of advocacy of policies on the other, since the latter problem was so far reduced to the level of merely individual preferences.

By contrast with all three, Weber's position is one of a much higher level of differentiation. It is not an advocacy that the social scientist abstain from all value-commitments—for example the position taken in *Wissenschaft als Beruf* makes that entirely clear. The point is rather that *in his rôle* as scientist a particular subvalue system must be paramount for the investigator, that in which conceptual clarity, consistency and generality on the one hand, empirical accuracy and verifiability on the other are the valued outputs of the process of investigation. But the scientist is never the whole man, and the scientific community is never a whole society. It is as inconceivable that either a person or a society should be exhausted in these terms as that there should be a totally 'economic' man of society. Other value-components are naturally paramount in other roles of individuals and in other subsystems of the society. Value-freedom I thus interpret as freedom to pursue the values of science within the relevant limits, without their being overridden by values either contradictory to or irrelevant to those of scientific investigation. At the same time it involved the renunciation of any claims that the scientist *qua* scientist speaks for a value-position, on a broader basis of social or cultural significance than that of his science. Thus from Weber's point of view such a phrase as 'scientific socialism' is just as unacceptable as 'Christian Science' would be if the term science there were meant in an empirical sense. The policy-orientations of political movements are *never* simple applications of scientific knowledge, but always involve value-components analytically independent of the sciences, natural or social. Value-freedom, furthermore, implies that a science need not be bound to the values of any particular historic culture.

2. *Wertbeziehung*

Secondly, there is a sense in which the doctrine of *Wertbeziehung* is the obverse of that of *Wertfreiheit*. The latter I have interpreted in the sense of stressing the *in*dependence of the role of scientists from other roles. The former may be interpreted as stressing their *inter*dependence. This, above all, seems to be directed against the kind of naïve empiricism, according to which scientific knowledge is held to be simply a 'reflection' of the reality of the external world, whether this empiricism be understood in the more historicist sense of involvement in the particular cultural system itself, or in that of British empiricism with its relations to utilitarianism and to cultural trait-atomism. It is an implication of the differentiation of roles between scientist and other bases of participation in both the cultural and the social systems, that the bases of interest for the posing of problems for a science should be carefully distinguished from the canons of procedure in the solution of those problems, and of the validity of propositions arrived at through following those procedures. Scientific investigation is never purely an occupation of the ivory tower and its products are not 'immaculately conceived'. Values for Weber may in this context be said to constitute the extrascientific source of the scientific 'paternity' by virtue of which 'mother-science' can be fruitful. This doctrine is of course related to a number of considerations. First it may be noted that the scientist himself, as a total human being, must find his commitment to his science meaningful in terms of *his* values—it must be his calling (*Beruf*). But, secondly, science is only in a limiting case a purely individual isolated activity—it must in the nature of the case be socially organized. In this connection it is essential that it should be integrated to a degree of the value-consensus of the community in which it takes place, not totally absorbed, but accorded the kind of place which is essential to its support in a broadly political sense. Without such consensus for example anything like a modern university system would be unthinkable. Contrary, then, to much naïve cultural 'isolationism' we can then say that *of course* science, including the socio-cultural science, is oriented in terms of and dependent on the total value systems of the society and culture of the time. This almost follows from the fundamental fact that science is a human enterprise. But as noted, the interdependence is not incompatible with its essential independence.

3. *Causal explanation and generalized theory*

In the above two primary references of Weber's methodology of social science the problem has been that of relation to the wider culture. The next problem I wish to take up concerns a problem internal to the sciences, namely the relation between the status of natural and of cultural science. Here it seems to me that the crucial points are essentially very simple. Weber took very seriously indeed the proposition that *knowledge* in the empirical sense clearly implied the *causal explanation* of phenomena and events. Causal explanation, in turn, is simply not possible unless the particular facts are related, not merely in an historical sequence, but through analysis by means of a generalized theoretical scheme which is in the nature of the case abstract. Very bluntly, the conception of generalized *theory* as has been developed in the great tradition of the natural science is an essential component of *all* empirical science. This includes not merely definitions of generalized concepts, and classificatory schemes, but substantive propositions about the *relations* among abstractly defined variables.

The basic fallacy of 'historicism', if I am correct in interpreting what I take to be Weber's view, was the idea that, through emphatic 'understanding' of the cultural orientations of a system alone, either it was possible to *explain* action within it without reference to any analysis in terms of generalized theory, or explanation itself was thought irrelevant. Weber's position in repudiating both doctrines means that, in *this* crucial sense, there is not 'natural' or 'cultural' science, there is only science or nonscience and all empirical knowledge is scientific in so far as it is valid. It is not possible here to take the space to ground this view—only to state that it was very clearly asserted by Weber, and is of the very first importance. In particular it may be noted that Marxism still adheres basically to a position of historical relativity which is incompatible with Weber's position.

The new thing in Weber, beyond this position itself, was the claim that not only was it methodologically essential, if causal knowledge of value-oriented human action was to be achieved, to develop general analytical theory in the social sciences, but it was entirely feasible, a proposition which had been vehemently denied in the historicist tradition. Indeed Weber himself tackled this task at its very core. This seems to me to have been one primary aspect of the significance of his embarking in the famous series of comparative studies in the sociology of religion. In the essay on the Protestant Ethic he cut into the centre of a major problem of 'historical' explanation. In the older tradition the indicated procedure would have been to delve even more deeply into the specific historical antecedents both of Protestantism and of capitalism in the West. Instead, Weber quite deliberately chose to develop an 'experimental design' by which he studied the negative cases where 'capitalism' had failed, under what he showed to be comparative circumstances,[1] to develop. My essential point is that Weber chose this method not only in order to help to demonstrate his thesis about the relation between Protestantism and capitalism, but *also* to show the importance and the feasibility of generalized analytical theory in the cultural sphere. His most developed product in this respect was the section on the Sociology of Religion in *Wirtschaft und Gesellschaft*. This is elementary theory, but for more than a generation it has been far in advance of anything else in the field. Such propositions as that stating the intimate relations between a religious ethic and the phenomenon of prophecy, or with reference to the dispositions of different kinds of social strata to different religious orientations are examples of the propositional content of this scheme. Indeed there is a sense in which this was the major 'pay-off' of Weber's new orientation, the commitment to and development of a generalized analytical science in the field precisely of the cultural content which the historicist tradition had declared completely inaccessible to such methods. This, essentially, was what Weber meant by sociology as a theoretical discipline.

4. *Verstehen*

There was, however, one essential component of his methodology which has not yet been treated. Weber, that is to say, had to cope with the doctrine that the methodological dichotomy between nomothetic and ideographic orientations coincided with that between observation of 'external' realities in almost the physical sense and participation with the object of observation through *Verstehen*. It is necessary to discuss this problem briefly in order to complete the methodological picture.

It can, I think, correctly be said that Weber dealt with this

---

[1] The two studies of religion and society in China and India respectively. The study of Ancient Judaism belongs in a different category.

problem area as an integral part of his general methodology. First it was essential that he should make clear that *both* the understanding of cultural meaning-systems as such—e.g. mathematical-propositions—and of motivational meanings 'intended' by individual actors should be included. Without clarity on this point the essential bridge between cultural levels and those of the concrete actions of individuals could not have been built. The concept of *Verstehen* was, however, also intimately connected with all three of the other methodological doctrines which have just been reviewed.

First, let me suggest an important relation to the concept of *Wertbeziehung*. Not only are the non-scientific values of the investigator himself and his culture involved, but also those of the persons and collectivities which are the object of his investigation. At the level of *Verstehen* scientific investigation is basically a process of meaningful *communication*, even though, where for example the objects are dead, it is a one-way process. In principle, however, it would always be desirable to have the object available for interviews, and taking his written expressions, accounts of him by others, etc., is always second best—thus to be able to interview Brutus about Caesar's death would, from the point of view of certain definitions of that event as an 'historical individual', have been highly desirable.

We can now say that effective communication in human cultural–symbolic terms, *always* involved the sharing of values at some level and in some respects. At the same time, however, the values shared in the nature of the case cannot be those of a total cultural *Gestalt*. If this were the case the investigator would be enclosed within a basically solipsistic system, as that problem has been outlined above. What must be conceived to be shared are value-components, which are relevant to the particular investigative problems and are in principle isolable from others of the investigator's own culture. If anything Weber seems to have underestimated the possibilities of extension of understanding on these bases, as some of his remarks on the impossibility of understanding very primitive peoples seem, in the light of the development of anthropology, to indicate. From this point of view *Verstehen*, of course, is both a method and a result of the investigative process. As method it is as noted inherently dependent on the sharing of values and motivational meanings between investigator and object.

The relation of these conditions to value-freedom in turn is patent. *Only* the investigator who is capable of differentiating his role from that of simply a participant in his general culture can attain the perspective and the objectivity necessary to select out those elements which are essential to his scientific purposes from those of his own culture which are irrelevant to it. The science itself, that is, must have its *own* value-system which articulates both in that of the culture in which the investigator participates and in that of the objects he studies. The clear implication is that of a basic *universalism* of values involved in social science, which are not particular to any cultural complex. This seems to point to the grain of truth in Karl Mannheim's well-known doctrine about the special status of the 'free intelligentsia' who were not fully bound into their cultures—however inadequate Mannheim's analysis of this phenomenon. This is a crucial sense in which Weber, as comparative sociologist, *could not* be a radical relativist with respect to values.[1]

If, however, the *Wertbeziehung* of the social-scientific investigator is emancipated from boundness to any particular cultural complex, how is it to be conceived to be controlled by standards of genuine relevance? There is an entirely clear answer in Weber's scheme, namely by virtue of the generality of theoretical conceptualization and of the canons of empirical validity. Science is, precisely, one of the primary elements of a generalized cultural system which is most specifically governed by general norms, the familiar norms of objectivity both in verification of statements of empirical facts, and in logical inference and analysis. Thus once again the central importance of Weber's break with the particularism of the historicist tradition becomes evident. The general loosening up of his methodological position through differentiation keeps leading him back to the view that, if the values of science are to be differentiated from the diffused general value complex, then if their interdependence with others in defining relevance, both in the direction of the object observed and the observer himself, is taken into account, and finally if the crucial facts are to be accessible through *Verstehen*, then the process as a whole must be subject to control through general theory of the *logical* type already established in the natural sciences. In *this* crucial respect Weber aligned himself with the basic 'utilitarian' tradition,

[1] Cf. Dieter Henrich, *Die Einheit der Wissenschaftslehre Max Webers* (Tübingen, 1952).

ry, against both historicism
the basic *autonomy* of both
eory of science, relative both
r value-commitments of the
ese considerations over any
lar complexes of meaning or

sketch of some problems of
would like to endorse em-
y Professor Henrich that these
t the level of the methodology
. Basically Weber is not con-
nds on which valid empirical
g and motivated action is or is
es this for granted. What he
f the structure of such know-
the more general culture of
re concerned with the episte-
rn physicist with the question
lly' exists, or the biologist of
rence between living organism
ps the most fundamental of all
d through a basic *differentiation*
hich he started.¹

IVE SOCIOLOGY

of the immense importance of
s I have sketched it. Yet had his

cially if he is schooled in the German
osition taken in the whole of the dis-
s very considerably from that of Karl
eidelberg in the summer semester 1929
of historicism and to Marxism it seems
etrogressive as compared with that of
dgment of von Schelting (*Max Webers*
ugh I would extend the criticism over a
It seems to me that Mannheim mainly
pes of position more explicit rather than
dition to the scheme of empirical proof
should emphasize the role of general
never really faced this issue; rather than
ltural complexes in which ideological
tive thought, were rooted.

writings been confined to these questions, the occasion we are here celebrating would have been far less significant than it is. Weber's methodology was meant, and in fact served, as the framework of a *substantive* contribution of the first importance. Its importance cannot, however, be properly assessed without seeing the connection between the two.

Of course Weber had laid very extensive and substantial foundations for his substantive sociology before the methodological revolution which began with the essays on Roscher and Knies. This phase of his work was, however, as is well known, concomitant with an equally new set of substantive investigations and analysis, the first of which was the famous monograph on the *Protestant Ethic and the Spirit of Capitalism.* There is, I think, an exceedingly important set of relations between these two parts of his work.

1. *Sociology of law*

I should like strongly to suggest that the core of Weber's substantive sociology lies neither in his treatment of economic and political problems nor in his sociology of religion, but in his sociology of law. It is thus striking that, in *Wirtschaft und Gesellschaft*, after the very condensed statement of his methodological position, he begins immediately to outline his classification of the types and components of *normative order* in society (Sec. II, Par. 4, beginning with the concepts of Brauch and Sitte). He comes furthermore very quickly to the concept of *legitimate* order, which is the nodal point where the concepts of law, of political authority and of the social role of religious ethics come together.

This central emphasis is, of course, thoroughly understandable in the light of Weber's personal history, his training and early academic career in the field of jurisprudence. The tendency to dichotomize emphases as between *Idealfaktoren* and *Realfaktoren*, however, seems to have operated to obscure the continuing importance of this node, since law cannot be nearly allocated either to the one or to the other, but is the principal mediating structure between them. It is, however, very clear that Weber, precisely as a sociologist rather than a political scientist or economist, considered political and economic structures, and processes, not to be understandable without full analysis of their relation to normative order—witness the crucial role of the concept of authority in his political analysis and, on the other hand, he did not think the analysis of religious values and meaning systems could be made relevant to understanding concrete social action without understanding how they affected conceptions of normative order and the legitimacy of its different types.[1]

It is then the very centrality of the problem of the relation between the two sets of factors in human socio-cultural action which, in my opinion, underlies the centrality of the topic of law as, in advanced societies, the focus of practically significant normative order in Weber's work. It was above all by virtue of this emphasis and the substantive analyses he presented, that Weber was able to develop a fundamental resolution of the dualism which kept, figuratively speaking, the Marxes and the Hegels perpetually 'setting each other on their heads'.[2]

Without attempting to discuss the complex problems in detail, I may suggest that the crucial focus of Weber's sociology of law lies in the concept of *formal rationality* which, though by no means confined by Weber to the field of law, was certainly particularly strongly emphasized there. The criterion of formal rationality designates a level of differentiation of the normative order at the societal level by virtue of which it can become relatively independent in both directions in the ideal–real series. Legal decisions then are no longer a simple application of *ethical* orientations as, for example, has tended to be the case in systems of religious law such as the Jewish or the Islamic supplemented by casuistry, which often became very elaborate, while on the other hand they can become also relatively independent of more particularistic politics and economic interest-constellations.

The implication of this is that, for its full effect to be felt, the

---

[1] It is perhaps worth noting here that a primary focus of ambiguity in Marxian thought lies in the problem of the relation of legal order to the famous concept of the *Produktionsverhältnisse*. It has long seemed to me that Marx was simply unclear on the problem of how far the element of legal order in such structures, e.g. the *authority* of management in the firm, was a simple epiphenomenon of either his economic interests or his power position or a combination of the two. Weber's analysis came directly to grips with the core of this problem.

[2] It is of course clear that the logic of this dichotomy is essentially the same as the one of heredity *versus* environment in the history of biological thought. To my mind arguing whether the 'ideal' or the 'real' factors ultimately determine human action is today exactly as futile as arguing whether hereditary *or* environmental factors ultimately determine the nature of organic life. In both cases it is clearly a matter of complex interdependence among equally essential but differently operating factors.

D

system of legal norms itself must become relatively *universalistic*. It must be organized in terms of general principles when related to more particular facts. Another particularly important point is the development of procedural institutions, which emancipates the legal system from boundness to particular precepts so long as it provides procedures for arriving at legal solutions—thus though English Common Law has been less highly rationalized than Continental Roman Law in systematization of legal doctrines, it has been even more highly developed on the procedural side. Finally relative independence, both from political and from religious authority, both of the judiciary and of the private legal profession, have been very important phenomena, slowly becoming more prominent in the course of legal history.

2. *The sociology of political and economic life*

As I suggested above, Weber's sociology of law is an essential key to the understanding of his analysis of political and economic phenomena. The most important single link is perhaps the conception of rational–legal authority. This conception incorporates all the essentials of a highly developed legal order as just outlined, in specific relation to the organization of governmental authority and power. Under this pattern of authority political leadership is itself legally bound in the framework of something like a constitution, but equally by virtue of this legal framework it is in certain respects independent of ethical and religious control in either the traditionalistic or the charismatic senses.[1] It is then a characteristic of rational–legal authority that legitimation applies first to the legal or constitutional order itself, and only through it to the particular positions of authority which operate under it and then to their incumbents. The concept of legitimation therefore is the primary link in the other direction between the legal order, and through it the political system, and the cultural system, particularly values and religious orientations. In this respect the hallmark of both traditional and charismatic authority patterns is that neither presupposes the same order of differentiated legal system as does the

[1] On a previous occasion I have attempted to show that Weber's three famous types of authority do not lie on the same level, but that the traditional and the charismatic are developmentally different from the rational–legal. Cf. my article, 'Authority, Legitimation and Political Action', which appeared originally in *Nomos I: Authority* (C. J. Friedrich, ed.) and is reprinted in my volume *Structure and Process in Modern Societies* (Free Press, 1961), chap. V.

rational–legal, but rather a much more direct legitimation of political action, on the one hand by virtue of a traditionally given diffuse status, on the other of a non-traditional assumption of moral authority. Both are, so far as they are in Weber's sense 'rational' at all, cases of 'substantive' rather than formal rationality.

Similar considerations apply to the economic field. As contrasted with the utilitarian tradition it is first notable that Weber never dealt with economic problems without careful attention to their political context. Of course, in many organizational contexts, the degree of independence of economic processes and interests, on the one hand from conditionalized and diffuse *Gemeinschaft* structures, on the other from political authority, is low. Weber was, however, particularly interested in the situations and conditions where this independence did develop and this was to him a primary aspect of modern capitalism.

Here again the legal reference was very prominent, in particular to the institutionalization of property and contract at legal levels. In terms of Weber's empirical interests it is somewhat overshadowed by his concern with the more direct effects of commitments to a religious ethic on economic behaviour, as above all in the case of the Protestant Ethic. There are, however, two things to be said in this connection. First, quite clearly the development of legal systems in the Western world, particularly perhaps in England, was closely connected with various conditions of economic development, and Weber repeatedly lists a firm legal order among the most important conditions of markets and of capitalism. The keynote here is the calculability of market chances. Secondly, where this kind of condition is not present, the orientation of action to economic considerations is in the nature of the case severely limited because of its diffuse ascription to non-economic elements such as ethnic and kinship groupings or religiously motivated collective solidarity.

One further important conclusion emerges. This is that, in the substantive sociological sense, Weber's theoretical scheme is inherently evolutionary. The comparative emphasis is legitimate and essential. There is no simple linear process at the level dealt with even by a Comte or a Marx, and many outcomes are dependent on highly variable contingencies. Nevertheless Weber was committed to the attempt to set forth a general picture of a 'modern' type of social organization which, as it happened, emerged in its later phases primarily in the Western world, and which was qualitatively different in an evolutionary sense from anything found in other civilizations. He tended to characterize this as rational bourgeois 'capitalism', but the economic stress in the designation is not sufficient or even crucial. It was, at the very least, conceived as a very comprehensive complex of institutional components, in which universalistic law and rational–legal authority, as well as profit-oriented economic enterprise play a central part.

3. *The sociology of religion*

The third primarily important part of Weber's substantive sociological contribution is in the cultural area, centring, of course, his famous studies in the sociology of religion. Since they have already been mentioned a number of times only a few points about them need to be made. The first, of course, is to repeat that, however important Weber's historical interest in ascetic Protestantism and its relations to the rest of Christianity and to the political and economic order of Western society, the primary thrust of his concern with religion is comparative and systematic, including in the latter a pronounced evolutionary reference; I have suggested above that the programme of comparative studies in this field was meant in part as a demonstration not only of the importance but of the feasibility of generalized analysis in the cultural field, a field which had tended to be accepted as the citadel of historicist particularism.

Secondly, there is an important problem which concerns the relative priority of Weber's treatment of religion as compared with law and with the political and economic spheres. With respect to the primary differentiating influence on the development of types of culture and society, there is no doubt that Weber assigned priority to the systems of religious orientation. Incomplete as was his study in final execution, this conclusion emerges clearly from the design and findings of his series of comparative studies in the sociology of religion. Given his evolutionary perspective, this primacy with respect to the differentiation of types of socio-cultural system must of course be linked with the evolutionary strain in his thought. It seems to follow that it is in the religious sphere and subject to that, other spheres of culture like ethical conceptions and science, that we have to seek the primary loci of the major creative innovations, whether they operate, as Weber tended to feel, by charismatic 'breakthrough' or by other types of process.[1] It should, however, be made clear that this assertion of the priority of the cultural elements in certain contexts of control and differentiation of type, does not imply a reversion to an idealistic emanationist point of view, which denies the independent causal significance of the 'real' or 'material' factors. Weber is perfectly clear on the significance of the latter in general terms, and has probably made larger contributions than any single writer of his generation, if not since, to the understanding of a wide variety of detailed problems of just how they operate.

This sense of the priority of cultural factors, and hence of the sociology of religion in Weber's work, must be carefully distinguished from the sense in which I have contended that the sociology of law, as the centrally significant aspect of normative order in social systems, is the nodal centre of his sociology as a whole. There is a very important and subtle relation here between the conception of the universalism, and at the same time the independence, of law, and the theme that the analyst of social systems should both be objective in the sense in which its relation to the concept of *Wertfreiheit* has been discussed, and that in order to do so he should operate with generalized theoretical categories.

Law, that is to say, is, as both Weber and his great French contemporary Émile Durkheim recognized, the primary structural focus of societies, the more definitely so the more advanced they are. The cultural legitimation of legal systems, however, lies in their grounding in the religious orientations of their populations and their historic antecedents. Law is thus the primary focus of the comparative and developmental analysis of societies. Interpretations of its deeper meaning, however, must rest on analysis of the cultural systems in which these meanings are grounded.

Social science, like any other rational discipline, is in the first instance grounded in culture; it is an enterprise of the human investigator in his quest for interpretation of the meanings of the

---

[1] This general point of view is in accord with the conception that, to use the terms of current cybernetic theory, cultural systems, as primarily systems of 'information' in a specific sense are, given the requisite conditions, capable of controlling the higher 'energy' systems of political and economic action. A succinct and illuminating account of the relevance of cybernetic theory to social and political systems is given in Karl W. Deutsch, *The Nerves of Government*, chap. V.

human condition which are relevant to him. As such there is a reference, both to the values of scientific investigation itself, in its essentially autonomous way, and behind that to the more general value system.

The structure of the scientific discipline itself, however, the more so the more mature it becomes, is defined in terms of its theoretical uniformities and generalizations. Precisely in so far as the social sciences become autonomous relative to their philosophical and other cultural groundings, this autonomous structure is to be found in the first instance in the structure of its generalized conceptual system. Weber stood somewhat hesitantly before this conclusion, and definitely did not present a 'theoretical system' in a fully developed sense. He did, however, point a direction which to me is unmistakable. In any case the congruence between the structure of his methodological position and the structural relations among the components of his substantive sociology seems to me to be of first-order significance.

WEBER AND THE PROBLEM OF IDEOLOGY

The body of this paper has been couched at the level of relatively technical, though by no means detailed, discussion of Max Weber's ideas in the fields of the methodology of social science and of his substantive sociology. We began, however, with certain major problems of the state of Western society in the present century and the relations of the prevailing patterns of social thought to these problems in the role of ideologies. In conclusion I would like to return to these themes.

First I would like to emphasize again that the three main patterns of social thought which together constituted Weber's reference system, were at the same time more technical positions on the framework of social science and foci of ideological orientations. Ideologically the idealist–historicist position may be treated as at least closely related to conservative ideologies in the European sense. These have been on the whole those which were more favourable to the old Europe and its civilization, with a certain, though by no means complete, presumption that its primary trustees should be the older aristocratic classes, particularly in their role of cultural élites. On occasion this could shift over, as in certain respects it did with the Nazis, to the view that a total 'people' should become the bearers of (in a severely vulgarized version) the great tradition.

In any case, this historicist–conservative base can plausibly be contrasted with not one, but two, directions of challenge to it and, from the point of view of its proponents, threats to its integrity. The older of these, which most Germans, and indeed Continental Europeans, felt to be basically 'foreign' to them, was what I have called the utilitarian system, especially in the form of the ideology of 'economic individualism', or more pointedly 'capitalism'. Here a particularly salient point is the *common* antagonism of continental conservatives *and* socialists in this ideological sense, to capitalism. The second direction of course was the socialistic, which came more and more to focus in the Marxian system.

I have already spelled out the principal respects in which Weber took a technically intellectual course which rejected acceptance of any of these three traditions, though he adopted important elements from all three. Broadly the same can be said ideologically, with an important qualification. He was almost unequivocally antagonistic to what he conceived, in the intellectual–political situation of his time in Germany, to be both the conservative and the socialist positions, though for the former he did not un-equivocally repudiate nationalism, nor for the latter the theme of 'social justice'. Toward the capitalistic alternative, on the other hand, he seemed to be much more markedly ambivalent. He re-garded 'capitalism', including bureaucratic organization, both private and governmental, as essentially the 'fate' of Western society, yet he had grave misgivings about its implications, especially in 'humanistic' contexts.

I wonder whether it is going too far to suggest that this indicates a rather definite attempt to break out of the idealist–materialist, or historicist–Marxist dilemma, but with a good deal of indecision as to whether it was advisable and where it could lead. Clearly to him 'capitalism' in some sense had to be accepted, but equally on a variety of grounds, scientific and ethical, the prevailing inter-pretations were on the one hand inadequate to the phenomenon itself, on the other out of accord with his feelings of rightness and appropriateness.

On the level of the more technical aspects of his thought, Weber clearly broke out of what I have called the 'trilemma' presented by the structure of the principal currents of social thinking of his time. His resolution of the trilemma pointed in the direction of a new pattern of thinking in the area, of which an autonomous theoretical sociology was an essential ingredient. On this level Weber clearly converged with other parts of a major intellectual movement of his generation. Taking his contribution—which I regard as the most crucial single one—along with many others I think it can be said that the whole intellectual–social situation has been redefined in a way that makes the principal categorizations of the late nineteenth century, many of which are still widely current, basically obsolete.[1]

I would go farther to suggest that Weber's 'fourth position' could not be absorbed simply into another ideology, to compete on the same level with the other three. It is, from this point of view, no accident that it is impossible to classify Weber politically as a 'conservative' in the older German tradition, as a 'liberal' in the economic individualist sense, or as a 'socialist'. His intellectual breakthrough meant, however, more than a 'neutral' personal position as among these ideological positions it was an implied assertion that the time would come when these old alignments would no longer be meaningful. To use the phrase made current in the United States recently by Daniel Bell, Weber heralded 'the end of ideology' in the sense in which that concept has been so prominent in the earlier part of the present century.

It may very well be that there is a relation between this situation and the political and social situation of our time. I noted that the outbreak of the First World War, just a half-century ago, marked the beginning of the end of the European system of national states as that had taken shape in the nineteenth century, and of its dominance in the world. The most important single source of that loss of dominance of course has been the emergence of the two supranational units, the United States to the West, the Soviet Union to the East, which are of an order of magnitude and power altogether different from the classical national state. The rapid

---

[1] The most comprehensive treatment of this movement so far available is, to my knowledge, H. Stuart Hughes, *Consciousness and Society*. My own *Structure of Social Action* (1937) dealt with the more directly sociological aspects, especially, besides Weber, Durkheim and Pareto, and some of the relations to the tradition of economic individualism. Now it seems to me particularly that Freud, and the American pragmatists and social psychologists, such as G. H. Mead and John Dewey, have played a very important part.

decline of 'colonialism' can in turn be related to these changes, as can the European unification movement.

It is surely notable in this connection that the three principal intellectual positions which figured in the background of Weber's work, and which have been the foci of the principal modern ideologies, are very clearly related to the structure of the Western systems. First, the idealist–historicist pattern of thought has been characteristic of the centre in the first instance of Germany, particularly western and southern Germany, and in different respects of France. Then clearly the utilitarian system and the ideologies of economic individualism have been most prevalent in Great Britain, and from there the United States, at least for a considerable time. The case of Marxism may seem not to fit. With, however, its very strong emphasis on primacy of political organization, within that of authoritarianism and bureaucracy of certain types, there seems to me to be more than a little affinity between Prussianism and Soviet Marxism. It is perhaps not stretching a point too far to suggest that there is a certain symmetry between the wings of the system and that as one moved from the cultural centres of Continental Europe eastward there has been an increase in centralized political authoritarianism which is in some sense 'socialistic', whereas moving westward, the climate became increasingly 'capitalistic'. At any rate the ideological polarization of the cold war period has certainly been on the basis of the intellectual conflict between utilitarian individualism and Marxian socialism. I am inclined to regard this, however, as part of a still more general aspect of the situation of Western society in which Prussian authoritarianism has also been involved.

In the light of these considerations Weber's achievement, in the crucial field of the intellectual analysis of social and cultural phenomena, of a position which clearly transcended *all* of the three ideologically central positions in such a way as to include in relativized form contributions from all of them, takes on a special significance. It seems to me that Weber stood at a very crucial juncture in the whole development of Western civilization. He understood, as hardly any of his contemporaries did, the fact and nature of the break-up of the older system, and he contributed more than any single figure to the outline of a new intellectual orientation which promises to be of constitutive importance in defining the situation for the emerging social world.

With respect to my own country I have long felt that the designation of its social system as 'capitalistic' even in Weber's highly sophisticated sense, was grossly inadequate. It seems increasingly probable that trends in the Soviet Union will make the more stereotyped conception of it as the 'socialist' society just as inappropriate. In any case I cannot refrain from feeling that the emergence of the science of sociology, of which I regard Max Weber as one of the very few true founders, is a harbinger of these great changes, and that our science may well be destined to play a major role, not only in its primary task of understanding the social and cultural world we live in as object of its investigations but, in ways which cannot now be foreseen, in actually shaping that world. In this sense it may possibly turn out to be the most important heir of the great ideologies of the turn of the last century. This possibility is perhaps the truest measure of the greatness of Max Weber.

Value-freedom and Objectivity

MAX HORKHEIMER

I learnt about value-freedom in Max Weber's sense of the word when I was a student of his in 1919. Like many of my comrades I was deeply interested in understanding the Russian Revolution. In 1917 the Bolsheviks had been the first to call a halt to the war with their cry of 'Peace and bread!' Thus it appeared that backward Russia was to devote her energies not to final victory but to setting up a better society. The question for us was to understand what these events signified for world history, what attitude the peoples of the West, particularly Germany, should take to them. Was it possible to strengthen the positive impulses of the process and limit the negative ones, to avoid radical isolation and retrogression into a new and dangerous nationalism? The politically alert were already aware of the first signs of a development which in Russia tended towards Stalinism, and in Germany to National Socialism.

Max Weber lectured on the Soviet system. The auditorium was crowded to its doors, but great disappointment followed. Instead of theoretical reflection and analysis, which, not only in posing the problem, but in every single step of thinking would have led to a reasoned structuring of the future, we listened for two or three hours to finely balanced definitions of the Russian system, shrewdly formulated ideal types, by which it was possible to define the Soviet order. It was all so precise, so scientifically exact, so value-free that we all went sadly home.

Even later the theory of value-freedom did not become wholly clear to me. It is probably connected with the aim of philosophy. Sociology and psychology, as the last great disciplines of philosophy, have freed themselves from the attempt to look at the world as embodying meaningful behaviour. Philosophy itself, apart from restorative ontologies, became epistemology, methodology, logic and historical imitation of systems. With the resignation of philosophy, which formerly was extensively motivated by the effort to support or supersede religion, the need necessarily arose for a guiding line for action, for a basis for correct value-judgments.

51

This conscious or unconscious need was further strengthened by the decline of liberalism after the turn of the century. At a time when the economy was characterized by a relatively large stratum of independent employers, the form of behaviour considered the best for any individual's enterprise was also widely held to be the best, indeed the correct form for the whole of society. Today, in the day of great multiple concerns, fewer and fewer decisions made by the individual concerning himself and society depend on his own free judgment. Value-judgment has become questionable in two senses. The objective toward which it might have been directed, which in earlier centuries was the behest of a divinity and later that of one's own enterprise and of the existing social whole, had disappeared.

Max Weber wanted to eliminate value-judgment from sociology. Freud explained it, and thereby eliminated it. The inner voice, the conscience, is not a final, nor as Blaise Pascal taught us, a reliable arbiter. Truthfulness, efficiency, readiness to answer for others, are according to him conditions for existence in bourgeois reality at a time when the idea of the family was to some extent still intact. This idea, handed down by the father, internalized finally by the child, was in the last resort a scientifically understandable mechanism, not some kind of obligatory idea.

Weber's doctrine of value-freedom, no less than that of charisma, is an expression of his own times; he is wholly with them, not against them. Value-judgment should be justified by the setting of the task, not by its execution. Countless sociological investigations actually make a clean break with the purpose they are supposed to serve. Once the order is given by oneself or someone else, it is carried out according to the most progressive, independent rules and techniques. So it should be, according to Weber's conception. On the other hand, in that theory of society which is concerned with what is right, what Weber meant by the concept of value— and which has since then become a mere cliché—enters into every phase of cognition.

To measure bourgeois society by the ideas to which it subscribes —freedom and justice, respect for the individual—to express the discrepancy between idea and reality; and to promote the possibility of overcoming such discrepancy requires us, not less than in the time of Condorcet and the Saint-Simonists, to define autonomous and responsibility theory. The more refined apparatus

of investigation nowadays could make such thinking more penetrating, whereas actually it is threatening to disappear. How social
phenomena are structured, which kind of autonomous sociological
investigation is decisive, and which inconclusive, depends on the
continuing interaction between those ideas and the course taken
by the investigation. If by value-freedom is not meant the obvious
platitude that the scientist wears neither pink nor black glasses,
and is not misled by his followers or by hate, then it means
inhibition of thought—not at all a likely presupposition. In the
whole, as in each detailed part, theoretical study consists everywhere equally of unerring devotion to the actual, and of constantly renewed value-judgments.

As we left the lecture-theatre that day with such disappointment,
we thought that Max Weber must be ultraconservative. This conclusion was however over-hasty. Soon afterwards in his lectures, as
Professor Parsons has said, Weber came into conflict with the
old-style conservative students, the guilds. I was not against this,
but think his explanations were not always so value-free as they
seemed to him. Perhaps today—after a period marked by charismas
and much else—he would have agreed with me that sociology
cannot be completely divorced from philosophical obligation, and
that sociologists must still make value-judgments even after their
research subjects are already decided upon.

LEOPOLD VON WIESE

In our present-day interpretations of the problems of evaluation in
sociology, two points seem to be worthy of special consideration:
firstly, that the intellectual situation has altered considerably in the
fifty years since Max Weber's time, and secondly, that we must
make a sharper distinction between evaluating in daily life, which
is ruled by moral and aesthetic norms, on the whole, and the
value-judgments which are pronounced in works of scientific
literature. A value-judgment in communication between men is
different from such a judgment in print.

To the first point—what was valid half a century ago has today
only a diminished validity. Let us compare the intellectual situation
at the first German Sociological Congress in October 1910 under
Tönnies's chairmanship, when Weber gave his so-called business
report. He then proposed to make the Press the subject of a value-

free investigation. The warning contained in that suggestion was just as relevant as the actual topic of that first congress, the race question. I had to make my modest maiden speech in the discussion and said: 'While one may be in doubt as to whether the exclusion of all value-judgment is appropriate to the discussion of many sociological problems, at least in discussing the race question any value-judgment must be absolutely ignored'.

If we transpose that situation to the present time, we will more easily grasp the vehemence with which Weber's demand for value-freedom was advocated. During and after Alfred Ploetz's speech on the race question it became obvious how sharply moral and political conviction split the theoreticians. For some, sociology was a new philosophy, and a modern confession of faith. They were opposed by the sceptics, who doubted precisely this function of sociology. They preferred to see the young discipline principally as the method of a specialized science. But even in the narrow circles of the specialist sociologists there were considerable differences of opinion, for instance between Simmel's strictly defined specialist science or Tönnies's conception of sociology as the same as social philosophy. Gothein saw it more as historical–psychological research: for Ploetz it was a natural science.

Then came Weber's demand: above all no mingling with philosophies, no subjective evaluation. This was even more evident at the Second Congress in 1912, where such temperamental orators as Franz Oppenheimer and Robert Michels spoke.

Today the situation is very different. Principles have withdrawn into the background. Statistics is more of an example to many writers than are philosophy and ethics. In view of this the warning today should be: Do not forget that sociology must be above all a basis of ethics; or rather, the basis. Thus before one sets up hypotheses, the relevant facts should be extensively tested, and probed from many angles. The facts provide men with the points of departure and constant bases for norms and obligations. That is to say that neither is sociology a part of ethics, nor ethics a part of sociology, but each is dependent to a great extent on the other.

This brings us to our second point. Weber never made the claim that we, the intellectually trained, should become so objective, so liberated from our own personality that we only explain logically, but do not assess comparatively. He was too much a man of will for that, and always took sides.

In short, to turn intellectuals into mere reporters and to deprive them of any function of judgment was completely alien to him. But he also held 'sociology and psychology which strive for objectivity' as the bases of ethics. Yet to do justice to this task, it was in his opinion necessary within the realm of these sciences (and so for research proper) to limit oneself to the logical categories of analysis and systematization. One must above all reject the practice of interlacing the apparently quite objective and logically constructed web of thought with more or less concealed prejudices and thus present the subjective contents as ostensibly objective.

This veiling of value-judgments should even today be sternly rejected. It is not a question of exercising pressure to avoid any value-judgment, but of clearly separating the two parts, the objective and subjective parts, in so far as practicable—a necessary addendum, since a complete separation is impossible. Even the objective part will show a certain dependence on subjectivity.

Even in the choice of topics to be treated and the manner of fundamental observation, inclination and aversion on the part of the investigator come into play, in so far as he possesses freedom in the choice of subject and the manner of treatment. In relation to the confusion of experiences his sights are directed only to certain complexes of phenomena—he chooses from among them—and he will necessarily strive towards a definite aim, which is also influenced by his desires and aversions.

As so often in life, it is a matter of keeping a sense of proportion. Science must never impose mere dogma either overtly or covertly. But the demand for a limitation of value-judgments must not lead to a position where the scholar would have to admit he had no firm standpoint of his own: that he was only repeating what the world around revealed to him, that his ideal was photography.

HANS ALBERT

Since I am in substantial agreement with the views put forward by Professor Parsons, I should like just to make a few supplementary remarks relating particularly to the problem of values in the social sciences.

As Professor Parsons has emphasized, Weber's importance for the social sciences can be seen in his contribution to overcoming the methodological dualism of arts and sciences, and of related ideological thought. I am of the opinion that we today can go further in many respects than he thought possible, particularly regarding the condition and role of nomological knowledge in the social sciences, and the structure and application of theories. Theoreticians who claim to derive immediately from Max Weber, generally overlook the fact that scientific doctrine has developed much further since his time.[1]

His solution of the value-problems in social science, containing the method and principle of value-freedom, seems to me however to be essentially tenable, apart from certain utterances concerning the problem of so-called value-involvement (*Wertbeziehung*),[2] which stress unnecessarily the extent of remove from the natural sciences.[3] His principle of value-freedom has become one of the essential starting-points for those attempts to defeat Max Weber which *de facto* involve not so much the critical adoption and development of his findings, as a regression to views which he himself had already discarded. It is very interesting to observe how these attempts often concern themselves affectionately with biographical details in order to show the origins of his opinions, and then without any methodological analysis worthy of the name, demonstrate the untenability of his opinions in the light of modern research, and hint at their dangerous influence. The display of biographical work bears no relation to the amount of objective analysis of the problems. Sociology is not so much concerned with Weber's biography as with the question of a serviceable methodological conception.

We are in no way obliged to consider as particularly important the somewhat undifferentiated methodological views expounded in the inaugural speech at Freiburg, which many of his present-day critics mention prominently, nor to prefer this in any way to his later works, based on fundamental consideration of methodological

[1] Cf. e.g Karl R. Popper, *The Poverty of Historicism* (London, 1957); also Ernest Nagel, *The Structure of Science* (London, 1961) (particularly the last three chapters) and the works of Carl G. Hempel, Paul Oppendheim, and Jürgen V. Kempski.

[2] 'Value-relevance' or 'reflection to values' was a term used by Weber to emphasize that there were necessarily criteria for the selection of factual data in any scientific enquiry. The study of culture he saw, as in this respect, more circumscribed than natural science because the investigator had an interpretative role in forming the values of own culture—Eds.

[3] Cf. e.g. Ernest Nagel, 'Problems of Concept and Theory Formation in the Social Sciences', reprinted in *Theorie und Realität* (Tübingen, 1964).

questions. Of course it is relatively easy to criticize his idea of freeing science from endogenous evaluations in order to make it open to exogenous evaluations when applied in practice, and easy to show that this idea is genetically connected with his very problematic nationalism, his ideal of the national power-state. This can be linked with speculations on the dangers of subordinating science to politics, speculations only very indirectly connected with his views. In any case this is simpler than trying to argue with the differentiated solution of the problem of values which he put forward later and which does not offer any starting-points for broad-sweeping counter-arguments.

Despite zealous reading, I have not encountered any attempt to overcome his principles of value-freedom that was not open to relatively simple objections. At the back of such attempts one can discover time and time again (1) a lack of discrimination between the different aspects of complex value-problems, and (2) an underestimation of the possibilities of a social science which is in any certain sense value-free, in which there may be a partial connection with the idea that the principle of value-freedom in some way means a limitation of the possibilities of knowledge, an idea which arises sometimes from older philosophical traditions, but often from mere confusion.

Like Professor Parsons I am also of the opinion that Max Weber's solution of the problem of value has proved to be in essence an element of a useful methodological conception. On the one hand it makes it possible to examine and report on the actual state of values in every relationship. On the other hand it calls to account the value-basis of social scientific research itself, and points out quite correctly that the solutions of social scientific problems, i.e. the theories of these sciences, do not need to contain any value-judgments. The effective resources of the social sciences can be seen in the solution of actual problems.

Moreover the solution of practical problems, the examination of factual relationships on a theoretical basis, should be of great significance even in a practical respect. This is perhaps a point where we can go beyond Max Weber who inclines to emphasize the role of inflexible final evaluations with regard to norms. The results of the investigation of practical relationships are by no means only technologically relevant in a very narrow sense, as those theoreticians are wont to impute who do not ascribe to the

E

conception of a value-free social science the responsibility for an irrationalism otherwise present in the field of aims. Examples of this, such as that the examination of factual links can be significant for normative orientation, without the involvement of value-judgments, are to be found in scientific teaching itself.[1]

As for the importance of the social sciences for social living, the fact is often overlooked that it does not depend on the production of value-judgments but on the choice of the practical problem to be examined. However, we cannot treat relevant practical problems only from some point of view of values, but we can in the analysis neutralize to a great extent the so-called value problems, i.e. by a value-free approach, however paradoxical that may sound. The unbridgeable gap between final inflexible positions ought also to play a much smaller role than one might assume from Max Weber's emphasis.

Those who have decided to carry his scientific programme further in modern form would do well to give up the sometimes emotional trimmings of heroic positivism. This is possible without in the least detracting from the importance of Max Weber and his achievements.

One can moreover defend the view that the principles of the scientific method itself can be relevant to a certain degree for all social spheres, especially in so far as they are geared to the idea of critical examination.[2] This idea can be applied not only to propositional systems, but to social realities of the most diverse kinds. Even the critical investigation of propositional systems is a task which can be of great significance for social development, for such systems, if they are effective, are themselves social realities. One need only point out the importance of institutionalized ideologies to find evidence for this. The critical examination of propositional

[1] Professor Parsons has correctly pointed out that even value-free social science is subject to normative regulation, a fact which Max Weber takes into consideration. An examination of the methodological discussion shows that the airing of practical problems can considerably influence the orientation of research. The analysis of logical connections leads for example to the revision of our criteria for the relevance of theories, their examinability and verification, ideas as to possible modes of application, and so at the same time to a normative reorientation in the sphere of knowledge.

[2] Cf. Karl R. Popper, 'On the Sources of Knowledge and Ignorance', *Proceedings of the British Academy*, 46, 1960; William Warren Bartley, *The Retreat to Commitment* (New York, 1962); Paul K. Feyerabend, *Knowledge without Foundations* (Oberlin/Ohio, 1961); Hans Albert, 'Rationalität und Wirtschaftsordnung', in *Gestaltungsprobleme der Weltwirtschaft, Festschrift für Andreas Predöhol* (published by Herald Jürgensen, Göttingen, 1964).

structures is a feasible task for sociology, which itself belongs to the realm of social criticism. It is evident that it would be a serious misunderstanding if a social science which incorporates the principle of value-freedom in its methodological conception were to be considered neutral in every respect. A value-free social science can obviously be regarded as an instrument of enlightenment, as Ernst Topitsch has clearly shown in his paper.[1] Thus it is not at all consistent with the dogmatic notions of conservative forces which today are trying to turn to account isolated findings of social research. At a time when anti-enlightenment still dominates official thinking to a great extent, a sociology of Max Weber's stamp could well unsettle this state of affairs.

JÜRGEN HABERMAS

In the argument about value-judgments, Max Weber took up a position which unmistakably allots to the social sciences the task of producing knowledge capable of being utilized technically. Like all strict empirical analytical sciences they should provide information which can be translated into technical recommendations for a choice of means to a particular end. Conditional prognosis or causal explanations presuppose the knowledge of empirical uniformities. A social science suitable for that purpose will develop theories and test the validity of hypotheses with the aim of finding out reliable general rules of social behaviour. As far as required by the subject, the analysis can be facilitated by an understanding of motivation. The aim of this knowledge is however not the understanding of social facts but the causal explanation by means of ordered relationships. In this respect Max Weber accords methodologically subordinate status to the understanding of meaning. Parsons therefore claims with good reason that Weber was interested in knowledge as a part of a general theory of social behaviour. But Weber's interest in knowledge was wider than this.

For the student of Rickert, a cultural science cannot derive its interest from the investigation of empirical regularities. Its questions are not only directed to the analysis of the relative nature

[1] Cf. also his works in his volume of essays, *Sozialphilosophie zwischen Ideologie und Wissenschaft* (Neuwied, 1961).

of cultural phenomena but also to the explanation of their significance. From this point of view the deduction and verification of
hypotheses concerned with laws, from which technical recommendations can be made, lose their value: they form preliminary
studies, which as such do not lead us straight to the 'knowledge we
are striving for'. The analysis and orderly presentation of the
historically given, individual grouping of those factors and the
concrete interaction determined by them and significant in its own
way, and above all the clarification of the basis and the nature of
this significance would be the first task, admittedly to be solved by
application of this preliminary work, but 'completely new and
independent of it'.[1] Here it is not the understanding of the meaning, but the explanation which is given a methodologically
subordinate status.

My first question to Professor Parsons is this: Does not Max
Weber's interest in knowledge, going beyond the production of
knowledge which is technically usable, also aim at the explanation
of the significance of social processes? Three further questions may
clarify this first one. They are concerned in order with the methodological meaning of the three categories which Professor Parsons
has rightly distinguished: understanding, value-relativity and
value-freedom.

Understanding. Max Weber distinguished the motivational
understanding of a subjectively intentioned sense of action from
the so-called value-interpretation, related to the significance
objectivized in cultural values. In this sense single texts and entire
epochs both have 'significance'. Value-interpretation comprises not
a real linking but the ideal relationships proper to an evaluated
cultural object. It reveals in them the areas capable of objective
evaluation and discovers the concrete value-relationships to which
an historic object owes its individual meaning. Max Weber can
leave this task to the historic–philological sciences, for sociology
can find another approach to social realities. It approaches
subjectively the meaning of actions, and in so doing tends to
select hypothetically purposeful actions, governed according to
pure maxims of behaviour. A strict social science which 'seeks
to observe and understand behaviour and thereby explains its

---

[1] *Gesammelte Aufsätze zur Wissenschaftslehre,* 2nd revised and enlarged edition (Tübingen, 1951; subsequently quoted as W.L.), pp. 174 f.

course causally',[1] proceeds by normative analysis, as shown by the example of the theory of mathematical economics.

If, on the contrary, one makes sociology as Parsons does, a strictly empirical analytical science, social roles no longer coincide with a subjectively intended meaning which can be reconstructed in the form of pure maxims. Value-structures and chains of motivation go their separate ways. The understanding of motivation cannot open up the way to these value-structures. Approach to social realities of this kind can only be provided by a hermeneutic understanding in the manner of value-interpretation. If this is so, then the social sciences are burdened with the problem of *Verstehen* inherited from historicism. Parsons supersedes this problem by demanding a universalism of values: the meaning-contents objectivized in value-systems are to consist of elementary value-components, valid for all cultures and all epochs. Therefore my second question to Professor Parsons is this: does a *Verstehende* social science extend beyond the understanding of motivation to the dimension of a hermeneutic adoption of handed-down meaning-contents, for which Max Weber had provided something like value-interpretation?

Wertbeziehung. Rickert tried with the help of this concept to separate culture as the object of the historic–interpretative sciences from the concept of nature. The historian certainly does not communicate with his subject at sight alone: he fits it inevitably into the value-relationships of his own cultural situation. The transcendental sense of this category is also present in Max Weber: it is not related in the first place to the *choice* of scientific problems, but to the *constitution* of possible objects of cultural–scientific knowledge. Otherwise a firm distinction could not be made between natural and the cultural sciences.

Parsons, who rejects this distinction with regard to sociology, understands the methodological *Wertbeziehung* of the social researcher simply as obligation to the value-system of science. This dictates a strict division between the role of the investigator and the role of the member of a certain society. The cultural-specific values should guide the investigator in the choice of problems but not in the method of their treatment. Obviously in

---

[1] *Grundriss der Sozialökonomik*, vol. III, *Wirtschaft und Gesellschaft*, 2nd enlarged edition, 1st half-volume (Tübingen, 1925), p. 1.

Weber's conception *Wertbeziehung* enters more radically into the methods of the cultural sciences. In the natural sciences the theoretical points of view which guide the course of research are subject to control by the outcome of the research itself: they prove heuristically fruitful or yield nothing from which to educe useful hypotheses. The value-relationships, however, as guides to method in the cultural sciences remain transcendental to research as such: they cannot be corrected by the outcome of the investigation. When the light which had fallen from value-ideas onto the great problems of culture retreats, then the cultural sciences prepare to change their position and their apparatus of concepts, and make towards 'those constellations which alone are capable of giving meaning and direction to their work' (W.L. 214). Sociology owes to this constitutive *Wertbeziehung* its ability to place the causal–analytical knowledge of empirical stereotypes at the service of a more extensive interest in knowledge. 'We want to understand the nature of the reality of environment: the cultural significance of its various phenomena on the one hand, and the reasons for its having historically become thus and not otherwise' (W.L. 170 ff.). Max Weber himself was guided in his historical–sociological research by an idea which was decisive in his construction of concepts and his formation of theories: the idea of the rationalization of all social fields. It has often been remarked that the ideal types for the forms of authority, for the order of procedure in economy and law, for urban settlements and the forms of education are always formed and arranged in accordance with the private philosophy of history, from whose visual angle Weber interprets the whole development of society. This also explains the central position, emphasized by Parsons, of the sociology of law, which displays above all the concept of formal law: a system of general and abstract norms mediates between the purposive exchange between private owners of goods and the bureaucratic exercise of authority of a rational state institution. Even the preference in method, accorded by Max Weber on logical grounds to the model of purposive action, only has any prospect of making empirically substantial hypotheses possible beyond normative–analytical purposes, if that tendency is realized as a general rationalization.

My third question to Professor Parsons therefore is this: does the *Wertbeziehung* which is inevitable in the social sciences in regard to method, extend only to the selection of problems, or does it influence the formation of theories as such?

Value-freedom. Even if we start from the point that the bases of social scientific theories are dependent on general interpretations, without these being refutable according to criteria existing in the empirical sciences, such presuppositions can be explained. *Wertbeziehungen* are at one and the same time methodologically unavoidable and objectively not binding. We are therefore bound to declare the dependence of descriptive pronouncements on premises of normative content. In particular Weber explains the meaning of value-freedom in method in connection with the socio-technical devaluation of empirical–analytical knowledge. The knowledge of empirical ascertained patterns in social activity lends itself to technical recommendations for a purposeful choice of means, wherein the purposes themselves are merely hypothetical. The postulate of value-freedom is to be taken for granted in scientific theory. There is obvious ground for discussion in the scientific and political aspects connected by Weber with this postulate. He used it in order to restrict the social sciences to a cognitive interest, valid for the production of knowledge which can be utilized technically. The meta-theoretical assertion that this knowledge must have an exclusively descriptive content is scarcely worth our notice. The positivists' claim, however, that sociology's scope should be limited to this, has evoked doubts and protests. I will limit myself here to asking how this scientific–political claim is explained by Weber himself, although it contradicts the type of his own investigation, for instance the hermeneutic intention repeatedly stated: that is, to clarify the cultural significance of historical connections and from them to make the present social situation understandable.

It seems to me that we cannot separate Max Weber's methodology from his general interpretation of the tendencies in development which are relevant for the present time. In this respect we can learn from older researchers into Weber's work, from Löwith, Lanshut, and Freyer.[1] Weber took the increasing rational re-organization of the conditions of living as the guide for his analysis:

[1] K. Löwith, 'Max Weber and Karl Marx', in *Ges. Abhandlungen* (Stuttgart, 1960), pp. 1 ff.; S. Landshut, *Kritik der Soziologie* (Leipzig, 1928); H. Freyer, *Soziologie als Wirklichkeitswissenschaft* (Berlin, 1930).

A capitalist economic order, formalized legal procedures and bureaucratic hierarchy form the structures of a society, the institutionally independent spheres of which uniformly comprehend social behaviour. You know how Weber judged the steel-rigid container of this rationalized world we live in. It is precisely the form of organization intended to ensure the purposefulness of behaviour, i.e. to allow an optimal use of means for autonomously posited purposes, which limits the autonomy of individual choice. Max Weber finds the irrationalities of rationalization all collected in bureaucratization. The autocracy of bureaucratic ideals of life lead to the 'dividing up of the soul',[1] to the professional man without intellect and the pleasure-seeker without heart,[2] Weber conjured up a vision of a house of bondage, 'in which man will perhaps be forced to submit weakly, like the fellaheen in the Egyptian state'[3] and then formulated the cultural problem of the present-day thus: 'in view of this overwhelming power of the tendency towards bureaucratization, how is it at all possible to save any remnants of any kind of individual freedom of movement?' Weber's philosophical answer is this: decisionist self-assertion in the midst of a rationalized world: his political answer: scope for a leader, strong-willed and with an instinct for power—scope for the strong politician whose use of the expert civil servant is both authoritarian and rational, and for the private employer, who uses his business similarly.

The 'leader with a machine' is thus the social role which in a partially rationalized society appears to allow subjective purposefulness without the price of a heteronomy of aim. In this context the scientific–political claim of value-freedom also deserves a place. The experiential sciences are in an ambiguous way part of the general process of rationalization. They have disenchanted the world, and have taken away their claim to objective validity from the values and norms which orientate behaviour. Thus they make way first of all for an individual discrimination between subjectivized forces of belief. On the other hand, they too, like bureaucracy, follow the tendency to usurp the scope of decision, having

---

[1] *Gesammelte Aufsätze zur Soziologie und Sozialpolitik* (Tübingen, 1924), p. 414.

[2] *Gesammelte Aufsätze zur Religionssoziologie*, vol. I (Tübingen, 1920), p. 204 (cited hereafter as R.S.).

[3] *Gesammelte politische Schriften*, 2nd enlarged ed. (Tübingen, 1958), p. 320 (cited hereafter as G.P.S.).

first cleared the way. They must therefore be restricted to function as technical aids. So far as the postulate of value-freedom aims at restricting the social sciences to the production of technically utilizable knowledge, it is analogous to the political claim for protection of the decision-making authority from the competent expert's arrogance.

It is ironical, however, that, as we have seen, this recommendation of a restrictive concept of science rests on an interpretation of developments in the whole of society: an interpretation which, if it is to have validity, presupposes a more pretentious concept of sociology. In his own work Max Weber did not keep within the limits set by positivism: he was, however, in agreement with the Neo-Kantians, positivistic enough not to allow himself to reflect upon the connection between his methodological perspectives and rules, and the results of his social analysis.

My fourth question to Professor Parsons is therefore: how far can methodological decisions, which are obligatory for empirical analytical procedures in the social sciences, be discussed in connection with social processes?

In the same connection I should like to put a further question to the previous speaker, Professor Albert. He stressed the point that the value-free operation of social science not only produces knowledge of empirical patterns but can also be utilized for purposes of criticism. It is beyond doubt that the social sciences can examine accepted value-systems logically, and, in a given situation, also technologically. But does a normative definition of science, in this case in its application to social criticism, depend on the choice made by an individual scholar, or, as Popper thinks, on a choice influenced by a critical tradition—or does it arise simply from natural interest? However that may be, we are always obliged to account for such methodological principles and decisions. As sociologists we should not be afraid of judging those who determine the rules of analysis together with the social process that they analyse. Statements of this kind are not to be found within the bounds of strict empirical science. The business of an ideologically critical examination of the methodology of sociology cannot be relegated to the sociology of knowledge.

Please allow me a final intellectual historical observation. Professor Parsons has claimed that Max Weber's teaching is a development towards bringing about the end of ideology. Weber is said to have broken the trilemma of historicism, utilitarianism and Marxism, and to have led the way into the free field of discussion beyond the European fronts of civil war. I envy our American colleagues their political traditions which permit such a generous and (in the best sense of the word) liberal interpretation of Max Weber.[1] We here in Germany, who are still seeking for alibis, would only too gladly follow them. But Weber's political sociology has had a different history here. At the time of the First World War he outlined a sketch of Caesar-like leader-democracy on the contemporary basis of a national-state imperialism.[2] This militant latter-day liberalism had consequences in the Weimar period which we, and not Weber, must answer for. If we are to judge Weber here and now, we cannot overlook the fact that Carl Schmitt[3] was a 'legitimate pupil' of Weber's.[4] Viewed in the light of the history of influences, the decisionist element in Weber's sociology did not break the spell of ideology, but strengthened it.

DIETER HENRICH

In the following remarks I should like to try to confirm one of Professor Parsons's theses by a chain of thought which is very different from his, and yet leads to similar conclusions. I too think that Max Weber's work is based on a theory of empirical science in its relation to possible practice, which could lead beyond the traditional alternatives, even though in a form which does not allow us to accept it without any mediation, but compels the interpreter to expose and develop its principal features.

In order to carry out this task, may I remind you of the current image of Max Weber's position? It is common to those who in their judgment of this position are most unlike each other, the positivist and the Marxist interpreters of Weber.

When he formulated the postulate of value-freedom, he radically separated empirical research techniques (operations which enable one to make correct predictions) from the decisions taken by people in their everyday actions. In so doing he conceded to empirical research into social processes just that measure of objectivity which

[1] Cf. R. Bendix, *Max Weber—An Intellectual Portrait* (New York, 1960).
[2] Cf. W. J. Mommsen, *Max Weber und die deutsche Politik* (Tübingen, 1959).
[3] See above, p. xx.
[4] Following a friendly piece of advice Professor Habermas said he thought afterwards 'a natural son' of Weber's to be a more appropriate expression.

makes it possible to put it to the service of action which stems from an irrational decision, but which is dependent on the rational choice of means.

Positivist sociology sees in this separation a conclusive and double protection; the protection of research against hypotheses which cannot be tested empirically, and the protection of society against ideologies. For ideologies refuse rational control of their practices and incline to give arguments in favour of their interpretations of the world, which are imaginary and must therefore be forcibly excluded from discussion. On the other hand Marxist sociology complains that neither form of protection is strong enough to make rationality dominant in politics and society. For research techniques need orientation to goals of knowledge which depend on questions no longer worth considering in the research itself. And these aims can be arbitrary and obscure, not so much in holding rigidly to theory, which can be criticized, as in the act of decision from which they stem. Far from criticizing this act of decision itself, the positivist theory rather promotes it, just as Max Weber had done.

One could appeal to Max Weber himself in asserting that the independence of the formal means of empirical cognition does not yet sufficiently guarantee the objectivity of empirical science. He took more account than anyone previously of the significance of value-decisions even for empirical knowledge, if not for the manner of its progress, then for its outcome, its length and aim. If one wishes to ascribe to empirical knowledge an autonomous midway position between the ideal and the real in society, the bases for this are not immediately clear, at least in Weber's methodological work. He seems to concede to it no movement of its own, but one dependent on the whole movement of human culture. And his refusal to accept that empirical knowledge can be developed into an independent theory by using the concept of function is not only implicit but explicit. This is obvious from marginal notes in his copy of Schumpeter's book on the nature of political economy, in which such a theory was propounded.

The following conclusion seems obligatory: if objective empirical science could ever become a control for decisionist arbitrariness, it would have to be at least a sub-value system independent of acts of decision of the type put forward by Professor Parsons. In so far as it is conceived as a research technique used for knowledge of the means, it can never become this, at least in Weber's sense. He found no objection to the dependence of the course of research nor to decision-taking as an act of choosing an objective.

As a criticism of Max Weber this conclusion rests on the premise that in his work the relationship between objectivity of experience and the act of decision is of the same kind as that which his commentators have already imputed to him when they hold that this relation can be completely interpreted as that between object in view and choice of means.

The test of this interpretation can begin with a few observations arising from an analysis of Max Weber's text: in the presentation of two basic themes of the methodological essays Weber constantly avoids the restrictions he himself set up: e.g. with Rickert he has defined the concept of cultural significance—*Kulturbedeutung*—as the basis of the interest from which empirical science turns toward certain phenomena in the history of mankind. In this sense *Kulturbedeutung* is also an element in the structure of those concepts which connect empirical knowledge to subjective value-discrimination.

In direct contrast to this and yet in the same context Weber uses the same word to indicate the connection in which past culture has influenced present culture. An empirical science which investigates cultural meanings in this second sense must indeed proceed from a pre-scientific consensus of what is important. This consensus may, however, be controlled retrospectively in the light of experience, to see whether it accounts for the structures on the basis of which it came into being, or whether it is only an arbitrary and therefore partial and subjective reaction to them.

For others of Weber's basic methodological concepts this reversal of their meaning from logical to ontological can also be demonstrated. It means a limitation of the subjective points of departure of his methodology.

The second deviation of Weber from his own theorems is more obvious: his postulate of value-freedom does not prevent him from raising claims for clarity and consistency in decision even where he speaks as an empirical investigator. These claims do not simply arise *modo ponens* from the rationality proper to each empirical science. For there is no contradiction in the assumption that one might be taught by experience that it is no good directing one's actions to unequivocal ends. One would be happier in settling for compromise each time according to the exigencies and evidence of the situation as it changes. And if Weber himself did not presume that most men in fact come to this conclusion, he would not need to propagate his ideal of consistency so passionately.

The obviousness and persistence of this twofold self-revision prevent one from regarding them as chance defect in Weber's theory. In view of these there remain two possibilities of interpretation. They can be seen as the expression of the collapse of Weber's theory. Then the interpretation would have to say that the doctrine of subjective evaluation itself leads to the admission that value-judgments are based on knowledge through experience, and that decisionism itself acknowledges that its principle is only the product of an arbitrary decision. The only alternative to such interpretative criticism can be the attempt to explain Weber's inconsistency as a relaxation of the meaning of his theory from an implicit to a possibly explicit form. And I am prepared to plead for this alternative, in the event being in fundamental agreement with Professor Parsons.

Both inconsistencies seem to be relevant to each other. Even if this is so, one will have to say: 1. Empirical science must possess a relative independence regarding the consensus of a culture, because this consensus itself needs a rational control of its premises. 2. One can speak of an ideal of consistency in value-discrimination in connection with empirical science, even if not by virtue of its own authority, because this science serves not only the technique of the realization of aims of action, but itself comes into the definition of criteria for a possible decision.

If these two propositions are to remain in agreement with the simplest elements of Weber's teachings on method, they must not imply that value-judgments are provable from experience and that an empirical science of history and society proceeds without an historically conditioned posing of problems.

An interpretation of Max Weber's work on the basis of these propositions would have to satisfy the following three theses considered together.

1. In the course of its history empirical social science accumulates possible points of view for the continuance of research. Without these it would not be in a position to put into practice any causal analysis, weighing one against the other the importance of different causes in a complex operation, and not merely seeking for interesting

but ephemeral causes. Every possible theory can justify itself empirically by showing that it furthers the discovery of such connections.

2. Such causes can and usually do possess the quality of claims of significance. Therefore empirical social science, thanks to its relative independence, is in a position to examine the consensus of interest from which it began. It does so with regard to questions such as the following: Does the consensus contain an adequate understanding of the existing situation and its own interests in relation to it? Is it capable of perceiving the implications of meaning it has absorbed through its origins, in order either to accept these implications or eliminate them? Besides such questions, the one about means and possible opponents in the pursuance of interests is only one among others.

3. The postulate of the consistency of action in a decision, which deserves to be called reasonable, implies more than logicality and a survey of necessary means. A reasonable decision must, in its content, be in accordance with the historical situation of the society whose diagnosis empirical social science is in a position to make. Such agreement is reached if men's aim in life and explanation of life are a possible answer to all that they could know of their real situation. The theodicy of the main religions and the this-worldly asceticism of the different sects have been previously answers of this kind. The process of rationalization to which they themselves belong and which they have extended has, according to Weber, reached a stage in modern times where the old possibilities of explanation fail. Science itself cannot create such possibilities. And thus mankind experiences the conflict of gods, who have all lost their power over the world, and can only legitimately claim a place in the most private spheres. In political activity a consensus orientated to science can only be formal and provisional, even if for a foreseeable length of time: it has as goal the prevention of the danger of becoming fixed in a state of indifference to interpretation and the unmasking of the fanaticism which intrudes with substitutes where there is dearth of interpretation. Such a substitute is recognizable in that it misrepresents the situation, does not understand the damage it does, and has no means of realizing its illusionary programme. These are the criteria with which Weber criticized the October Revolution. He would certainly have used them in the same way for the totalitarianism of the following era.

If such an interpretation of Max Weber were to succeed, the meaning of the value-freedom of the sociological sciences would be put forward in a way that differentiated it from a decisionism which glorifies the consistent act purely for itself, and presses empirical science into its service. Man's experience and his shaping of the world are here complementary processes, each being the premise of the other. Empirical science is not a technique of the exercise of power, but the diagnosis of a situation. Its origin is in the consciousness of a problem which is explicable by this situation. And its aim is to be the premise for an interpretation and a transformation which remain in harmony with that which is real. It cannot itself perform both. But thanks to its definition, it possesses criteria which allow the arbitrary to be adequately differentiated from the suitable. Only with the help of such a theory of the meaning of objectivity and of the value-freedom of social scientific knowledge does it seem possible to interpret Max Weber's work in its entire scope and its manifold ramifications as a unified, connected whole.

Finally it must be noted that even this theory leads us into many difficulties which arise from the Kantian-like formalism on which it is based. For its nature and solution we can learn most from Emil Lask. He was close to Weber, and followed a path which is of no little significance for the real appreciation of Weber's theory. It may be that these difficulties are not removable, and especially that Weber's theory is no longer right for the course of social scientific knowledge, half a century after he helped to found it. In this case we derive from the consistency that exists in it between philosophical consciousness and social scientific analysis the supposition that no theory will be feasible in which the basic ideas are not integrated and no previous theory will be in a position to outstrip it— least of all a return to Aristotle's doctrine of man's natural happiness, nor to Hegel's ideas, according to which mankind's goal is only the concept of our development up to the present time.

In this sense Max Weber's theory is a part of the beginning to which Professor Parsons has attributed it.

PIETRO ROSSI

In his very comprehensive paper Professor Parsons has tried to define the position of the problem of objectivity in the social sciences in Max Weber's work. He dealt with the relationship of Weber's posing of problems to the most important trends in method, with which he was connected, or to which he took up a position: historicism, the development of social science in the framework of positivism, historical materialism. In my contribution, unlike Professor Parsons, I should like to consider the problem from a more limited point of view. In other words, I want firstly to establish the relationship of the concept of value-freedom to Weber's attempt at an objective foundation of the social sciences: secondly I should like to examine whether this concept is still applicable today (and eventually to what extent). My remarks remain therefore in the purely methodological field, without express reference to Weber's historical and sociological work.

The concept of value-freedom, as we know, is linked with the fact that science in general and the social sciences in particular are confined to a purely explanatory task, and are not permitted to determine men's behaviour nor to set up political, economic, ethical or religious norms. One can even say that the exclusion of value-judgments from historical research and the social sciences represents the 'external' condition of their objectivity, while the 'internal' condition consists in the possibility of an explanation, or —more precisely—of a causal explanation. These two conditions express the general rules of scientific method and must therefore also be applied to the social sciences. The first condition of objectivity in the social sciences, according to Max Weber, consists in the exclusion of all value-judgments: as in the natural sciences, so, too, in the social sciences norms of behaviour or evaluations based on these norms, can never be deduced from identifying the facts of the case. The substantial difference between science and the normative function of value-judgments is justified by the thesis (in which Weber follows the distinction made by Windelband) that value-judgments cannot be derived from factual judgments. The second condition of the objectivity of the social sciences consists in causal explanation: these disciplines too must establish the connections between facts empirically, and determine the conditions under which processes take place. The distinction between legal and individual causation (in which Weber follows Rickert) allows us to transfer to the social sciences the task of causal explanation, whereas Dilthey and his followers had limited this to the natural sciences, in order to allow the arts a more intimate understanding of historical structural connections. Thus the first condition limits the task of science in relation to the tasks which are foreign to it: the second condition defines the specific task of science and confirms the general value of the concept of causality as a category applicable to all sciences. Therefore value-freedom can only be correctly understood in relation to the explanatory task of the social sciences and by means of the distinction between this task and the task of setting of norms, which is alien to science.

It is equally well known—and I will remind you of this only *en passant*—that excluding value-judgments from the social sciences does not mean for Weber that these sciences have no concern with values. The opposite is the case. Not only can the social sciences make values an object of their research, but it is one of their main tasks to determine the conditions for their realization. They cannot determine the normative validity of values, i.e. they cannot determine whether a certain value shall be valid as a rule of behaviour and as a basis for evaluation. But they can and must determine the appropriate means for the realization of values and the consequences arising from this realization and the use of the means appropriate to it. Thus the observation on the one hand of the relation between means and end, and on the other of the relation between realization and consequences, voluntary or involuntary, foreseen or unforeseen, becomes the basis for a technical criticism of values, which is concerned with the possibility of their realization and enables us to compare differing or opposing values.

This question was already expressly dealt with in the essay on 'The objectivity of socio-scientific and socio-political knowledge' (1904) and was developed in the essay, 'The meaning of the value-freedom of the sociological and economic sciences' (1917) in which Weber worked out a logical scheme for a scientific discussion of values. The logical steps for criticizing values, and thus for comparing them, are as follows: reduction of specific value-judgments to their basic axioms: deduction of the consequences arising from these axioms: determination of the means necessary for realizing an attitude to values, and the factual consequences connected with them: the determination of the degree of probability of the impossibility of this realization: and finally the establishment of other values connected with the use of certain means or with secondary consequences. The fact that no value-judg-

F

ments are used in this criticism is proof that it is purely scientific.
In other words, it is not a position for or against certain values, it is
not a proposal of certain values, resulting in the negation or rejection of other values. It is exclusively a question of the conditions
for the realization of different values.

But the relation to values is still closer, for it constitutes just the
substance of the social sciences which distinguishes them from the
natural sciences. In order to define this relationship, Weber
appealed to Rickert's differentiation between value-judgment and
Wertbeziehung, and indicated the latter concept as an elective
principle, which enables us to delineate the field of research in the
social sciences from one case to another. Thus defined, *Wertbeziehung* is identical with the point of view from which the investigation is undertaken, i.e. in the direction of interest or
knowledge. It identifies social sciences in contrast to the natural
sciences, whose striving for knowledge is aimed at determining
general laws in systematic form. Since his essay on 'The Objectivity of socio-scientific and socio-political knowledge' (1904)
Weber has defined the methodological function of values in the
social sciences as follows: Values are elective criteria for determining the direction and scope of research. From its relationship
to values arises the significance of the processes which are the
subject of these sciences. The social sciences always start with
certain presumptions of value, which are extremely variable and
historically conditioned by the cultural situations from which the
research stems. These presuppositions are 'subjective' in the sense
that they are an extra scientific point of departure and not a
product of research. Within the sphere defined by these presuppositions one reaches conditions which can be empirically established, i.e. causal connections of objective validity. Thus causality
must guarantee the objectivity of the investigation and its results
within the bounds drawn by the value-presuppositions. Historical
conditioning and the relativity of elective criteria and the resultant
bias of the investigation—which are necessarily linked with the
acceptance of certain value-presumptions—do not prevent the
social sciences from fulfilling their task of explanation. The
relationship of facts can be determined objectively on the basis of
experience, independently of the acceptance of these or those
value-assumptions: within a certain field of research causal explanation can give results of universal validity.

The return to causality is therefore in Weber's view the means of neutralizing the subjectivity inherent in value-assumptions. If, however, one examines the scheme of explanation which Weber formulated mainly in the second part of his essay, 'Critical studies in the sphere of cultural–scientific logic' (1906) it is easy to establish the fact that *Wertbeziehung* also determines the explanatory procedure of the social sciences. The acceptance of certain value-assumptions determines not only the direction and the sphere of research, but also the tendencies of the relationships being studied for the sake of the explanation. This means that the social sciences can never give a complete and exhaustive explanation of a process, but only an explanation from certain points of view, and this explanation can only be partial. In other words, they cannot establish determining factors, but only a particular series of conditions which in turn are connected with other series of conditions, which for their part can become objects of research. This causal explanation frees itself from the determinist model of nineteenth-century positivism and becomes a conditional explanation. The social sciences can recognize the conditioning factors which make possible the processes with which they are concerned, and thus can determine the conditional relationships between facts. But they cannot maintain that they estabish necessary relationships. Not necessity, but objective possibility— ranging from adequate to fortuitous causation—is the modal category at the base of the scheme of explanation.

It is therefore clear that the direction of the process of explanation depends on the value-assumptions which are appropriate to the investigation. These premises become explanatory hypotheses and so lead the investigation to the establishment of certain conditional relationships.

One can therefore conclude from the above remarks that the 'neutralization' of value-assumptions remains a claim not realized by a return to causality. The conditioning of values turns the causal explanation into a conditional one. But the concept of *Wertbeziehung*, as Weber has expressed it, is thus put in question. *Wertbeziehung* cannot be confined merely to the first stage of scientific procedure, and exhaust itself in defining the area for research. On the contrary, the link with value-assumptions is evident at all subsequent stages of investigation. These determine the general direction as well as the methodological decisions arising

from it: and in the form of explanatory hypotheses they also
influence the sequence of explanation. If this be true, the acceptance of certain value-assumptions directly or indirectly conditions
the results of the research—but that is precisely what Weber
would deny.

Thus a new formulation of Weber's concept of value-freedom is
necessary. The exclusion of value-judgments from the social
sciences does not free them from value-assumptions which are
operative in the course of investigation itself. If we want to guarantee the scientific character of the social sciences, we must stipulate
conditions of objectivity relevant to the effective use of value-
assumptions, without taking for granted a 'neutralization' which
is not possible. These assumptions are inevitable in any investigation, but their use can be subjected to exact rules. It is generally
possible to give three rules for the use of value-assumptions, which
are valid for all social sciences. I would formulate them as follows:

1   The value-assumptions must be expressly named, so that their
    evaluative nature can be recognized.
2   The value-assumptions must be used as working hypotheses
    and be put to the test during the course of the research.
3   The value-assumptions must become explanatory models, to be
    retained or rejected on the basis of experience.

These three rules have certainly different values and different
functions, but they are all indispensable. This would of course
require a much more thorough and detailed discussion than I have
time for here. The first rule is of a purely formal nature and is
insufficient in itself, since the mere recognition of a value-assump-
tion does not make it valid. But it does prevent the confusion of
value-assumptions with facts and the delusion that one's research
has neither premise nor direction.

The second rule concerns the methodological function of value-
assumptions and establishes their hypothetical character. It
demands that value-assumptions be considered not as postulates
divorced from control by research, but as premises which may be
invalidated by research. The third rule determines the relation
between value-assumptions and the process of explanation, and at
the same time recognizes that their relation to experience is of
decisive importance for the retention or rejection of an explanatory
hypothesis. Together these three rules give Weber's concept of

value-freedom a new form and set down the conditions for the
utilization of value-assumptions.

Thus the exclusion of value-judgments from the social sciences
which Weber had demanded acquires a different significance. It can
certainly be concluded that the social sciences have neither the
task of proposing norms of behaviour, nor pronouncing evaluations
with reference to these norms, and that the social scientist—like
any other scientist—must not present his personal opinions as if
they were the result of research. All sciences, even the social
sciences, have a duty to explain, and even to predict: their operational function is based on this capacity for prediction, and not on a
normative claim. The social scientist is for his part bound by rules
which are just as strict as those binding the physicist, the chemist,
the biologist. Even when he acts as an expert, and works in a certain political or economic direction, the guiding impulse for the
choice of this direction is to be distinguished logically from the
impulse behind the programmatic employment of the means
necessary for its realization. But this in no way implies that the
social sciences cannot express any evaluations: on the contrary
they must do so, for these evaluations are contained in the acceptance of value-assumptions. Each operational choice demands an
evaluation of the situation—of the various possibilities for development and alteration contained therein. This evaluation belongs also
to the competence of science: this does not mean, however, that
science must establish which possibilities correspond to which
political, economic, ethical and religious ideals, but that it must
determine by comparison the conditions for their realization.
But then it is no longer a problem of whether the social sciences
can in general pronounce evaluations, or not: the problem is to
decide from one case to another which evaluations are legitimate
for any particular discipline. The exclusion of evaluation is thus
only a ban on certain kinds of evaluation, which are not legitimate: it is not a ban on evaluation in general.

Weber's structure of the concept of value-freedom seems hardly
tenable today. The ban on value-judgments in the social sciences
loses its significance in face of the recognition of the fact that even
scientific research must end in evaluation. On the other hand even
causality is no intrinsic guarantee of the objectivity of the social
sciences, for the simple reason that the explanation it provides is
not a causal one. The distinction between science and value-

judgments has to be formulated on a new basis, i.e. as a distinction
between different kinds of evaluation. In the same way the explanatory process of the social sciences must be defined independently
from certain value-assumptions which are used as a working
hypothesis. And yet the relationship which Weber set forth between
value-freedom and objectivity remains, in spite of the inadequacies
we have mentioned, a basic principle of method for the social
sciences. Weber's formulations must be modified and corrected,
just because this principle has neither exhausted its function nor
lost its value. The concept of value-freedom must be adapted to the
new interpretation of science, which has produced present-day
methodology, and to the new tasks of the social sciences. This has
been the purpose of my exposition and my conceptual proposals.

PROFESSOR TALCOTT PARSONS

Perhaps—in spite of the very high level and the very impressive
competence of these discussions—I may be permitted to open by
stating a disappointment. This disappointment is that only in one
connection was the relationship between Weber's methodological
work and his substantive sociology mentioned by any of the dis-
cussants. There were general references to the kind of thing that
ought to be done or that Weber did. But no actual analysis of what
he in fact did. The one exception is his political attitudes toward
his own time from which two or three of the speakers have taken
off. Now, I am very much aware of the great importance of this
problem for Germans, and the ambivalences which necessarily are
attached to this subject, and that Dr. Mommsen's important book
has focused this discussion. As an American rather than a German
citizen, I should like not only to stay aloof from these discussions
but I should also like to say that I think that they should be seen in
a perspective of the broader set of problems that Weber was concerned with as philosopher of science and as substantive analyst of
social phenomena in the broadest historical and comparative
perspective. I hope these perspectives are not going to be lost sight
of.

A second theme that seems to be exceedingly important began
with Professor Albert and was continued through pretty nearly
the whole set of discussions and that was that Weber made a beginning rather than presented a complete accomplishment. I very

much concur in this view. There is a sense in which Weber's own tragic death at the early age of 56 is symbolic of the incompleteness of his work; but I think, given the intellectual situation of his time, it is exceedingly unlikely that Weber would have presented a work of symmetrically rounded perfection at all. In my opinion it is not his primary significance that he created finished products, but that he began things. And he began things by digging very deep indeed, so that, in the longer run, in the requisite fields (I leave out philosophy which our chairman mentioned and other fields), I think, it can be said that as a result of his work and those of others in his time many of the positions of the nineteenth century which tended to be taken for granted in that century are no longer tenable. He burnt the bridges of the social sciences to its past, he created a situation which forced us to attempt to progress. In my paper I presented a sketch of the three principle frames of reference which had dominated that situation in the Western world. I think that one of the most significant things about Weber was his clear opposition to all of them. He did not polemicize against one in favour of a second. And this is a very critically important point and it applies to both the methodology and the substantive contributions, I think.

I think I would prefer not to attempt to answer particular points in detail, but just to mention two or three further ones. Now, I agree in particular with Professor Albert (and the same theme was brought up by Professor Henrich), that precisely in the area of theory in a technical sense—the way I would like to formulate is pretty close to Professor Henrich's formulation—Weber created a situation which could not lead to further progress unless a level of theory was created which he himself thought was impossible or inappropriate. And here I mean theory in a technical sense. It seems to me this is a crucially important point. I know this is not accepted by any means by all social scientists today. But I think substantial progress has been made since Weber's work. In his area many of its foundations were laid not only by Weber himself, but by others. I think very notably of Durkheim, I think of the American social psychologists, I think of certain of our neighbouring disciplines; Freud, whom my chairman mentioned, and the economists, to take two groups who are not ordinarily associated with each other, but who I think have made very essential contributions. Indeed in spite of wars and disturbances, the past half-century has not been an altogether unproductive era in these various aspects. But I very much appreciate that two of the discussions have focused on this central problem of theory.

Now, I should like to make a very brief comment on one or two of the other points which Professor Habermas made, even though I cannot take the time to run through his questions one by one. First I would like to say that it seems to me that he presented a picture of Weber's work which is not so much specifically incorrect as that it selects certain trends that are clearly there but, I think, do not stand alone in Weber, and if one appreciates what Weber was polemicizing against perhaps he is less inclined to give as much emphasis to them as Professor Habermas did. For example, I think here of what he called the positivistic trend in Weber's thinking and as one aspect of that, the emphasis on *Zweck-rationalität*[1] as the understanding of strictly *zweckrationales Handeln* being that on which empirical social science, in Weber's sense, concentrated. Now, I would just like to relativize this to another intellectual world, namely the English-speaking intellectual world. And there of course exactly the opposite is held to be the prejudice of Weber. It is alleged that Weber did not really appreciate the kind of thing the technical economist would be concerned with. That is, according to this line of argument, that he was much too much influenced by German Idealism and Historicism and that sort of thing. This is exactly the opposite criticism of Professor Habermas who seems to be afraid that Weber and my interpretation of Weber are in danger of too great a loss of the great traditions of German thinking in the *Kulturwissenschaften*. I think it is very important that a careful balance should be held here. I would say first that I don't think *Zweckrationalität* figures as prominently in Weber's own work as Professor Habermas has suggested, at least not in my reading. Secondly, however, precisely the kinds of theoretical developments which have been going on since Weber and which for example can be carried out in attempting to synthesize Weber with Durkheim, take the emphasis away from that. They do not accentuate it. I think for example of Durkheim's very strong emphasis on the problems of solidarity

[1] [Usually translated as instrumental rationality or purposive rationality, and distinguished principally from Wertrationalität (value or substantive rationality) —*Trans.*]

and social integration and their relation to normative structures
and this type of thing. I think this is wholly consistent with
Weber's main position but it brings out aspects which Weber
himself did not.

Now, I think one final word here touches the *Wertbeziehung*
problem and I am not quite clear—I did not have a chance to read
his statement in advance—whether I am in disagreement with
Professor Rossi on this point or not. Hearing him speak and following his text left me a little bit uncertain—this was the first time I
have heard this position. But I clearly think that Professor Habermas imputed to me an unduly narrow interpretation. One of his
questions explicitly asked: do I confine the relevance of the concept *Wertbeziehung* to the posing of problems. I would say most
definitely not, because I think the crucial thing is that objectivity in
social science must balance and integrate the values and standpoint
of the investigator and of the objects of his investigation. The fact
that values are on the one hand accepted by the objects and on the
other are accessible to understanding by the observer is the crucial
thing. If you take values as the focus of the culture of a society—
and I think the sociologist more than any other social scientist must
do this—treating them as the institutionalized focus of the normative order of the society, we may assume that the values state the
premises on which the more detailed normative order rests in a
complex set of interdependences. In another direction of course
this normative order is interdependent with situational factors of
various sorts. But it seems to me that the crucial thing is treating
culture, including the value system of the culture, as a manageable
object of objective study.

Now, let me make just one more point: Weber broke with
Historismus above all in his insistence on the importance of comparative study and he linked this very closely with the problem of
causality. Without comparative study the isolation of variables
which is necessary for the imputation of causality is not possible.
Whether it be done experimentally in the laboratory, whether it be
done by *Gedankenexperiment* as in his famous discussion with
Eduard Meyer, or whether it be done by explicit comparative
study of actual historical cases, the basic logic is the same. And the
thing that I would say there is simply that the comparative method
and the aspect of *Wertbeziehung* which is involved in the comparative method preclude the denial of the possibility that values can be

analytically studied. That is they must be capable of being analysed into components which with limits are independently variable. Without this I think one is caught in the solipsistic position of pure *Historismus*.

PART II

Max Weber and Power-politics

RAYMOND ARON

The task which you have entrusted to me has set me a problem of conscience, or, if I dare at this stage use an expression of Weber's, a problem of both science and politics. Max Weber, as we know, was not only the sociologist and philosopher whom we all admire, he was a political thinker, a publicist, who on several occasions thought of becoming a politician. Even if he never did enter active politics, he was nonetheless throughout his life the friend, counsellor and inspirer of men engaged in the day-to-day political struggle (e.g. Friedrich Naumann). I cannot therefore present or discuss certain of Weber's ideas and positions without suggesting judgments on Wilhelminian Germany or even German nationalism of that time, even if I do not formulate them in detail.

At another period in time, a Frenchman would have been able to refuse, and indeed ought to have refused, to write such a report: he would have been afraid of being tactless if he expressed himself frankly, and would have been less than frank if he had tried not to hurt any tender feelings. Personally I have not felt that I should be guided by such national considerations at this time and in these circumstances.

It is true that Max Weber does not belong to a past which is over and done with. The controversies aroused by W. Mommsen's book, *Max Weber und die deutsche Politik* are not purely scientific. They are also concerned with the significance we now attach to Wilhelminian Germany, to the First World War, to the Weimar Republic, and, by the same token, to Hitler and the Second World War. As a 'power politician', Max Weber belongs to a past whose interpretation influences our awareness of the present situation. In this sense a Frenchman's participation in the discussion might appear indiscreet, if there were not three good reasons for waiving possible objections.

83

First of all, I am not personally suspected of being anti-Weber, even if I could no longer express myself today exactly as I did thirty years ago in the Deutsche Soziologie der Gegenwart. Secondly some of the problems posed by Weber now appear strangely to present-day France. Mommsen was not wrong to point out the relationship between the constitution of the Fifth French Republic and Max Weber's ideas on constitution. Finally —and this is the decisive reason—the European community has become a real experience for us to such a point that it behoves us all, sociologists and laymen, to think hard about nationalism (or yesterday's nationalisms) and about power-politics. Nevertheless, I would not forget Weber's distinction between science and politics, although the way in which he himself practised this distinction was not always exemplary. It is a good thing not to confuse facts and values, reality and desires. Furthermore, one should take care to see the world as it is and not as one would wish it to be, or as one fears it may be: for a pessimistic distortion, inspired by the desire to show that power-politics are inevitable and indispensable, is no less to be feared than an idealistic distortion.

What exactly do we mean here by 'power-politics'? It seems to me that two definitions can be put forward; one narrow, the other broad. Either one calls 'power-politics' politics as practised between states, politics subjected to competition between powers because it is not subject to any law, any tribunal, any supra-national authority. In this sense, all foreign politics, up to and including our own times, has always been power-politics, however diverse the conditions of the political units, and the relations between these units. Or else one can term 'power-politics' any form of politics even within one state, which has power as its objective and/or its principal means. In this second sense, all power is at least partially power-politics. Politics seems to be all the more 'power-politics', the more analysis emphasizes sovereignty (*Herrschaft*) and struggle (*Kampf*).

Whether we keep the first or second definition, Weber, both as a politician and sociologist, is a typical 'power-politician'. He belongs to the posterity of Machiavelli as much as to the contemporaries of Nietzsche. He would have rejected as meaningless the question: 'Which is the best form of government?' The struggle for power (*Macht* or *Herrschaft*) between classes and individuals seemed to him the essence, or if we prefer the constant theme of politics. A people or a person without the will to power was, according to him, outside the sphere of politics. Liberal and parliamentary institutions became under his pen necessary conditions for a nation's role in the world. He sometimes recommended them so that they should be proof that one people, the German people, was capable of playing the part of a great power.

Only master races have a vocation to climb the ladder of world development. If peoples, who do not possess this profound quality try to do it, not only the sure instinct of other nations will oppose them, but they will also come internally to grief in the attempt. By 'master-race' we do not understand that ugly 'parvenu' mask made out of it by people whose feeling of national dignity allows them to be told what 'Deutschtum' is by an English turncoat like Houston Stewart Chamberlain. But surely a nation which only produced good civil servants, estimable office-workers, honest shopkeepers, efficient scholars and technicians and faithful servants, and furthermore submitted to an uncontrolled hierarchy of officials using pseudo-monarchic phrases—could never be a master-race, and would do better to go about its daily business, instead of having the vanity to concern itself about world destinies. Let us hear no more about 'world politics' if the old conditions return. And writers who are addicted to conservative phrases will wait in vain for Germans to develop real dignity abroad, if at home they remain exclusively the sphere of activity of a mere bureaucracy—however purely technical or efficient—and are even pleased when learned clerics discuss whether the nation is 'ripe' enough for this or that form of government. The will to impotence at home, which the scholars preach, has nothing to do with the 'will to power' in the world, which has been so noisily proclaimed.[1]

I have quoted this passage because it contains all the main themes of Weber's concept of 'power-politics'. Theoretically all politics, home and foreign, is above all a struggle between nations, classes or individuals. Only those individuals animated by the will to power take part in this struggle, and are therefore fitted for politics. Weber never indicated explicitly any difference of character between the internal and external struggle. Like Machiavelli, he found struggle everywhere, but again like Machiavelli, he put external politics first, and set as his goal the unity of his nation (in this case the German nation) so that it could influence the course of universal history. A people of citizens and not of subjects, a people

[1] *Gesammelte politische Schriften*, 1st ed. (Munich, 1921), p. 259 (cited hereafter as G.P.S.).

which has given itself liberal institutions, and takes part in the struggle for power instead of submitting passively to traditional or bureaucratic authority—only such a people can aspire as a 'master-race' to take part in world politics, and this union of parliamentarianism and imperialist nationalism is certainly typical of Weber's thinking. However Weber would not have granted it more than circumstantial value, or should not have done so. In the period of capitalism in Wilhelminian Germany, because the patriarchal authority of the emperor and the junkers was thenceforth anachronistic or ineffective, because civil servants by profession had no feeling for politics, i.e. for struggle, Max Weber demanded the democratization or parliamentarization of the regime. But I think Weber was too much of a historian and a pessimist to declare that master-races are always free races. It is possible that a synthesis of liberalism and imperialism might have corresponded to Weber's scale of values: to justify parliamentarianism by national interest, by the nation's power-interests, ought to lend an instrumental nature to spontaneous feelings of preference or perhaps even more to violent antipathies.

If I keep to the second and broader meaning of power politics, this paper would to some extent deal with the whole of Weber's political sociology. As such an undertaking is out of the question, I propose to retain the first meaning of the concept of power-politics, i.e. external politics, the rivalry of states which being beyond the authority of common law or a tribunal, are obliged to execute justice themselves, and so to depend for themselves, their security, their existence, on their own strength, and on their alliances: if we abide by this definition of power-politics, we must immediately make this first observation. Max Weber as sociologist wrote little about the struggle between states, about nations and empires, about the relations between culture and power. To be sure, the chapter in *Wirtschaft und Gesellschaft* which would have been devoted to what one might call a sociology of international relations remained unfinished.[1] If he had had time, Weber would probably have enriched this section by using his historical erudition. One unrivalled fact is nevertheless incontestable. Weber's nationalism was anterior to his sociological research, anterior to his scientific work; he found it while living at the heart of Wilhelminian Germany, while he was studying, and he absorbed it and

[1] *Wirtschaft und Gesellschaft*, 3rd ed. (1947), part 3, chap. III, pp. 619-30.

made it his own, unhesitatingly, and it seems, without profound reflection. On many points Weber retained the teaching contained in Treitschke's famous lectures on politics, though his philosophy is more pessimistic and possibly more tragic.

He had decided once and for all that the supreme value to which he would subordinate everything in politics, the god (or demon) to which he had sworn loyalty, was the greatness of the German nation. I use the term greatness (*Grösse*) although it is not Weber's own: he more often speaks of *Macht* (power), *Machtinteressen* (power-interests), *Machtprestige* (power-prestige), and *Welt-politik* (international politics). My reason for choosing the equivocal term 'greatness' is that Weber always suggests a link between power and culture. The German people are a people of culture (*Kulturvolk*). Power is certainly the aim, but is also the condition for the dissemination of culture. Germany as a great power is responsible to future generations for the kind of culture mankind will have.

It is not the Danes, Swiss, Dutch or Norwegians, whom future generations, our own descendants, will hold responsible if world power —that is, the power to shape the nature of culture in the future—is shared between the regulations of Russian officials on the one hand and the conventions of Anglo-Saxon society on the other, with perhaps a touch of Latin *raison*. It is we, the Germans. And rightly so[1].

Weber admitted unhesitatingly the double solidarity of culture and nation: 'All culture is national and remains so today, and all the more so, the more democratic become in extent and kind the external means of culture',[2] and of the power of the nation and the diffusion of culture. To be sure, in the unfinished chapter of *Wirtschaft und Gesellschaft* he points out the interdependence of the extent or prestige of culture on the one hand, and military or political power on the other. He does not conclude from this that this power is favourable to the quality of the culture. Here is the passage as it figures in a footnote:

The prestige of culture and the prestige of power are clearly linked. Every victorious war promoted the prestige of culture (Germany, Japan, etc.)—whether it does the development of culture any good is another matter, incapable of value-free solution. Certainly not un-equivocally (Germany after 1870) nor according to empirically palpable

---

[1] G.P.S., pp. 60–1   [2] Op. cit., p. 47.

signs: pure art and literature of a German nature did not arise from the political centre of Germany.

Two observations on this passage: history which claimed to be 'value-free' to the point of not passing any judgment on the quality of works would be strangely impoverished. It is striking that power, being the cause not of the quality, but of the diffusion or of the prestige (once again!) of culture, should be kept by Weber as the ultimate goal.

Weber's originality does not consist in adhering to this nationalism, which was fairly common at the end of last century, nor in the passion with which he proclaimed the need for 'world-politics', as an inevitable consequence and ultimate justification of Bismarck's work. Weber seems to me original and different from his contemporaries, when he insists on the diabolical character of power and on the sacrifices demanded by the power-State. Treitschke, in his lectures on politics, found small states somewhat ridiculous. Weber is glad that a Germanism exists outside the Germany which has become a 'national power-state' (*ein nationaler Machtstaat*).

We too have every reason to thank Providence that there is a Germanism outside the national power-state. Not only simple, middle-class virtues, and genuine democracy, which has never yet been realised in a large power-state, but far more intimate and lasting values can only bloom on the territory of communities which renounce political power. Even those artistically inclined: such a true German as Gottfried Keller could never have become so original and individual in the midst of an army camp such as our state is inevitably becoming. (G.P.S., p. 60.)

As far as the relations between nation and State, nationalism and imperialism are concerned, Weber belongs to his time, he shares its conceptions and its uncertainties. On the one hand he recognizes and underlines the strength of national claims, the aspiration of all self-conscious nationalities towards autonomy, even independence. On the other, he indignantly opposes the idea of compromise agreement about Lorraine. As for a plebiscite in Alsace, the very idea seems to him ridiculous.[1] Weber did not want non-German or hostile peoples to be absorbed in the Reich. But at the same time he was very far from subscribing unreservedly to the principle of nationalities, whatever form this might take.

[1] Letter to R. Michels, quoted by Wolfgang Mommsen, *Max Weber und die deutsche Politik, 1890–1920* (Tübingen, 1959), p. 258.

The splitting-up of Central Europe into states called national (but which would inevitably contain some national minorities) seemed to him neither desirable nor capable of realization.[1] He was led to conceive of a policy both national and imperial which would have reconciled the power-interests of the Reich with certain claims of other nationalities.

Having submitted that Russia was the chief enemy of the Reich, the only one who could question its very existence, he recommended during the First World War a German polity favourable to Poland, less out of sympathy with Polish claims than from concern for the German national interests.[2] Autonomous states protected militarily by the Reich, linked with it economically, would constitute the best protection against the threat of Grand Russian Imperialism. However—and this is indicative of the spirit of the times—Weber never went so far as to admit total independence of the Polish state, any more than he thought of sacrificing to the explicit desires of the people military guarantees or political advantages in the West. Characteristic of Weber on all these points is the almost total absence of ideological justification. It seems to me he was indifferent to the Franco-German dialogue about Alsace: should the German character of this imperialist province over-rule the actual wishes of the people of Alsace? In the same way he abstained from any complex and subtle analysis of the 'principle of nationalities'. He recorded the variable strength of national feelings[3] and from this deduced quite realistically the danger of annexations in Europe and also the chances of mobilizing national feelings in Eastern Europe against the empire of the Tsars and for the Reich. He rarely advanced moral and idealist arguments in favour of any particular diplomacy—and when he did it was implicitly rather than explicitly. The final aim was arbitrary in the sense that no one—not even a German—was obliged to take as his supreme objective the power-interests of the Reich. As these power-interests were supposed to be inseparable from the interests of culture (at least of culture-prestige) they were surrounded by a sort of spiritual halo. Once the choice has been made, politics should consult reality at every moment in order to determine what

---

[1] Perhaps he was right.

[2] He had then abandoned his earlier ideas of a German colonization of the East, and his opposition to the immigration of Polish workers.

[3] *Wirtschaft und Gesellschaft*, pp. 227–229 (cited hereafter as W.G.).

G

is possible, with a view to reaching the ultimate goal, without caring too much about the morality or immorality of the measures it takes or recommends. If it does not care about them, it is not because of immorality but because of intellectual honesty. 'For everything which shares in the possessions of the power-state is involved in the legality of the "power-pragma" which dominates all political history.'[1]

If this analysis is correct, Weber's national and imperial ideas must have been typical both of his times and his generation,[2] moderate in their objective and devoid of any phrase-making in their formulation. Germany was exposed particularly to peril from the East, the Tsarist empire of Grand-Russian imperialism: he hoped therefore until the final catastrophe of 1919 that the peace terms would be such as not to exclude the easing of relations with Great Britain and France. He probably had illusions as to what this easing would entail, but there again, if he was perhaps lacking in clearsightedness, he had more of it than most of his contemporaries.

It would be easy, but in my opinion without interest, to go into Weber's opinions in detail, to follow their variations from the famous 'Inaugural Speech' to the pro-Polish writings during the war. These have often been studied and would distract us from fundamental problems.

Western political thinkers have always recorded as an obvious fact the heterogeneity of internal and external politics. When Hobbes, in his *Leviathan*, looks for an illustration of the state of nature and describes relations between the Sovereigns, he gives a radical expression to a classical idea. Weber, who defines the state as having the monopoly of legitimate violence should logically recognize the heterogeneity between the violent rivalry of states and the rivalry, which is subject to law, between individuals and classes within a state. Now the fact is that Weber who obviously admitted this heterogeneity has rather blurred the distinction. It seems to me he was impressed and to some extent influenced by Darwin's vision of social reality. For example:

Whoever draws even a penny income which others have to pay—

[1] G.P.S., p. 63.

[2] I do not think Weber ever said clearly what he understood by international politics, nor what amount of colonial possessions would have satisfied the ambitions of the Reich.

directly or indirectly—whoever possesses any commodities or uses consumer goods produced by the sweat of another's brow and not his own, owes his life to the waging of that loveless, pitiless struggle for existence, which bourgeois phraseology terms 'working peaceably for culture' (*Kulturarbeit*)—another form of the conflict between men, in which not millions, but hundred of millions decline and waste away in body and soul, year in, year out, or lead an existence to which any kind of recognisable 'meaning' is really infinitely more alien than it is to responsibility which everyone has (and this includes women, for they too are waging 'war', if they do their duty) for honour and that means simply—for the historical duties of the people, which depend on fate.[1]

This passage comes from his writings during the Great War. But more than twenty years previously, in his Inaugural Speech, similar ideas are expressed with the same force.

Even under the guise of 'peace' the economic struggle between nationalities goes its way: the German peasants and labourers in the East are not being driven from the soil by politically superior enemies in open battle: in the silent barren struggle of everyday economic life they are on the losing side, even though faced by an actually inferior race, and leave their homes and proceed towards decline in an obscure future. There is no peace in the economic struggle for existence: only those who take the appearance of peace for the truth can believe that the future holds peace and enjoyment of life for our descendants. (C.P.S., pp. 17–18.)

And again:

In place of the dream of peace and human happiness, there stands over the doorway to the unknown future of mankind's history: 'Abandon hope, all ye that enter here'.

Not how the men of the future will feel, but what they will be like, is the question which occupies our thoughts about the time coming after our own generation, the question which actually is at the base of every economic task. It is not well-being we want to cultivate in men, but those qualities which we feel to constitute human greatness and the nobility of our nature.

And yet again:

It is not peace and human happiness that we have to hand on to our descendants, but the eternal struggle for the maintenance and cultivation of our national characteristics. And we must not yield to the optimistic hope that the work may be done in our case with the highest

[1] G.P.S., p. 62.

possible development of economic culture and that selection will then by itself help the more highly developed to victory in a free and 'peaceful' economic struggle.

Our descendants will not hold us responsible before history primarily for the kind of economic organisation that we hand down to them, but for the measure of elbow-room which we win and bequeath to them. In the last resort processes of economic development, which are a nation's power-interests, are also struggles for power, when they are in question. These are the final and decisive interests of a nation to whose service its economic policy has to be harnessed. The science of economic policy is a political science. It is a servant of politics, not the day-to-day politics of those individuals and classes possessing power at any particular time but of the nation's permanent interests in power-politics. And the national state is for us not an indeterminate something, which one thinks should be all the more highly regarded, the more it is wrapped in mystical obscurity, but is the nation's temporal power-organisation, and in this national state the final criterion of economic consideration is the *raison d'état*. (p. 20.)

I think these frequently quoted passages reveal what one must call Weber's *Weltanschauung*, with a Darwinian component (the struggle for life), a Nietzschean component (not the happiness of mankind, but the greatness of man), an economic component (the persistent scarcity of wealth—the ineradicable poverty of peoples), a Marxist component[1] (each class has its own interests, and the interests of any one class, even the dominant one, do not necessarily coincide with the lasting interests of the national community), and finally a national component, i.e. the interest of the nation as a whole, must outweigh all others, since nationalism is the result of a decision and not of deeds.

When I read Max Weber for the first time thirty years ago, I was particularly struck by the lesson of intellectual courage and modesty contained in his work. I still believe that his work contains a lesson which remains valid for us. But today I also realize that this thinking, which claims to be free of all illusion, stems from metaphysics, and a pessimistic vision of the world.

Power-politics between nations—of which wars are a normal expression and inevitable sanction—does not seem to Weber a

[1] In *Wirtschaft und Gesellschaft* there is yet another component: imperialism arising from capitalist interest (pp. 621 ff.). His exposition does not correspond to strict Marxism, since he thought a Socialist economic system would be driven into imperialism even more violently. In another passage Weber explains the motives of imperialist expansion as not being exclusively economic.

survival from past ages or a negation of man's striving towards culture but one form among others all basically equally cruel, of the struggle for existence or of the struggle between classes and nations. In other words, a metaphysics, partly Darwinian, partly Nietzschean, of the struggle for life, tends to reduce the extent of the opposition between peace and war, between the peoples' economic rivalry and the states' struggle for power. Violence is no less violent for being camouflaged. If the same word *Macht* denotes the stakes of the struggle within a state, and the struggle between states, this is because the stakes are basically the same. In the one as in the other, it is a matter of knowing who is winning, who is in command, what share of available space or resources each class or each people will snatch for itself. This philosophy is no longer fashionable, for various reasons. Vulgarized and interpreted by barbarians, it has led to orgies of barbarism. Also, modern economics has proved false many judgments which specialists did not hesitate half a century ago to dignify by the name of scientific truth. Max Weber, like many of his contemporaries, but unlike the liberal economists, does not seem to doubt that the political power of a state commands the economic development of the nation. He speaks and writes as if the standard of living of the working classes depended ultimately on the arbitrament of war. In this respect, Weber does not belong to our times. We know today—and it would not have been impossible to know sixty years ago—that military strength is neither a necessary condition nor a sufficient condition for material prosperity.

Please understand me aright. Weber had chosen the power of the national state as the ultimate value, and this choice was free and arbitrary. Even if he had known that Wilhelminian Germany had no need of colonies either for the development of its culture or the well-being of the working class, he would not necessarily have altered his decision: power-interests were a goal in themselves, and it remains true that the dissemination of culture has some connection with the power of the nation to which it is linked. But one's image of the world would no longer be the same if the struggle between classes and nations had as its main, if not exclusive, object control or power, and not well-being and life itself.

It is true that we are in danger today of committing the opposite error from Weber's. Within nations, as well as between them, social relationships contain an element of conflict which can be called respectively competition, contest, rivalry or struggle. The object of conflict is varied and sometimes the honour of winning is the sole reward. But from the moment when neither existence nor wealth constitutes the stakes, when the struggle is essentially political, that is to say it decides primarily who is to be in command, the distinction becomes more decisive between the modalities, the means, the rules of the various conflicts. A world without conflict is effectively inconceivable. A world in which classes and nations would no longer be engaged in a struggle for existence (*Kampf ums Dasein*) is not inconceivable. In any case, the difference between violent and non-violent forms of combat is regaining its full implication. The victor on the *Wahlschlachtfeld*, the electoral battlefield, differs in nature, not in degree, from the victor on the military battlefield.

The Darwinian–Nietzschean view of the world constitutes a framework within which Weber's conception of *Machtpolitik* is integrated. Polytheism, the plurality of incompatible values, constitutes the other basic idea in Weber's philosophy of power.

Weber, as we know, started from the Kantian or neo-Kantian opposition between what is and what should be, between facts and values. He did not reduce what should be to a moral system but he made morality itself one sphere of values among others. He added that the spheres of values are not only independent of each other, but are in irreconcilable conflict. A thing can be beautiful not *although* but *because* it is evil (*Les Fleurs du Mal*). From there he passes to two propositions both connected with *Machtpolitik*: the first, according to which there is no tribunal capable of deciding the relative values of German culture and French culture, the second according to which it is impossible to be at the same time a politician and a Christian (at least if Christian morality is that of the Sermon on the Mount), or again that each of us, in our actions, must choose between the morality of conviction and the morality of responsibility, and that the same action, according to the choice of one or the other set of ethics, will call forth a radically different appreciation.

These two propositions continued and are continuing to arouse impassioned polemics. The formula of polytheism is to some extent obvious. The artist is not as such a moral being, and a work of art is beautiful, not good. Each sphere of values contains a specific finality, a proper sense. The warrior's morality is not that of the saint or philosopher. Each obeys his own laws. Each nation expresses itself in a certain scheme of values, is proud of certain achievements. Who could be sufficiently detached and just to decide between these schemes of values and these achievements? Up to this point we all follow Max Weber. Beyond it there arise questions and objections. Let us look again at the famous passage in *Wissenschaft als Beruf* (Science as a Vocation), (p. 545).

The impossibility of 'scientific' representation of practical attitudes—except in the case of the discussion of ways and means for a purpose assumed to be definitive—follows from reasons which lie far deeper. It is in principle meaningless, because the various value-systems of the world are in insoluble conflict with each other. J. S. Mill, with whose philosophy I do not otherwise agree, said once, and correctly: if one starts out from pure experience, one arrives at polytheism. That is flatly expressed and sounds paradoxical, and yet there is some truth in it, which we still recognise today: that something can be holy not only *although* it is not beautiful, but *because* and *to the extent* that it is not beautiful—we can find proof of this in Isaiah, chap. 53 and in the 21st Psalm—and that something can be beautiful not only *although* but *to the extent* that it is not good, we know since Nietzsche, and earlier still we find this embodied in Baudelaire's *Fleurs du Mal*, as he called his poems—and it is a commonplace to say that something can be true, although it is neither beautiful, nor holy nor good. But these are only the most elementary examples of this 'war of the gods' between individual systems and values. How one will ever be able to decide 'scientifically' between the respective values of French and German cultures, I do not know. Here different gods are in conflict and for all time. It is as it was in the ancient world, when men were not yet disenchanted about their gods and demons, but it is so in another sense: just as the Greeks sacrificed to Aphrodite and then to Apollo, and particularly to the gods of his own town, so it is still today, disenchanted, and divested of the mythical but inwardly sincere form of that behaviour. And over these gods and in their struggle fate rules, but certainly no 'science'.

It is true that no one can decide scientifically between French culture and German culture. But has the question any significance? Is it legitimate to pass from a fact—French and German cultures are different from each other—to the idea that gods are fighting each other till the end of time? I cannot help thinking that Weber, obsessed by the vision of struggle everywhere and at all times, came thereby to transform an incontestable but temporary rivalry of power into a war of the gods. There are circumstances in which power rivalries engage the very fate and soul of man. But such is not always the case.

Is it so obvious that 'something can be beautiful not only *although* but also *to the extent* that it is not good'? Is it consonant with the wisdom of nations, that something can be true *although* and *to the extent* that it is neither beautiful nor holy nor good? The beauty of *Les Fleurs du Mal* has sometimes evil as its subject, but it does not originate in any intention of evil which might have inspired the poet: and if one can say that, thanks to the poet, vice assumes the appearance of beauty, it does not follow from this that vice is the cause or condition of beauty. Likewise, he who sees and says the truth, sees and says 'that which is neither beautiful nor holy nor good'. But the search for, or the expression of, truth is not therefore in conflict intrinsically, inevitably, inexplicably, with the search for beauty, holiness, or goodness.

But let us leave aside the wars of the gods which are only indirectly relevant to our subject, power politics, and come to the opposition which dominates the whole of Weber's philosophy of action, the opposition of the two ethics of conviction and responsibility. No one is obliged, he tells us, to become involved in the sphere of politics, but if he does so, he must accept its inexorable laws. Since what is at stake in politics is power, and the division of power between classes and nations, he who claims to guide his companions, other members of his class or nation, must submit to the relentless exigencies of the struggle. It cannot be left out of account that this may require ways and means which, even if not evil, are at least dangerous. The ethics of responsibility are obviously not to be confused with *Machtpolitik*, and in an oft-quoted passage of *Politik als Beruf* he criticizes the cult of *Machtpolitik*.

For although, or precisely because power is the inevitable means, and the striving for power one of the driving forces of all politics, there is no more harmful distortion of political strength than the 'parvenu' boasting about power and the vain self-mirroring in a feeling of power, in short any worship of power itself. The mere 'power-politician' as glorified by an enthusiastic cult, may make a strong impression, but this impression is in fact empty and meaningless. Here the critics of *Machtpolitik* are perfectly right. In the sudden inner collapse of typical protagonists of this attitude we have seen what inner weakness and impotence are concealed by this ostentatious but completely empty gesture. It is the product of a paltry superficial sophistication towards the meaning of human activity which is in no way related to the knowledge of the tragedy in all activity, particularly political activity is really involved. (G.P.S., p. 437.)

The ethical code of responsibility is defined not by the cult of power, nor by indifference to moral values, but by the acceptance of reality, by submission to the exigencies of action, and in extreme cases by the subordination of the salvation of one's soul to the salvation of the state. On the other hand, he who chooses the ethics of conviction, obeys the commands of his faith, whatever the consequences.

In fact, Weber more or less confused two sets of antinomies: on the one hand that of *political action* with its necessary recourse to ways and means always dangerous, sometimes diabolical, and that of *Christian action* as suggested by the Sermon on the Mount or the teachings of Saint Francis (turn the other cheek, renounce the goods of this world): on the other hand, the antinomy of *thoughtful decision*, taking account of the possible consequences of the decision, and *immediate irrevocable choice* without any consideration of possible consequences.

These two antinomies do not entirely coincide. No politician can ever be a 'real Christian' if the Sermon on the Mount contains the whole of Christian morality. No one has the right to ignore the consequences of his actions, and no one, in certain circumstances, can evade an inner exigency, whatever the risks of a decision dictated by a categorical imperative.

Weber, as a theoretician, claimed to follow the ethics of responsibility; as resolutely, and as practically and as soberly as possible he accepted *Machtpolitik*; that is to say, the use of ways and means required, within nations or between nations, by the struggle for power. He chose the ethics of responsibility and the obligations of power-politics from conviction, not out of personal interest, but out of devotion to the supreme value to which he had decided to adhere—the power of the Reich. For the politician who wants power for its own sake, or because of vanity or personal ambition, is a mere caricature of the true leader who only fulfils himself in the service of a cause greater than he.

In this political activity, Weber hardly behaved as a realist, and I am not sure whether, despite his knowledge and clearsightedness, he was really destined to become a leader of men. He more easily accepted in theory and in abstract than in fact the mediocre compromises, schemings and intrigues which are an integral part of effective politics as practised under all regimes and particularly in democracies. Very often Weber appeared more sensitive, on his own and on others' behalf, to the value of a gesture, to the exemplary significance of a refusal than to the foreseeable consequences of his own decisions.

Weber was right to refuse illusions: politics are not carried on without conflict, non-violent conflict, and the ways and means of the conflict are not always compatible with the laws of Christ or simple morality. Two things however in this theory disturb me:

The first is the extreme and somewhat radical form given to the antinomy between the two moral codes, of responsibility and of conviction. Is it ever possible to ignore completely the consequences of a decision which one takes? Is it ever possible to disregard the moral judgment passed on a prevailing decision? I think Weber would have recognized this himself, but in declaring real an alternative which only becomes so in the most extreme circumstances, he runs a double risk: the risk of justifying on the one hand the false realists who scorn the moralist's reproach, on the other the false idealists who condemn indiscriminately all policies which do not correspond to their ideals, and who end by contributing consciously or otherwise to the destruction of the existing order, to the advantage of blind revolutionaries or tyrants.

What is more, Weber is right to remind us that the eternal problem of justifying the means by the end has no theoretical solution. But in affirming not only the heterogeneity of conflicts but their irreconcilability, he prevents himself from founding his own authentic system of values. Although he wrote that we could not live without a minimum of human rights, he devalued his own values of liberalism and parliamentarianism, by reducing them to mere ways and means in the service of the Reich.

In the same way, I come to another objection: by setting the power-interests of the German nation as the ultimate goal, is not Weber slipping towards some kind of nihilism? The nation's power, he says, is favourable to the prestige, not the quality, of culture. If that be so, can the power of the nation be an ultimate goal, the god to whom one sacrifices everything? There is no question of denying the rivalry between nations and one's duty to safeguard the nation's position on the world's stage. But if the power of the nation, whatever its culture, whoever governs it, whatever the means employed, is the supreme value, what reason have we for saying 'No' to what Weber would have rejected with horror?

That, I think, is the main point we must think about. Weber affirmed and described the rivalry between European nations. If today he seems to us to have over-estimated the importance of these conflicts and under-estimated the repercussions of a great war on the future of the European nations as a whole, he has at least, compared with many of his contemporaries in Germany as well as in France, the advantage of not having lost the sense of moderation and decency. He never lent his voice to the ravings of propaganda which were rife on both sides. He did not question the national State as the supreme form of political community. (Perhaps this form has not been ousted even today.) In any case, he belongs to his time in this respect too. On the rights and duties of the great powers, on the diplomatic rules of *Machtpolitik*, he expressed himself in the same way as his contemporaries.

It remains to say that Weber, who as a sociologist is as up to date today as yesterday, was not always, as a politician, in advance of his times. Thus, he did not understand the implications of the Bolshevik revolution nor foresee the totalitarian despotism of single-party rule. Anxious to spare democracy the reign of politicians without vocation, he emphasized the plebiscitary legitimacy of the charismatic leader, unaware of the dangers which the following generation was to experience and suffer. He, who better than any other had understood the originality of modern civilization, did not understand the gap, at least potential in the technical age, between the power of arms and the prosperity of nations. As a bourgeois anti-Marxist, he invoked against Marx either the fate of bureaucracy or the efficacy of religious beliefs, but not the fact, common to all modern economies, of growth due to increased productivity.

True, it has not yet been proven that Weber's pessimistic Darwinian–Nietzschean view is the false one, and our view today the true one. The future lies open, and we do not know whether humanity will decide to destroy itself or to unite. But we do know that we can never again recognize in a nation's power-interests the final goal and a sacred value. Weber did, or believed he did, because the culture accumulated throughout the centuries seemed to him acquired for ever and immune from the accidents of history. If he had known that in the name of power culture itself was in danger of being sacrificed, he would have realized that he was both too confident and too pessimistic—too confident when he put his trust in the elected leader and did not separate power from culture: too pessimistic when he could not imagine mankind at peace, or at least capable of submitting to rules the inevitable conflict between classes and nations. Weber after all betrayed himself in his theory of politics for power was never his aim, neither for himself, nor for the nation. His thought and his life obeyed two values: truth and nobility. The man and the philosopher leave us an inheritance undiminished by the mistakes of the theoretician of *Machtpolitik.*

Max Weber and Power-politics

CARL J. FRIEDRICH

Power-politics is a decidedly important topic. The discussion of it
will be all the more difficult, since Weber did not develop an
unambiguous concept of power—in spite of his enthusiastic
participation in many discussions about *Machtpolitik*. Thus for
example his ambiguous concept of sovereignty is stamped with
many strange ideas about power, particularly in the sense of force.
In any case power is for Weber a value, and one which ranks
relatively high.

While listening to the discussion of value-freedom I was
exercised by one particular question. Some say Weber is right to
demand value-freedom, then they qualify this by saying that he
recognized the role of values and value-judgments. Others say
Weber is wrong, but then they make the same qualification, that he
recognized the role of values and value-judgments. It seems to me
then that the fact is generally admitted that Weber did recognize
the role of values and value-judgments, whether one agrees with
the claim for value-freedom or no. It amounts to this, that Weber
in many spheres conducts an allegedly value-free discussion with
value-concepts which now seem to us liberal. One has only to
think of the typology of sovereignty and legitimacy, contained in
the concepts 'traditional', 'rational–legal', and 'charismatic'. The
discussion about bureaucracy is also thoroughly value-laden, and
interlaced with his dislike of bureaucracy on the one hand, and his
esteem for its achievements on the other. Add to this that he
brings to life ideas of norms in the ambiguous concept of the 'ideal
type' as the expression itself indicates. It becomes apparent in
dealing with precisely this topic of bureaucracy, how Weber, with
his 'ideal-type' method of observation, brings evaluation in through
the back door, having first thrown it out of the front door by
ostensibly value-free definitions.

With specific regard to power, there is a complete lack in Weber
of clarification oriented to the stuff of experience. Power is simply
defined: this is the basis for the erection of a castle in the air of

derived concepts. This is the reason for the treatment as identical of such different types of leader as Eisner and Mohamed, a treatment hard to understand in the context of the last forty years. The concepts of charismatic leadership, born of a clearly rationalistic misunderstanding of the really religious, the numinous (Rudolf Otto), has been more and more falsified and rendered shallow and has given rise to more and more extensive misunderstandings. I believe with Aron that it is in complete accord with Weber's understanding of science for me to indicate these politico-scientific mistakes of his sharply and clearly. This is not to impair any discussion of the greatness of his achievement but to endorse it. For 'those who proceed through error to truth are the wise, those who linger in error are fools' (Rückert).

Today's topic is up to a certain point proof that discussion of power-politics is basically concerned with a definite question of values, and you will see in the discussion that there are considerable differences of opinion as to whether Weber rated power too highly or not highly enough, whether he rated it falsely or correctly. The whole thing revolves around a specific problem of values, and much more around a problem of values than of causal nexus, although it is constantly maintained that Weber was chiefly concerned with questions of historical causality.

One further point. I have mentioned value-freedom. In the discussion about this complex of problems no clear distinction was made between freedom of value-judgment and freedom of real values—a distinction which also plays an important part in dealing with the problems of power-politics. That power-politics are value-orientated lies in the nature of the matter, and if Weber understands and recommends parliamentarianism as a form of government which advances the power of a modern state, this is a matter of real values. There can be no question of a value-freedom consisting in the fact that Weber had conducted an empirical research to find out whether there was any better order. But even freedom of value-judgment, as long as it does not merely signify matter-of-factness and impartiality, is not only *not* Weber's scientific position, but he is directly concerned with developing and proving such value-judgments.

In this connection the first task would be to clarify why there is in Weber such a confusion of the problems of authority and legitimacy, which proved so disastrous in its consequences, and to show that this arises from his vague concept of power, which involves an overestimation of power as force. From this false premise arises Weber's misconception of justice and government, which gives too much weight to command and the sanctions of the use of physical force. This shows again a lack of empiricism linked with inexact philosophical assumptions. For it is simply not true that the state possesses a monopoly of the legitimate use of force: this may arise on occasion, but is not universally valid, and the excuse of an 'ideal type' confuses still further the actual way in which things are linked.

In my opinion all this is not dealt with sufficiently by my friend Aron in his paper, although it would have contributed to a more profound substantiation of the point of view he has expounded.[1]

HANS PAUL BAHRDT

In Professor Aron's paper we heard a series of quotations from Max Weber. We can no longer speak today as he did about 'power', 'nation', 'world politics'. And we think the Germans of the Imperial Reich would have done better to have prejudged the possibility of the development of Germany's power more modestly than even Max Weber did. We can only do him justice if we point out, even when he overestimated Germany's chance of becoming a Great Power (which was often the case even in the second half of the First World War), how far removed he was from the much more unrealistic opinions of his contemporaries.

In many of Max Weber's pronouncements we think we recognize Darwinian or Nietzschean modes of thought. Yet it seems to be more probable that his own heroic pessimism arose from a specific lack of solution in his own thinking.

I think therefore that for Max Weber, at least when he was older, the nation as such was not an ultimate irreducible value. If at the time of the Inaugural Speech in Freiburg a hint of unreflecting emotional nationalism clung to his criticism of contemporary Germany, later on (and I refer here to passages in Vol. I of *Wirtschaft und Gesellschaft*) he describes and completely exposes

[1] I should like to have dealt with all this in more detail, but can only refer to my latest book *Man and his Government* (New York, 1963), in which I try to outline a general theory of the connections between power, authority legality, and the state (government) on the basis of the experience and facts available to us today.

by analysis the typical progress of ethnic communities and then, where definite historic assumptions are available, the development of these into nations. It is indeed scarcely credible that a blind worshipper of national power as the essential basis of a nation could allow for neither the actual community of origin (let alone racial homogeneity) nor the mystery of language-community, but should declare nations to be wholly the result of historical and social processes, in which an erroneous assumption, only subsequently made, of common ancestry, plays a part, and common language is only one factor (sometimes not even present) beside other social and cultural factors. The significance of the common language is explained characteristically quite plainly by its quality as a commodity of mass-culture, i.e. as that part of culture which reaches all members of the society.[1] In this context he names a whole series of complicated 'degrees', sometimes differing on the basis of historical circumstances, 'of the qualitative unequivocality of the national "belief in community" '.[2]

Just as the 'nation' is not a final thing beyond which one cannot go, so too 'power' is not an ultimate value for Weber. If one considers the many passages in which he speaks emphatically about power (*Macht*), power-states (*Machtstaate*) and power-politics, one must be quite clear in what milieu and for what readers these political statements were made. He lived in a country obviously lacking in the feeling for power-relationships indispensable in politics. Some are intoxicated by unreal dreams of power, like the Pan-Germans and later the annexionists in the First World War, and thus lose the sure eye which Weber considered one of the most important assets of a politician. Others, the bourgeois liberals, whom Weber would gladly have seen stronger, lack the instinct and the will to get the power they need for success.

Weber finds himself in the complicated situation of a political thinker impelled by liberal motives, but having outgrown the categories and lines of thought of classical liberalism. So to a bourgeoisie, to whom a concrete liberal policy appeals, but who do not understand its altered assumptions, his desperate attempts to make himself comprehensible appear tortuous, ambiguous, even cynical. I do not think it is cynicism—and Professor Aron did not

[1] Cf. *Wirtschaft und Gesellschaft* (Tübingen, 1956), p. 243.
[2] Ibid., p. 242.

say it was—when Weber speaks of parliamentarianism and democracy as if they were only instruments of power-politics. Behind Weber's struggles for parliamentarianism there is ultimately a quite simple liberal motive, concern for the citizen's freedom. As for this freedom, Weber could no longer argue as classical liberalism had done. He could not expect it to come merely from limiting the power of those at the head of institutions. The power-factors of capitalism and bureaucracy, hardly open to the influence of institutional forms, were too strong and indispensable for that. A certain measure of freedom could only be obtained and held if there were competing forces.

It is doubtful whether Weber ever seriously hoped that the general process of bureaucratization, in view of its technical superiority above all other forms of government, would be checked. In any case he believed that only an enormously strong opponent, its equal in inner rationality, could provide a counterforce to it, and thus maintain that dynamic quality of society that was itself the prospect of freedom. In Weber's conception such opponents could only be capitalism, and the economically creative and entrepreneurially disposed bourgeoisie which sustained capitalism.

He asks: 'In view of this preponderantly bureaucratic tendency how is it possible to save any remnants of that freedom of movement that is in some sense "individualistic"? For in the end it is a gross self-deception to believe that we, even the most conservative of us, can even live today without these acquisitions from the time of the Rights of Man.'[1] The obvious answer to this is: the introduction of parliamentary democracy. The actual answer, behind the demand for democracy, can be read in the same work. A little earlier he talks of the consequences arising from the nationalization of employer-run business and says: 'If there were no private capitalism, governmental bureaucracy would reign alone. Private and public bureaucracies, which now work alongside each other, and when possible, against each other, thus to some extent keeping each other in check, would then be fused in a single hierarchy.'[2]

Socialism, according to Weber, is not a partner capable of arresting the process of bureaucratization, for it encourages the rise of a monolithic total bureaucracy: so only capitalism remains

[1] *Gesammelte politische Schriften* (Tübingen, 1958), p. 321.
[2] G.P.S., p. 320.

H

as a sufficiently powerful opponent. We can see why Weber constantly found it necessary to return to problems of power.

He certainly foresaw dangers ahead for bourgeois industrial capitalism. He thought he observed a strong leaning to the safety of a static investment capitalism.[1] But primarily he reproached the German middle class for not taking up the political tools corresponding to their dynamic economic role. He criticized harshly their bourgeois tendencies to ape aristocratic behaviour, and their preference for the older gentry out of fear of threats from the proletariat. He approved a middle-class struggle against the upper class, as well as the class struggle of the workers against the capitalists. All tendencies and ideas for reform which aimed at abolishing this struggle he thought either utopian or dangerous, not because he thought 'struggle' to be the 'meaning' of life—although many of his statements might lead one to think so—but because he saw a chance of freedom only if the dynamism of the social process was maintained. I believe Wolfgang J. Mommsen is right in thinking that even Weber's support of imperialist foreign policy is connected with his concern for the bourgeois–industrialist development of Germany which could not remain aloof from the world political struggle for power in this phase of history.[2]

Let us ask another question: was Weber really right when he foresaw as the greatest danger the general torpor and stagnation resulting from increasing bureaucratization and the decline of productive industrial capitalism into investment capitalism? If so, was he right to think that only a healthy productive capitalism, borne by a middle class conscious of instincts for power, could stop this development? Was imperialist foreign politics (and colonial politics) a phenomenon bound to accompany this bourgeois expansion?

However exact and realistic his analysis of his own times and however logical the extrapolation of trends for the future, Weber was not a very good prophet. (Of course it is easy for us to say what ought to have been prophesied between 1900 and 1920.) It seems to me that Weber was capable, as very few others are, of thinking ambivalently.

He is obviously a man who thinks in historical processes, not

[1] For example, G.P.S., pp. 177 ff.
[2] Wolfgang J. Mommsen, *Max Weber und die deutsche Politik* (Tübingen, 1959), p. 420. Cf. also (in Mommsen) Weber's position with regard to the fleet.

in historical static, functional patterns. But he does not seem to have succeeded in developing out of his ambivalent thinking and thought-process, a style of thinking which I would unreservedly call 'dialectic'. This does not mean that Weber must be accused of not having a comprehensive dialectical philosophy of history. We mean rather that he did not apparently succeed in foretelling the qualitative change which highly ambivalent phenomena can affect in the course of their immanent development.

This is how he was thinking when he spoke of the power-politics of the Great Powers, completely within the system of the seven or eight great powers which in his day, but only for a very short historical period, held a rather shaky equilibrium. He did not see, or did not see clearly enough, that in the course of industrial and particularly technical development a few powers particularly favoured by special geographical conditions can become world powers of a quite different order of greatness, while the others at best only become moderately great.

Further, Weber has some very illuminating passages about the connection between capitalist expansion and imperialism, but as far as I can see, no prognosis that the introduction of industrial capitalism into colonies must abolish after so short a time the premises of colonial sovereignty.

Professor Aron has already indicated, and we agree, that Weber, who praised so highly the capacity for achievement possessed by capitalist economics and productivity, makes no mention of the fact that the enormous growth of production could lead to change in the style and intention of capitalist economy, and thus perhaps to other political possibilities. He did not foresee the chances of mass-welfare and consequent internal expansion, and the subsequent superfluity of a hierarchy supporting exploitation and utilizing all the opportunities of imperialist foreign politics.

But this picture of an industrial capitalist middle class, resisting the growing atrophy through general bureaucratization is in part too pessimistic and in part too optimistic. Weber does not discuss the possibility that the three great modern types of rational mastery of practical problems—rational bureaucracy, rational capitalist economics, and scientifically based production techniques, could some time, through immanent processes of change, reach the point of being in a new relationship with one another. For example he does not see that scientific and technical progress can generate such large long-term investments in the interests of both military and economic development, that rational economic thought, geared to calculable chances in the market, becomes incompetent. The latter, i.e. the rational in the sense of calculating, is only possible in a short-term context. This circumstance which can lead, on the one hand, to a relative diminution of the power of production capitalists in favour of technicians inside enterprises, can, on the other, lead to a call for aid from the bureaucratic state, which having longer periods of time at its disposal, can make longer-term investments than the capitalist dares to make. Which of the two is the more dynamic, the bureaucrat or the capitalist?

Nor does Weber see something closely connected with this, i.e. that the constant expansion of bureaucracy in new and more complex spheres must lead to a crisis and to internal change within the bureaucracies. He often speaks of the importance of professional qualifications and official expertise. In comparison with feudal forms of government this kind of expertise has also to be seen as an expression of the improvement of productivity by specialization. But it is easy to overlook the fact that it is becoming more and more obvious that official expert knowledge is insufficiently specialized for the range and heterogeneity of the objects of government. This is expressed not only in criticism of juridical monopoly, not only in specialist advances in communication and in the preparation of data: this would suggest that the formalization of justice and of methods of government, as described by Weber, is no longer sufficient to keep clear and manageable the conditions over which government is exercised. It is apparent, too, in the revival of those groups of notabilities, depicted by Weber as outmoded, but now appearing as groups of experts. These are composed of people with specialist knowledge not common to the middle class, and not built into professional activity in the bureaucratic machine.

Bureaucracies thus lose their monolithic character and become polygot. The Babel of specialist jargons and the infiltration of forms of work alien to bureaucracy cause rifts in the firmly enclosed structure of bureaucracy; these rifts reduce, at least from time to time, its capacity for achievement, and thus its technical superiority over other forms of organization. Yet Weber thought that bureaucracy was inevitable because of this technical superiority. These phenomena do not, indeed, imply de-bureaucratization, but possibly a transformation of the great bureaucracies, which would in the long run give them another role in society and politics. For example it is conceivable that a state bureaucracy, shaken by crises, at the same time expanding, attracting new tasks, compelled to accept new scientific expertise and scientific techniques of information, is more dynamic than industrial capitalism whose applicability to technological development is only limited. If that should happen—and the development of the relationship between economy and state in many highly industrialized countries would indicate this—then the question of the chances for freedom in the future is no less debatable than when Weber asked it—but it must certainly be answered differently. Certainly it is not to be separated from the question of the division of power any more than it was in Weber's time, or indeed than it has been at any time.

WOLFGANG J. MOMMSEN

Professor Aron's paper has impressively presented the particular power-pragma which determined all Max Weber's politics and social work and which fills with a mixture of fascination and discomfort all who read it more closely: he has described with remarkable clarity its historical and intellectual roots. Even from the standpoint of a historian who has specialized in these questions, there remains little to add in this respect. However, a few additions and observations may perhaps be useful: I should like to base these on some newly acquired material.

Professor Aron made the specifically national aspect of Weber's ideas on power the central point of his brilliant analysis. This aspect was especially linked in the pre-war period with an imperialist viewpoint, in the narrower technical sense of the word. Professor Aron has already pointed this out and Professor Bahrdt has also spoken about it. It seems to me appropriate to look more closely at the imperialist element in Weber's thinking, since there are only concealed traces of it in his work. Weber shared the view, not uncommon in his time, that in the process of an intensified economic contest of the great nations in the world market, following a period of relatively peaceful economic exchange, the world would be divided up into economic spheres each reserved for its own national economy. Unlike Hobson, but like contemporary Marxist interpreters, he did not believe that capitalism was of itself in a position to create a constantly growing home market by stimulating new consumer-needs. In other words, he saw in the indefinite but foreseeable future, the attainment of a saturation point for any national economy that was excluded from world markets by insurmountable customs barriers: this would inevitably cripple the dynamics of capitalist economics. What this meant for Weber's ultimate ideals can here only be indicated: a gradual silting up of individual employers' initiative, bureaucratic economy to meet basic needs, death by suffocation of free voluntary political life, in short 'the hollow shell of future bondage' of a second late antiquity. These views which reveal Weber's personal attitude form the foil to his harsh imperialist pronouncements, as for instance in 1897 in Saarbrücken, that 'German industry, the foundation of its existence and its development, is endangered if we cannot support our economic interests sufficiently emphatically with a strong armed force'.[1] In the pre-war period Weber was a supporter of the economic theory of imperialism in the narrower sense, even if he set great store by sociological and socio-psychological factors. But this conviction of his (which shows through those parts of *Wirtschaft und Gesellschaft* compiled 1911–1923)[2] caused him almost fatalistically, and long before 1914, to count on a great European war breaking out. The quotations made by Professor Aron from the Freiburg inaugural speech are essentially to be understood from this point of view. Weber himself wrote that he 'had aroused dismay at the brutality of his opinions'.[3]

Weber seems to have modified his views on the nature of imperialism during the war: economic factors retreated in favour of national and power-political factors: the First World War was for him a battle to decide the extent of the influence of German culture in the world, as Professor Aron has already shown. As far as the role of economic motives was concerned, 'elbow-room' in the territorial sense, and especially in the colonial sense, was no longer the decisive factor, but the size of national capital reserves and the economic productive capacity of the nation in the future economic struggle of the Great Powers. For Weber the real

[1] Report in the *St. Johanner Zeitung*, Year 37, No. 10, 13 January 1897, of Weber's lecture in St. Johann-Saarbrücken on 9 January 1897 on 'The development of Germany and its importance, for the movement of population'.

[2] *Wirtschaft und Gesellschaft*, 4th ed. (Tübingen, 1956), vol. 2, pp. 520 ff.

[3] Letter to Alfred Weber on 17.5.1895, quoted in Mommsen, *Max Weber und die deutsche Politik* (Tübingen, 1959), p. 41.

question was whether the German economy would be in a position after the war to produce the amount of its own finance capital necessary to assert an independent position in face of the Anglo-Saxon world.[1] To this extent claims of territorial annexation retreated further into the background. It would of course be a mistake to see this as a fundamental revision of his ideas on power-politics.

Professor Aron was in some doubt as to whether Weber was really serious about implementing the principle of nationality. This is not quite justified, apart from the problem of the legal affiliation of Alsace-Lorraine. Actually Weber thought that the victory of the principle of the nation-state was only a question of time. Allow me in this connection to deal briefly with one of Professor Bahrdt's points. He opposed the view that the nation-state, even in the later period, was a supreme value for Weber. This is not confirmed by our source-material: even in 1920 there are frequent records of Weber's consistent avowal of the German state as the ultimate target of his political activity. The analysis of the concept 'nation' in *Wirtschaft und Gesellschaft* is particularly difficult. In this connection perhaps I may point out that in later years, influenced by developments in Austro-Hungary, he recommended a return to the idea of 'nation' based on community of language. He thought emphasis should be laid not on the state, but on the nation.[2] He was now more sceptical about the future of a multi-racial Austria than at the beginning of the war. He was no longer convinced that one should uphold the extension of the principle of the nation-state to the whole of Europe.

On the other hand Woodrow Wilson's idea, that a mere division of Europe into autonomous democratic nation-states would automatically bring peace to the world seemed to him a great illusion; he thought the autonomy of small nation-states only

[1] Cf. G.P.S., 2nd ed. (Tübingen, 1958), pp. 137 ff.; also Weber's letter to Friedrich Naumann on 2.11.1915, quoted in Mommsen, op. cit., p. 211, note 1, and Weber's speech in Nuremberg on 1 August 1916 on 'An independent commission for a German peace', German Central Archives I, Chancellor's Office, 2448: 'A major post-war problem will be the provision of capital for further development of German industry.'

[2] Cf. Weber's speech on 1 August 1916 in Nuremberg as reported in the evening edition of the *Frankische Kurier*, No. 391 on 2 August 1916: 'If one says that the state is supreme, and the ultimate in the world, this is quite correct, if correctly understood. The state is the highest organisation of power in the world, it has power over life and death. . . . It would be contradictory and false, however, to speak only of the state, and not of the nation.'

lastingly possible under the protective cloak of the hegemony of the great powers. This is the starting-point for his ideology of a special German task in the historical explanation of the first World War, the maintenance of a German-determined central European cultural circle, somewhere between 'Anglo-Saxon convention', 'Latin *raison*', and the 'Russian knout'. In a speech on 1 August 1916 (which remained unknown for a long time) he spoke of the great responsibility which, unlike the smaller neutral states and North America, the Germans bore to history. This belief in Germany's historical responsibility inspired his words: 'In thousands of years, our descendants will still be talking about Germany's sufferings, struggles and achievements in this terrible struggle for existence.'[1] Apart from all national feeling, Weber could think both of Germany's national power-interests and supranational ideals: he thought Germany should have the role of protective power to the small nations in Central Europe (a role which the U.S. adopts to a certain extent today). Yet for us, in contrast to the way it was seen by those living then, this cannot be more than a valid argument for the justification of power-politics for big nations. Even Weber, despite his comparatively sober thinking, was not wholly free from immoderately over-estimating the possibilities of German power-politics, advanced in the numerous private and official programmes of the time.

So we must agree wholly with Professor Aron when he gives as the quintessence of his analysis that in certain features, as for example in emphasizing the idea of the national-power-state, Weber's ideas remain bound to his time, a time which is not ours. Yet I wonder whether we can be satisfied with such a historical relativization of his thought, without a more exact estimate of its consequences for his collective sociological work. Since I am not particularly competent in the realm of sociological theory, I will confine myself to some few remarks. The view that one can separate Weber's theoretical work from his 'private' political utterances I consider to be mistaken. It is rather a question of defining the historically determined coefficients which we must employ to be able to apply Weber's theory correctly to the solution of today's very different problems. As a historian I see here the possibility of Weber becoming a fruitful source study for modern sociology.

One of the material problems in this connection seems to me to

[1] Ibid.

be the question of the limits and the legitimization of the use of power in internal politics. In Max Weber's eyes the idea of a powerful Germany justified the use of power even in conflict with ethical norms; in certain circumstances he even regarded it as a duty. We can hardly accept this today.

The problem however is hardly altered theoretically by the elimination of the concept of nation. There is no adequate theoretical justification in Weber for this principle (again formulated emphatically in *Politik als Beruf*) of the primacy of power-politics serving material aims as opposed to ethical duties. An actual basis for this fact is to be found in the fact that Weber's formal definition of the state as possessing the monopoly of the legal use of physical force has its origins in the doctrine of *raison d'état*. In one of the earliest parts of *Wirtschaft und Gesellschaft* 'political community' is defined as a group whose common activity is directed to 'reserving a sphere and the activity of those permanently and temporarily in it by readiness to use physical force, and indeed normally also by force of arms, for orderly control by those concerned (and if the case arises, to win for them further areas)'.[1] It is worthy of note that in this context imperialist expansion is expressly mentioned as a possible component of a state's use of force. Foreign politics is chosen here as the point of departure for a definition of the nature of the state: to this extent we need not be so surprised by Weber's blurring of the distinction between home and foreign politics, which Professor Aron has already pointed out.

Weber's national–imperialist ideas contain one of the reasons for explaining all political phenomena almost exclusively as extremely multiform modifications of the exercise of power; an interpretation which found a one-sided radical extension in Carl Schmitt's decisionism as mentioned by Professor Habermas. Weber's sociology of government has been appropriately called 'a sociology of power, such as has not been so fearlessly advanced since Machiavelli and Hobbes'.[2]

Weber interpreted the winning-over of a political following by means of charismatic talents or on a rational basis of one's own aims (in the sense of the theory of rational authority developed by

[1] Ibid., pp. 514 f.
[2] Gerhard Masur, 'Max Weber und Friedrich Meinecke in ihrem Verhältnis zur politischen Macht', *Studium Berolinense, Aufsätze und Beiträge zu Problemen der Wissenschaft und zur Geschichte der Friedrich-Wilhelm-Universität zu Berlin* (Berlin, 1960), p. 716.

Professor Friedrich) equally as forms of the exercise of power as the orders of a commander to his administrative staff. A quotation in illustration: 'A command can direct its effect from one person to another by "empathy" or "suggestion" or "rational persuasion" or by a combination of all these main forms of influence'.[1]

Such a comprehensive use of the concept of power in the framework of the sociology of government would of itself give no cause for criticism if it did not result in a priority in the failure of efforts to determine the limits of the exercise of power, and/or a justification of the power-process in the framework of such a system. The problem could perhaps be stated, a little too emphatically, in the one sentence: that there is no concept of non-legitimate rule in Weber's sociology of government, and cannot be, apart from the idea (which appears once in *Wirtschaft und Gesellschaft* but is never systematically developed) of explaining the medieval town-government as a model of non-legitimate government. To the extent that the basis of the legitimacy of a government disappears, so does the chance of getting obedience to orders: thus Weber's definition of a government is purely formal. In Weber's theory of modern government there are as it were lucunae which make various interpretations possible. Still greater is the possibility of manipulation or distortion, as Professor Topitsch demonstrated yesterday with reference to the doctrine of natural law.

Weber's reasons for his harsh emphasis on ideas of power are finally those of universal history as well as national. Here I may refer to Professor Bahrdt's explanations with which I concur at many points. Weber's chief interest was in the institutional structure of modern government, but this did not affect his interpretation of all politics, even internal, as power-politics. In the formation of a legal form of government such as parliamentary democracy, he saw no possibility of limiting 'man's control over other men', let alone abolishing it: he saw it merely as a postponement of chances of getting 'obedience to commands' for the benefit of other people. He was not particularly concerned with the question, a burning one today, about the possibilities of limiting potential misuse of power, or of opposing it with 'immanent bounds of legitimacy'.[2] As is well known, Weber expressly denied that natural

[1] W.G., p. 545.
[2] J. Winckelmann studies these limitations in his survey *Legitimität und Legalität in Max Webers Herrschaftssoziologie* (Tübingen, 1952), pp. 41 f.

law, which in his time was the usual form of such a system of normative limitation, could be a suitable basis for a modern legal system or a theory of 'constitutional democracy'. For Weber, the opposite question was of exclusive immediate interest, how the exercise of power in the sense of the creative structuring of society could be possible for long in view of what he thought to be the increasingly rapid rigidification of all social group-relationships. The concern about a 'new bondage in the future', whose prison-cage he saw being built by his contemporaries, his concern about an atrophying society, permeates the whole of his sociological work. For there was no room left in such a society for his highest ideal: a race of men, free, creative, individualist, choosing on their own initiative the social forms corresponding to their own values in life.

Weber's vigorous support of power-politics even in internal affairs is only understandable against this background of universal history.[1] He agreed with Nietzsche that all great social and cultural structures are the work of great individual personalities. Here the Nietzschean aspect of his philosophy, already indicated by Professor Aron, is again evident. A markedly aristocratic individualism was characteristic of Weber's thinking during all his life: this was reflected in his sharp rejection of any collective concepts in sociology.[2] He was not very far removed from Nietzsche's interpretation of the natural character of history, which only gains any meaning from the creative activity of great personalities. Great charismatic personalities who erect values have a duty, especially in a world declining into routine, to win a following for themselves, and in the furtherance of their own aims not to be afraid to use

[1] Cf. also Nolte, 'Max Weber vor dem Faschismus', *Der Staat*, vol. 2 (1963), pp. 22 f.

[2] Weber expressed this most clearly in a letter written to Robert Liefmann on 8 March 1920 (and found posthumously). He writes: 'If I am now a sociologist (according to my employment documents) I am so essentially in order to put an end to the use of collective concepts, a use which still haunts us. In other words: even sociology can only start from the action of one or a few, or many individuals, i.e. pursue a strictly "individualistic" method. Your views on the "state" for instance are quite old-fashioned. In the sociological sense, the state is nothing but the chance of certain kinds of specific actions taking place, the actions of certain individual persons. It is nothing else. . . . The "subjective" element in it is that the actions are oriented according to certain presuppositions. The "objective" element is that we—the observers—make this judgment: the chance exists that this action, orientated to these presuppositions, will ensue. If it does not exist, neither does the "state".'

power if necessary even in conflict with moral law, in order to keep open a society threatened by uniformity and atrophy through the increasing enclosure of social activity in legal formulae.

It is obvious that this should not happen in sterile despotic forms, but in the framework and with the specific means of plebiscitary mass-democracy as being in the circumstances the optimal form of choosing the leaders of society. This is an enthusiastic aristocratic liberalism, changing into a formal democratic Caesarism, in the face of a mass society which had become anti-liberal. Weber coined for it in 1919 the concept of 'plebiscitary leader-democracy'.[1] Dialectically outstripping the positions of classical liberalism, Weber also mocks at outmoded negative liberalism, whose only claims from the state are freedom and an optimum 'diminution of control'.[2] In the same context belong his keen polemics against all who believe good administration to be the aim of all politics.[3] The transition to parliamentarianism was for Weber first and foremost a means of increasing the power of the German state. The traditional striving of continental liberalism to supersede 'man's control over men' by 'the control of the law', or at least to reduce it, he considered a complete illusion. He felt basically only scorn for such 'feeble ideals'. His position is better expressed by the formula: 'as much freedom as possible with as much control as possible'. The advantage of 'leader-democracy' over 'leaderless democracy' lay for him precisely in that the latter furthers the creative power-politics of great politicians, while the former tends to the 'diminution of control' or, more precisely, to a lightening of the burden of leadership.

KARL W. DEUTSCH

This morning we experienced the lively mind of Raymond Aron, and we shall always be grateful for this experience. But we must also ask how precise and balanced a picture of Weber's mind we found in this brilliant and fascinating paper. We ask two things of every scholar whose work we want to understand: one as to the origin of his ideas, with reference to place and time, and one, quite different, about the depth and range of his ideas.

---

[1] Cf. the writer's essay on Weber's treatment of the problem of 'plebiscitary leader-democracy', *Kölner Zeitschrift 1963*, part 2, pp. 255 ff.

[2] Cf. W.G., p. 157.   [3] Cf. G.P.S., p. 277.

Let us first ask: what did Weber mean? This is like asking: what did Newton mean? and is different from the question: what is the range and what are the limits of Newtonian physics? So we ask first about Weber's personal opinions. We find in Professor Aron's paper the statement: Weber's ultimate ideal was the prestige and greatness of the nation, heightened by parliamentarianism, but more possibly by charismatic plebiscitary dictatorship. This portrayal of Weber is a clever and profound parable, and perhaps not unconsciously, a parable also for French readers. But the quotations in support of this parable are, although not all, for the most part from Weber's writings during the First World War. In the printed copy of Professor Aron's paper most of the notes refer to the 'Political Writings'. If one follows these up, it appears that some of the most vehement passages come from a three-page letter written in 1916 to a women's magazine, in which he polemicized against pacifists. This is not improper: he was then writing in a particular climate. But it is questionable how much stronger or more biased his formulations became in the climate of the war-years 1915–16–17.

A second point: Weber writes as a lawyer, an advocate of certain political courses of action or strategy. It is not unknown for advocates to borrow, apparently uncritically, their opponent's arguments in order to represent their client's case according to the opponent's value-premises. If one reads carefully through the passages quoted by Professor Aron, it often appears that Weber employed the rhetoric of the power-politics of 1916 in order actually to persuade his readers to moderation. He proposed that they should not begin unlimited U-boat warfare; he warned them against repeating the fateful error of 1915, the false estimate of Italy's position, when it was first maintained that that country was bluffing, but, when they eventually entered the struggle, saying that they had always wanted the war. And he warned his compatriots not to commit this fatal underestimation of foreign opinion in connection with America.

Above all, Weber constantly proposed moderate aims, not exaggerated ones. And this he does often in the same passages where Professor Aron's quotations end with the words: 'Thus far Max Weber'. But Weber actually went further, and often spoke of the agreement, the consent, the interest of Germany, or else, like many of his contemporaries he saw his country engaged in a struggle for existence. We are not now concerned whether Weber's judgments were realistic. In 1916 he wrote that Germany was fighting for her life against armies of Gurkhas and Negroes, who would turn the country into a desert. The Allies were actually more interested in rebuilding the Germany they conquered than in laying it waste.

Things were not wholly as Weber saw them. But the idea of a country fighting for its life, the idea of a law of community of language is not quite the same as the unbounded worship of national power. I quote Weber (1916): 'Only the balance between the great powers guarantees the freedom of the smaller nations.' And again: the Germans were fighting the over-running of the world by the Russians and the Anglo-Saxons. That is nationalism, but it is not unlimited power-politics. It is the classical aim of a balance between the powers, including Germany, in contrast to the newer dream of a German world-hegemony, cherished by the extreme nationalists of his day.

Professor Aron has convincingly explained how far Weber was from our contemporary consciousness of internationalism, and from our understanding responsibility to the world, how far from that internationalism which Professor Aron himself has so often and so honorably represented. It is perhaps no more than just, not to ignore how much separates Weber also from the extreme nationalism and power-worship of so many of his contemporaries.

But what is the objective range of Weber's ideas? What untapped scientific possibilities do they contain? We owe Weber not only biography and philology but also the living continuation of his ideas, including our dissociation from some of them, just as the physicists who accepted Einstein's theory of relativity, proceeded to reject his ideas on quantum theory as being incorrect. In Professor Aron's paper we find a definition of power which aligns Weber with Machiavelli and Hobbes, the idea that there is no other order in the world than that introduced by some external power. Without a sovereign Hobbes saw nothing but chaos. But there is a second idea of the world, which we find in Locke, that there is a natural law corresponding to the state of nature, i.e. that the systems of the world, in the absence of sovereignty, are not completely chaotic but that it is also possible to imagine self-ordering systems. This is an old problem of philosophy and social science, but one can also say that there are often in Weber's ideas notions of balance, counter-balance, and development towards rationality, and that this rationality is an ideal for Weber. So the world is not a completely Hobbesian system for Weber—neither for his cognitive nor for his evaluative thinking—and the comparison of Weber's world with that of Hobbes is an over-simplification of his ideas.

Weber's distinction between fact and ideal does not therefore necessarily have to end in a blind alley. It can be developed further. Weber makes a correct distinction: he often defines facts as proba-bilities. He speaks again and again of *Chance*.[1] Values, he says, are chosen against the background of revealed facts and probabilities. But one could develop his ideas still further in two respects.

Firstly—men live, as Weber himself well knew, not only by single values, but each man lives by a multiplicity of values, none of which can be reduced beyond a certain degree. Weber's rational criticism is therefore applicable to the question of the compatibility of values. At any given time and place, this com-patibility can be empirically tested and scientifically established. Science can therefore very well decide whether a value-configura-tion belongs to the *class* of consistent and viable value-constella-tions. This conclusion is subject to error, being based on the strength of probability, but in this sense it is a scientific conclusion like any other. However, *within* the class of probable value-configurations that are viable, science cannot arbitrate; within this class possible strategies are determined in terms of ethical, rather than in terms of scientific values.

Value-consistency can even be expressed mathematically, since it can be conceived scientifically. Political economy disposes of a whole series of formulae by which the gain in one value and the loss in another can be expressed simultaneously and made com-prehensible. The factor-analysis of psychologists and many sociologists is another tool which could be used here. Weber's ethics of responsibility could be developed into a resultant gain of responsibility for secondary value-consequences: what effect does the pursuit of one value have on other values?

Let us apply these ideas to the problem of power. As Professor Aron reminded us, Weber puts the sharper, narrower concept of sovereignty before the concept of power. But government, for

---

[1] In a number of contexts: for example he sees social class as something that may be discussed in terms of individuals' life prospects, the probability of using goods *or* services in the market—Eds.

Weber, is the chance of getting obedience. A chance is a probability, and the answer to the question: what is chance? is a number.

So Weber's concept of sovereign power is quantitative. His concept of the chance of getting obedience is a probability and a probability is a frequency.

So Weber's concept of sovereign power is a matter of the frequency of men's compliance or submission. How often do men submit in their behaviour to the directions or orders of the government? or of their rulers?

This idea of Weber's can be operationalized. There are methods of measuring the rates of success of members of parliament in parliamentary voting. Robert Dahl has put figures to the names of a great number of American senators which show how often a particular senator voted for measures that were carried. It is possible to define the participation in decisions on important matters as power, and then calculate rates of participation. These ideas were put forward by the American theoretician Harold Lasswell, and I find both his and Dahl's method compatible with Weber's ideas.

One could go further. One could collate the rates of submission for whole countries and populations, especially for certain kinds of behaviour: how often do men comply with penal laws, taxation laws, taxation ethics? What are the rates of compliance, of infringement, of enforcement? We know that the rate of enforcement sometimes raises that of compliance, but sometimes decreases it by embittering the population. We know that the rate of submission depends, in general, less on that of enforcement than on other social, economic and cultural conditions. We can try to express this interaction of rates of submission, transgression and enforcement by a system of equations. Weber's theory, thus explained and enriched by the factor of the autonomous probability of relevant behaviour, forms a mathematical model of four equations which I regret I cannot show you here.

Weber tells us further that the rate of submission rests above all on legitimacy, on submission for internal reasons. He sees these internal reasons for submission in tradition, charisma and legality supplied by bureaucratic–rational routine. He says that in practice submission often stems from a combination of these three sources, but he also states very clearly that the proportions of these sources become altered in the process of development.

This offers three interesting starting-points for a further development of Weber's ideas.

Firstly, it is possible to measure legitimacy. The idea that legitimacy is measurable by the frequency of unsupervised submission is as old as the Greek sophists. How high is the rate of submission in the absence of supervision and how different is it in the presence of supervision and instruction? The higher the rate of unsupervised submission, the greater the legitimacy.

Secondly, Weber's theory could be expanded into a theory of sociological influence and social change of the super-ego. We will leave this particular development to our colleagues in social psychology and psychiatry.

Thirdly, there is the possibility of a more sociologically and politically oriented theory of the stage of economic and political development. Where tradition reigns unbroken, there is little room for charisma. Where tradition cracks under the pressure of economic development, or under the pressure of crisis or catastrophe, or of radical change in technology at each state of development there is again the possibility of charismatic leadership, the search and yearning for the charismatic leader grow in the hearts of men. It is also possible to develop from Weber's ideas a kind of 'market research for charisma'. The transition period, while the charismatic leadership is being sought, ends once again with the transition to bureaucratic routine, in which the frozen charisma atrophies in legality.

It would therefore be possible to construct from Weber's ideas a theory of the alternation of charismatic and non-charismatic periods in the history of the development of each people and each country. Charisma, thus viewed, is the source of legitimacy and form of government in periods of transition. Martin Lipset has tried to demonstrate this for the America of George Washington and the Ghana of Kwame Nkrumah. Significant aspects of these processes are measurable. The erosion of traditional authority is not independent of measurable social changes, which are comprised in the idea of social mobility. I cannot go into this in detail here. I should just like to say that these displacements nowadays in the developing countries are represented by a displacement of I per cent of the population each year out of the tradition-bound sector of society into the sector socially mobilized for mass-communication and potential political participation.

What is lacking in Weber's concept of power? Firstly, the idea of the autonomous probability of commanded behaviour. This is a dangerous lacuna. Secondly, the idea of the cost of power, the 'opportunity costs', as the political economist says. Thirdly, perhaps one could develop something which receives too little attention in Weber's thinking—but which I think is implicit in it, i.e. the notion of politics as an often decisively important instrument in speeding up social learning, in speeding up and guiding the learning of new forms of behaviour and new forms of social co-operation. In this sense power as such is of no substance. Talcott Parsons has explained that in this sense power can be compared with the idea of money; like paper money, it has no buying power of itself, but indicates human relationships. If one continues these ideas, force is analogous to gold, and prestige to credit. Professor Parsons, in some of his essays, and I myself in a chapter of my book, have further explained these ideas.

Let us come to a conclusion. In his *General Economic History* Weber has given us other ideas which are perhaps of the greatest significance for understanding him. In his view the West grew not primarily from power as such, but out of the self-governing town: this self-administering town grew from a feudal community, that community from the sacrament of holy communion, which first made these men capable of law and organization. The rise of the West, the greatest development of power in the history of the world, came about according to Weber from a chain of events, which in their nature are far more relevant to human communication and living together than to men's power to command, and these events had only secondary consequences in the sphere of forms of government. Weber was here thinking like Nietzsche who once said: 'the greatest changes in the history of mankind come not in our loudest, but in our quietest hours'. Nietzsche was speaking not of the displacement of power, but of changes in values, when he spoke of the revolving of the earth: 'It revolves inaudibly—we cannot hear it turn', he said. In this spirit Weber's sociological observation of history can also help us to understand better the hidden interaction of changes in value, power and knowledge in the development of social orders and of states.

EDUARD BAUMGARTEN

The organizers of the congress were kind enough to invite me to make some observations without any previous preparation, because

I was wholly occupied up to the last minute with another piece of work, which was indeed concerned with the same subject.[1] I have therefore the doubtful pleasure of using weapons which I have sharpened only while listening to Professor Aron and the other speakers: allow me to make a friendly use of these weapons under the motto of the lion, who in the coat of arms above our heads, holds open a book, on whose pages stands 'Semper apertus'. Professor Aron followed this motto in an exemplary way in his paper, notwithstanding several passages where Professor Deutsch thought that, if Professor Aron ended a quotation with 'Thus far Weber', the later part of the text *not* communicated to us showed instantly a quite different Weber.

That may well be: that has struck me too in several passages. And yet in principle—the whole of Weber *was* revealed to us by Professor Aron. He so arranged the sequence of abbreviated quotations that in every passage he quoted the whole range of Weber's position was apparent. I would say this was quite different from Professor Mommsen's paper: he appeared here—much more strikingly than in his excellent book—as the public prosecutor, under the pretext that a great man of genius should not be so much a child of his time as Max Weber was: Mommsen often actually concealed with the hand of a public prosecutor those passages in the defendant's speech which contained answers against his verdicts: if he had read them out, the verdict 'guilty' would have been more often refuted as invalid and unjust. I would have to prove that in more detail: it would be easy to prove. But that is not the point at this moment. A great man is like a visitor who has still not departed on the third day:[2] Weber will be still with us after these three days, and the difficulty is not so much that he was a child of his time, but that we are children of our fears which result from our experiences, and our reproaches to him would be better directed against ourselves.

Weber said in one place: 'No pedantry in the world can be too great to oppose confusion.' In Professor Aron's excellent lecture, there was still one confusion concerning a central point. Professor Aron said that Weber had reduced parliamentarianism and democracy to mere tools of the nation's greatness, and this national

---

[1] *Max Weber—Werk und Person* (documents chosen and commented on by Eduard Baumgarten), Tübingen, 1964.

[2] [There is a German proverb: *Am dritten Tag der Gast stinkt*. Eds.]

greatness was for him the supreme absolute value. The confusion lies in the word 'absolute'. The ideal of 'the greatness of the nation' was on the contrary conditionally qualified. So little is it true that he thought of democracy only as the sum of a number of tools, that the greatness of a nation in the modern world only consisted for him to the extent to which this nation developed real democracy. It is true that in his notorious inaugural speech in Freiburg, he said 'Human happiness? Abandon hope, all ye. . . .' But he went on to say: What interests us is that we should develop in men, first of all in our compatriots and ourselves, that kind of human character which our children and our grandchildren will still acknowledge. If one asks what he imagined this character to be, which our children will readily admit, he defined it first of all negatively. Our descendants will *not* want to recognize us if, as parvenus of power, we merely make loud noises on the world's stage: they will not want to know anything about German power, if it remains at the point where the present German will to power only knows the N.C.O.'s form of it: 'Commanding, obeying, standing to attention, boasting.' That is a passage where Professor Aron stopped reading before the end. Professor Deutsch's objection, 'Thus far Weber . . .' fits in here and the main point was still to come. [Interjection from Professor Aron: 'But I *did* quote passages about the perversion of power!'.] Certainly you did, but not as far as the point where it becomes quite clear how power, typically German power, was the actual object of hatred, of Weber's national self-hatred. Your quotations tended perceptibly in this direction, but you did not carry them to their full conclusion. For you and for us this conclusion would have been that Weber's concept of power was orientated not to Nietzsche nor to Darwin, let alone to the concept of the 'master-race' (Herrenvolk), but to the passionate, wholly unliterary, elementary, simple desire to be successful within the framework of the European tradition of power in the external and internal contest with the great bearers of political power, the English and the French. In 1917, in the middle of the war, Weber spoke of 'Herrenvolk'. In what sense? He had rejected these words of the Pan-Germans: 'We must be a master-race': and declared, 'We are not a master-race for we put up with our monarch.' Internationally considered, this was an unprecedented occurrence. I should like to ask which nation, priding itself on its national symbols, would have allowed in its midst during wartime a man who like Weber, would attack and pillory the monarch, their own Kaiser, in this casual way. But for Max Weber this was still possible in the 'authoritarian state' of Germany, and it signified this: that the greatness of the nation was for him not a sacrosanct and absolute value, but relative, and above all, open to, and needing, criticism. His article against the Kaiser, as well as the one against Bismarck (which had as little respect for a German symbol of national greatness as the article he wrote against the Kaiser) appeared in the national *Frankfurter Zeitung*. Many of his compatriots forthwith stopped taking the *Frankfurter Zeitung*, people of the extreme right and of the extreme left: 'Max Weber is a disgrace to the nation', they said. In the same way, Ludendorff said to me after the war, that Weber was a traitor to his country. It remains a fact that Weber was felt by his contemporaries to be a man who tended to scorn the 'greatness of the nation', at least in the sense of a conventional prestige, rather than to consider it sacred. It was during the war also that he wrote the essay on 'Value-freedom', which ends more or less as follows: the scientist as scientist has *one* unmistakable vocation: to keep a cool head even about the highest ideals, particularly during the war, i.e. particularly about the ideals of the state. In this connection it is the scholar's vocation to work in freedom, in certain circumstances to swim against the tide, not to surrender unconditionally to the ideal of national power.

In 1911, before the war, Weber wrote in a letter to Graf Keyserling: We Germans are not a people of culture because we have not had the nerve to behead at least one of our monarchs. Honigsheim, the well-known sociologist of religion, who emigrated to the U.S., certainly tended to isolate and overestimate in his memoirs the significance of some of Weber's emphatic pronouncements: and yet it did so happen that Weber once said, in the years before the war, to his young friends Honigsheim, Georg Lukács, and Ernst Bloch: 'if I ever hold a seminar again, I won't admit any Germans, only Jews, Poles and Russians'. His hearers did not sufficiently discount his anger at that particular moment. Lukács and Bloch were deeply disgusted to see and hear the same Weber who had once so impressively denigrated his country—now in a patriot's uniform—in the hall of his house in Heidelberg, at Ziegelhauser Landstrasse, on the first Sunday in August 1914.

The apparent contradiction, which annoyed Lukács and Bloch,

contains precisely that phenomenon which allows us to put our finger on the point which I previously indicated as a confusion. Professor Aron is perfectly right when he quotes Weber as saying: Political economy and the politics of economy must serve an absolute ideal, namely the nation's power-interests.

Political economy, economics, is not a terrain which includes the whole of mankind as 'humanitas'. For Weber, the existence of the nation and its chances of power were an ultimate point of orientation for economic policy. But from a human point of view the nation signified neither an absolute nor the supreme value. We are not splitting hairs when we assert that he ascribed to the nation a value, for man as human being, which was absolutely binding. A man belongs absolutely to his nation, in the sense of an unalterable inescapable loyalty. However negative or critical one's feelings about the cultural qualities of one's own people—permanently or at any given time—Weber thinks he still belongs to them in an absolute sense. He feels really responsible for the people of this nation as for those of no other. In this Weber is a scholar neither of Nietzsche nor of Darwin, but something much older; he is the Socrates of the *Crito*, who does not leave his prison, but answers to his 'freer' worldly disciples, who want to 'liberate' him: I do not want to live anywhere else: I want to die here as a slave and a native. There is a passage in a letter written in 1911 (to Frau Else Jaffé). 'For you see the vassals in olden times often said to their lord, "Lead us to hell if you must, and our hands and hearts belong to you gladly. Only know and hear this, master—you are wrong. Our heads tell us so, and they remain our own." ' Now this looks as if Weber had a vassal's loyalty to his country and yet kept his *head* free towards it. I would have no objection to this interpretation.

I think I have come to the end of my time, and turn towards you, Professor Aron. I can not only endorse a certain thesis of yours, but confirm it; this thesis is linked in my mind in a surprising way with 'value-freedom', or more precisely with what Weber always claimed as value-discussion. Certain values can, in his opinion, be made the subject of value-free discussion, i.e. of impartial, purely practical discussion. Then there appears something astonishing, a phenomenon which remains dominant in Weber from beginning to end. In 1893, in discussion with the Social Democrats in the Social Political Club, he declared that they should certainly return and take part in discussions, but not as if we thought we could convince them by our opinions or shake them in theirs. Nothing of the kind. But we need it as a criticism of us, so that we can stand so much more securely by our opinions. That was Berlin 1893. The close of his discussion of values was *Wissenschaft als Beruf* (Munich, 1919), in which he said that value-discussions carried on bitterly did not bring men together, but showed them the unbridgeable gap which necessarily separated them. It seems that a sovereignty of the unteachable individual and his convictions is postulated, which has a remarkable affinity with the sovereignty of the power-status. There is indeed a parallel here, which introduces a not only questionable, but obviously weak, point into Weber's otherwise strong positions regarding problems of the freedom of value-judgments. Here, above all, is criticism of Weber warranted. And at this point I should quickly come to far-reaching agreement with Professor Aron. The differences with Professor Mommsen, on the contrary, cannot be settled satisfactorily yet.

ADOLF ARNDT

In Professor Aron's masterly lecture of Cartesian clarity we found a Weber who is worthy of respect, 'not because, but although' his work contains a risk of evil. This risk of evil is the point I want briefly to deal with.

There are two decisive problems which I think cannot be left as Aron dealt with them. One is the point when he said that Weber had not made clear the heterogeneity of external and internal politics. Secondly I completely missed Weber's value-doctrine of power, concealed by his vaguely expressed concepts of legitimacy.

Firstly, Weber's view of the connection between home and foreign policies. However amateurish Weber's political activity often appears (excuse me if I say that so bluntly), his view of this connection holds something extraordinarily pregnant for the future. Today, I think the necessity of the co-ordination of home and foreign policies is no longer questioned. I would dare to say that one of the objective reasons for both world wars lay in the delayed, tardy and insufficient democratization of Germany. If one sees this, one cannot criticize Weber so strongly. His doctrine of legitimacy comes into play in the matter of the co-ordination of internal and external politics—particularly for foreign policy.

When he investigates the legitimacy and explains its three kinds, he is questioning the justification of power. Consequently Professor Mommsen's statement that Weber recognized no illegitimate power, cannot be correct. If someone asks how and by what means power becomes lawful and justified, and finds three kinds of legitimacy, then logic compels the existence of power which, in his eyes, is illegitimate. This can easily be seen in history. What did Weber meet with in his own times? What he found was an unlawful handling of power by officials who understood nothing about politics. Thus Germany's condition up to 1914, and again after 1917, was worsened by the fact that the military leadership, the supreme army command, unlawfully took over political leadership, the leadership of the Reich. This was the situation that Weber found. So he comes to his question: when exactly *is* power legitimate? He distinguishes, I would say, between two irrational and one rational form of the legitimate. The irrational or ideological forms of legitimization are the traditional which claim something as correct and valid because it always has been, and the charismatic, which bewitches us and demands belief. The rational way of justifying power is legality.

To be sure, Weber often stood in his own way, as for instance by his unfortunate decision which was due to a personal and political bias, not a scientific judgment; his claim that in the confusion of the transition period after 1918 one should strive for a charismatic government, a transition government to which he gave the unfortunate title 'plebiscitary leader-democracy (not however dictatorship!). Here I fall into the strange role of the lawyer having to defend a Nationalist, and must call attention to the fact that Weber did not appeal for global power or aim at a totalitarian regime. He advised a plebiscitary leader-democracy, as he unhappily named it, a concept which moreover twice contains the idea of democracy. One must however not ignore the fact that for him this so-called 'plebiscitary leader-democracy' was insolubly linked with two presuppositions: with a bureaucracy, working competently and reliably on the basis of stable legislation, and with a tight control of this bureaucracy through a strict right of enquiry on the part of parliament. Nor must we ignore the fact that the regime Weber recommended for the transition period of confusion after 1918 was to be democratically legitimized and founded, and that the civil service, stable legislature and a freely elected parliament with rights of enquiry should take collective decisions.

And so I would contradict Professor Habermas and Professor Mommsen: Carl Schmitt is not a pupil of Max Weber, not a really legitimate pupil. Carl Schmitt did what he always did: he made an arbitrary selection of certain elements; he knocked together a patter, for example, for his idea of parliamentary democracy, and used the conjurer's trick of incorporating before-hand the error he later found in it, which made it impossible to function; in this way Schmitt made it possible for himself to attack democracy, not as it is or should be, but the false model he made of it. We should not hang Weber with Carl Schmitt. That is unjust, as well as being historically inaccurate.

Back to the question of justifying power. This question contains the presupposition that power is not justified by itself, but needs justification. Weber enumerated the possible forms of justification descriptively and under the postulate of value-freedom: two irrational kinds and one rational. But the rational kind of legitimacy does not, for Heaven's sake, mean that he wanted to maintain any kind of law, no matter what! (and this is proved by his writings). To desanctify the law by reason is not arbitrariness, but reasonable practical justice. Perhaps for Weber's formulations it is a tragic circumstance that in his day German legal teaching reached its lowest point: it did homage to a positivism which had lost any meaning it could and should have. Perhaps, too, it is Weber's misfortune that single definitions of his become isolated, for instance the inadequate definition of the state as the community which successfully claims for itself within a certain sphere the monopoly of legitimate physical force.[1] This definition—in the sense of nation-state—is only meant for relationships with other states, and is simply an attempt to approach the phenomenon of 'state' under the postulate of value-freedom: yet in stressing the point that force must be legitimate, it admits its own limitations and points to the value problem, the question of how power may be invested with value—which contains the tacit recognition that there is no value in power alone. Only by realizing the inherent meaning of power by something which gives it a value, does the whole come into view, and new perspectives open.

Apart from the unhappy idea that Weber had of suggesting

---

[1] Cf. my criticism of this in *Staatliche Gewaltanwendung, rechtlich und politisch betrachtet* (Bad Homburg, 1961).

to politicians his so-called 'plebiscitary leader-democracy' as a transition solution for a time of confusion, his scientific position reveals the view that this man, who claimed justice in a capitalist period to be calculable ('like a machine'), therefore excluding chance and arbitrariness, considered rationality of the law appropriate for his own times. The irrational and the rational kinds of legitimacy are not timeless and indifferently interchangeable. The postulated stability of the law should not be based on chance nor rest on decisionism, but on an awareness of problems, on the practical consideration of their relationships and the reasonableness of their solution, since the best chance of winning obedience lay in reasonableness, i.e. moderation and understanding. At the heart of Weber's value-doctrine, contained in his question about legitimacy of power, we can glimpse the beginnings of the thinking-out of the problem, which meanwhile had been opened up and developed by basic research in jurisprudence.[1]

What Weber means by the category of legitimacy of rational purposefulness must not be misinterpreted by misunderstanding a positivism, no longer meaningful, which identifies power with law; i.e. not arbitrary law, but a form of law which legitimizes power by a convincing reasonableness, and which arises from an awareness of the problems considered. It is thus not deduced from a closed system of natural law, nor justified traditionally and charismatically, but achieves something new by insight into practical relationships. There can be no clearer formulation of this than the one Professor Henrich gave us yesterday.

So much for Weber's problem as to the justification that will confer legitimacy on power;—power that is of value. In wrestling with this problem Weber should be seen as a political pedagogue, not as a political practitioner. We should not forget that he put three questions to himself and to us: How can we make the people political? (not with the dreadful 'political education'! he wanted political people, not 'politically educated' people!). How can we instruct parliament? How can we find politicians of the right calibre? Weber formulated these questions out of his doubts about Germany. His direction was always towards disenchantment,

---

[1] Cf. Theodor Viehweg, *Topik und Jurisprudenz*, 2nd ed. (Munich, 1963); Josef Esser, *Grundsatz und Norm in der richterlichen Fortbildung des Privatrechts* (Tübingen, 1956), and my article, 'Gesetzesrecht und Richterrecht', *Neue Juristische Wochenschrift* (1963), p. 1273.

de-ideologization, towards awareness, the rational and reasonable. (It is possible that the 'eternal values' will come to us in new understanding through the portals of reason: it is certain that this direction of thought is the polar opposite from Carl Schmitt's and the ensuing totalitarianism.) In these three questions therefore lay Weber's pedagogical ideas. Perhaps this congress will recognize that we are still faced with these three questions today.

Conclusion

RAYMOND ARON

I have obviously not the time to defend myself against all your criticisms, not even to defend myself against my defender, Professor Mommsen, for he went so far in the same direction as I, that if I had time, I should have to start arguing with him. Professor Deutsch has told me more or less plainly that I translated Weber into French. That may be so, but he can be translated into American too, even with a certain 'German' thoroughness. But whether the American or the French translation is the better, is not to be determined in a 'value-free' way.

I would like to add one or two things on one point: when we deal with a great thinker, a great personality, and especially a controversial personality, it is of course possible to imagine several interpretations of this man's work and thought. I am not convinced that I would give exactly the same interpretation next year, and it is correct that such an interpretation should be discussed. But I should like to defend myself against one particular criticism: that I only quoted half of the relevant passages. Of course, if one is quoting one gives half the page: but even if one gives three quarters of the page one does not give four quarters. One can always argue like this. Anyway I tried to reproduce the different aspects of Weber's lines of thought. I said what he meant by power-politics. But I also quoted the passages where he censures power-politics. So I think I was not so biased as has been suggested. But of course my subject was a limited one. I did not develop all Weber's lines of thought, I only tried to establish what he thought in his time and in his situation. I believe, in spite of the discussion, that he was a nationalist, and I think it better to honour a great man, in accepting him as he was, and not as we would prefer to see him fifty years later.

It is quite possible that one can measure legality mathematically, but this lies beyond Weber's range of ideas. It is of course a fruitful development of certain directions of his thinking. But he was a philosopher: he believed in the distinction between command and obedience, and he would never have agreed that money and power are identical. In my opinion, that is Weber translated into American: it may be an improvement, but it is not the Max Weber I have read, and read several times, each time with renewed admiration.

PART III

Industrialization and Capitalism

HERBERT MARCUSE

Industrialization and capitalism in Max Weber's work are problematic in two respects: as the historic destiny of the West, and the present destiny of the Germany created by Bismarck. As the destiny of the West industrialization and capitalism are the definite reifications of that occidential rationality, the idea of reason, of which Weber was so aware in all its manifestations: open and concealed, progressive and repressive. As the destiny of modern Germany, Weber believed that they determined the policy of the Reich: first the historical task of the German bourgeoisie in overthrowing the conservative feudal state, then in democratization and lastly in the struggle against revolution and socialism. It is essentially the idea of such a combination of industrialization, capitalism and national self-preservation that motivates Weber's passionate and indeed malevolent attack on the socialist attempts of 1918. Socialism contradicts the idea of Western reason, and the idea of a national state, therefore socialism is a universal mistake, if not a universal crime. (We allow ourselves to ask what Weber would have said if he had seen how not the West, but the East is developing western rationality in its most extreme form—in the name of socialism.) Whatever capitalism may do to man, it is to be understood first and foremost and essentially as reason.

Weber's analysis of industrial capitalism combines indissolubly philosophical, socio-historical and political motives. His theory of the internal value-freedom of science is shown for what it is in practice: the freeing of science for the acceptance of evaluations imposed from outside. Since his inaugural speech at Freiburg, in which he openly and recklessly subordinated value-free economics to the demands of imperial power-politics, this function of Weber's scientific doctrine is clear. He expounded it himself very sharply

133

at a later date (at the conference of the Verein für Sozialpolitik in
1909).[1]

The reason why, on every occasion and with a certain amount of
pedantry, I oppose so extraordinarily sharply the use of the actual
[Seiend] to revive the ideal [Seinsollen], is not that I underestimate the
question of what should be, but exactly the contrary: it is because I
cannot bear to see problems of world-shaking importance, the most
far-reaching ideas, in a certain sense the greatest problems which can
concern mankind, are here turned into a technical and economic
question of 'productivity' and into the subject of discussion of a specialist
discipline.

The ideal, however, which is separated from science (which is
mere specialization) is at the same time protected from science and
scientific criticism: 'the value of that ideal itself can never be
deduced from the material of scientific work'.[2]

Weber's analysis of industrial capitalism shows that the concept
of scientific neutrality, or rather impotence, is not tenable against
the ideal: pure value-free philosophical–sociological conceptualization becomes a critique of values in its own development: and, on
the other hand, pure value-free scientific concepts conceal their
own valuations: they become a critique of the facts given in the
light of what these facts inflict on things and men. The 'ideal' is
revealed in the 'actual': the indefatigable dynamism of the concept
forces it into the open. In Weber's most value-free work (*Wirtschaft
und Gesellschaft*) where there are veritable orgies of formal
definitions, classifications, typologies, the 'sharp edge' is provided
by formalism. This authentic concretization is the result of his
mastery of an enormous amount of material, an erudition inconceivable nowadays, an intelligence capable of abstractions, because
able to distinguish the essential from the inessential, the real from
the apparent. Formal theory, with its abstract concepts, attains
what a pseudo-empirical sociology, hostile to theory, strives for in
vain, i.e. the true definition of reality. Thus the concept of industrial capitalism is concretized in the formal theory of *rationality and
control*—the two fundamental themes of *Wirtschaft und Gesellschaft*.

Let us try first to sort out the connection between capitalism,
rationality and control in Weber's work. In its most general form

[1] *Gesammelte Aufsätze zur Soziologie und Sozialpolitik* (Tübingen, 1924),
p. 419.   [2] Op. cit., p. 402.

it can be summed up as follows: the specifically Western idea of
reason is reified in a system of material and intellectual culture
(economics, technology, 'way of life', science, art), which is fully
developed in industrial capitalism, and this system tends towards a
specific type of domination which has become the destiny of the
present epoch—totalitarian bureaucracy. The *idea of reason* as
Western rationality is both the dominant and fundamental concept:
we will begin with that.

There is a rationality which has been effective only in the West—
it has shaped (or helped to shape) capitalism—and will determine
our foreseeable future: the attempt to define it in its manifold
(and often contradictory) forms constitutes a large part of Weber's
work. The 'Spirit of Capitalism' as described in the first volume
of the *Religionssoziologie* is one of these forms: the foreword to
this work explains programmatically how the rationality which
becomes word and deed in capitalism fundamentally distinguishes
the Western form of industrialization from all other forms of
economics and technology.

To enumerate the characteristic elements of Weber's concept of
reason: (1) Progressive mathematization of experience and knowledge, which, arising from the natural sciences and their brilliant
success, affect the other sciences and the 'way of life' itself; (2) insistence on the necessity for *rational experiment* and rational
proof in the organization of science and the 'way of life'; and
(3) the result of this organization, which according to Weber is the
birth and establishment of a universal organization of expertly
trained officials: this organization becomes 'an absolute clamp on
our whole existence'.[1] This last definition completes the transition
from theoretical to practical reason, to the historic form of reason.

The awareness of its specific *historicism* was contained from the
beginning in Weber's concept of 'ratio': we shall see that it is not
sustained throughout his analysis and fails at the decisive point. In
Weber's sociology formal rationality turns without a break into
capitalist rationality. Thus it appears as the methodical discipline
imposed on the irrational 'drive for gain' as typically expressed in
'this-worldly' asceticism. In this discipline Western reason becomes
the *economic* reason of capitalism—striving for constantly greater
profits in the continuous rational capitalist enterprise. Rationality
becomes a condition for profitability, orientated in turn towards

[1] Note to vol. I of R.S. (Tübingen, 1920), pp. 1 ff.

systematic methodical calculation, 'capital accounting' (R.S., pp. 4–5).

The main basis of this rationality is *abstraction*, which—theoretically and practically one in both scientific and social organization—determines the period of capitalism—the reduction of *quality to quantity*. Functioning universally (as expressed economically in exchange-values) it becomes a premise of calculable efficiency, in so far as functionalization makes possible control over all particularities (reduced to quantities and exchange-values). Abstract reason becomes concrete in calculable and calculated domination over nature and men. Thus the reason which is Weber's target is *technical* reason, production and transformation of physical and human material (objects and people) by a regulated scientific apparatus constructed on calculable efficiency, organizing and controlling things and people, factories and offices, work and leisure. Controlling for what? Weber's concept of reason was 'formal' up to this point: defined as the quantifying abstraction of all particularities, the abstraction which made possible the universally predictable efficiency of the capitalist apparatus. Now however the *limits of formal reason* appear—neither the aim of scientific technical construction nor the content of the construction (its subject and object) can be deduced from the concept of reason: they emerged before the formal 'value-free' concept of the 'ratio'.

In capitalist rationality, as analysed by Weber, these elements of reason, prior to but materially limiting it, appear as two historical facts:

1   Human welfare—the aim of the economy—is provided for within the framework of the calculable chances of gain in private enterprise, i.e. in the context of the *proit* of the individual entrepreneur or enterprise:
2   The existence of the people to be cared for is thus dependent on the chances of gain in capitalist enterprise—a dependence embodied in the 'free' labour at the employer's disposal.

These facts according to Weber's conception of formal reason are assumed to be given facts, but historically they delimit the general validity of the concept itself. According to Weber, capitalist rationality has the nodal point of its reality in private enterprise: the entrepreneur is a free person, responsible for his own calculations and risks. As such the entrepreneur is a bourgeois, and the bourgeois way of life has its characteristic expression in 'this-worldly' asceticism. Is this conception still valid today? Is the middle class, which Weber saw as the bearer of capitalist development, still the bearer of later capitalist development? Is later capitalist rationality still the reason originating in this-worldly asceticism? I think the answer to these questions must be 'No'. The forms which Weber ascribed to capitalist rationality have collapsed and become out of date even while being perfected and their decline shows up the 'ratio' of capitalist industry in another light—in the light of its *irrationality*. To take just one example; 'this-worldly' asceticism is no longer a driving force in later capitalism—instead it has become a fetter on the evolution of the system. Keynes denounced it as such, and in the 'affluent society' it becomes dangerous wherever it stands in the way of the production and consumption of superfluous goods. Later capitalism is certainly built on 'denial': the struggle for existence and the exploitation of labour have to be intensified, if the increased accumulation is to be at all possible: 'planned obsolescence' now becomes a methodical anti-reason, a social necessity. But this is no longer the way of life of the middle class as the class which develops productive forces—it is the advent of *productive destruction* under totalitarian administration. And capital calculation of mathematical profitability and efficiency celebrates its greatest triumphs in the calculation of collapse, of the risk of its own annihilation as against that of the annihilation of the enemy.

In the development of capitalist rationality, *irrationality* thus becomes *reason*: reason as the enormous development of productivity, conquest of nature, increase in the amount of consumer goods (and of their availability to broader sections of the population): irrational because higher productivity, the control of nature and social wealth become destructive forces: destructive not only figuratively in selling the so-called higher cultural values, but literally: the struggle for existence is sharpened inside the nation-states as well as internationally, and dammed-up aggression overflows in the legitimization of medieval cruelty (torture) and the scientifically planned annihilation of men.

Did Weber predict this development? The answer is 'No' if by predict we mean *foretell*. But it is implicit in his conceptualization and denunciation: it is bad reasoning which finally appears as the reason of capitalism.

K

The *value-free* concept of capitalist rationality becomes in Weber's complete analysis a *critical* concept—critical not only in the sense of 'pure scientific' but also 'evaluative' and purposive, a critique of reification and de-humanization.

But then criticism comes to a halt, accepts the allegedly inevitable and becomes an apologia—worse still, a denunciation of the possible alternative—a quantitatively *different* historical rationality. Weber defined very clearly the limits of his vision; he defined himself as 'bourgeois'—and identified his work with the historic mission of the bourgeoisie; in the name of this alleged mission, he assumed a bond between representative strata of the German bourgeoisie with the organizers of reaction and repression; he demanded that political opponents on the radical left be sent to the madhouse, the zoo or the firing squad; he, who was the most intellectual of sociologists, raged against the intellectuals who sacrificed their lives to the Revolution.[1] The personal aspect serves only to illustrate the conceptual: to show how the concept of the 'ratio' itself in its critical content remains bound to its origin: reason remains *bourgeois* reason—and just one part of it, i.e. capitalist reason.

Let us try to reconstruct the inner development of Weber's concept of capitalist reason. The Freiburg inaugural speech was directed against capitalist industrialization as a complex of power-politics, as imperialism. Only the development of large-scale industry can guarantee the nation's independence in the sharpening international contest. Imperial power politics demand intensive and extensive industrialization—and vice-versa. The economy must serve the *raison d'etat* of the national power-state and work with its instruments—instruments for realizing extra-scientific aims and values to which value-free economics has to be subordinate. As historical reason, the *raison d'etat* requires domination to be in the hands of that class which can carry out industrialization and promote the rise of the nation—domination by the bourgeoisie. It is dangerous when (as with the Junkers in Germany) an 'economically declining class holds control in its hands'.[2] Thus under the pressure of extra-scientific political evaluation, economic science according

---

[1] The documentation is excellently compiled and analysed in Wolfgang J. Mommsen, *Max Weber und die deutsche Politik* (Tübingen, 1950).

[2] *Gesammelte Politische Schriften* (Munich, 1921), p. 20 f. (cited hereafter as G.P.S.).

to Weber becomes a politico-sociological critique of the state set up
by Bismarck. And this critique anticipates the future: the historically chosen class, the bourgeoisie, in Germany is 'immature':
in its weakness it longs for a new Caesar to help it fulfil its role
(G.P.S., p. 27).

The taking over of power by the bourgeoisie meant the democratization of a state still *pre*-bourgeois. But the political immaturity
of the German bourgeoisie calls for imperialism: democracy
appropriate to capitalist industrialization threatens to turn into
plebiscitary dictatorship: bourgeois 'ratio' demanded the irrational *charisma*. The dialectics of bourgeois democracy, of
bourgeois reasoning, troubled Weber perpetually: he expressed
this concern very sharply in *Wirtschaft und Gesellschaft*. We will
come back to that later—meanwhile pointing out that Weber also
foresaw the later development of that other supporter of capitalism,
the proletariat, more correctly than most contemporary socialists.
'It is not in the masses that danger lies'—he said in his inaugural
speech (1895) (G.S.P., p. 29).—it is not the governed who frustrate
imperialist policy or bring about its failure, it is the 'governing and
rising classes' who present such a threat—a threat to the nation's
chances of survival in international competition.

The conservative character of the masses, the imperialist
tendencies of the ruling classes—Weber foresaw the changes in
later capitalism. Unlike Marx, he did not anchor them conceptually in the structure of capitalism itself. 'Political immaturity' is a
poor definition, if it omits the factors behind the fact—here the
incapacity of capitalist productivity to maintain a free market and
free competition. Capitalist productivity itself encounters barriers
in the democratic institutions of a trading society. Control is
concentrated in and above the bureaucracy, as the necessary apex of
representation. What appeared as 'political immaturity' in the
context of liberal capitalism becomes 'political maturity' in organized capitalism.

And the 'harmlessness' of those so controlled? Even in Weber's
lifetime they were—for one historical moment—to bring about the
collapse of imperialist policy. Then the political activity of the
bourgeoisie and the material and intellectual capacity of capitalist
productivity took things in hand and confirmed Weber's prediction.

Now let us look at the concept of capitalism where it is (apparently removed from the concrete context of imperialist power-politics and developed in its value-free scientific purity; in *Wirtschaft und Gesellschaft*. Here capitalism is first defined as a form of 'rational economic enterprise', as a 'special form of accounting':

> Capital accounting is the calculation and verification of profit, comparing the total returns, on the one hand, of all assets (liquid and frozen) at the beginning, and on the other of existing and newly-acquired assets at the end of the period, in the case of a single profit-earning enterprise: or in the case of a permanent concern, by the balance-sheet at the beginning and end of the period.[1]

The attempt (one could call it provocative) to give a purely scientific definition, apart from anything human or historical, is obvious even in the frightful syntax; it is a matter of business and nothing else. In view of this attitude it seems almost a shocking lapse when on the next page he emphasizes (W.G., p. 49):

> Capital accounting in its *most formally rational* structure presupposes the *struggle of man against man.*

What capital accounting does to man is more sharply expressed in the abstract definition than in its concretization: inhumanity is hidden in the rationality of the balance-sheet.

The 'most formally rational' form of capital accounting is that in which man and his aims enter only as variables in the calculation of probable profit. Mathematization in this formal rationality continues as far as a calculation of the actual negation of life itself. Those who possess nothing are stimulated into economic activity by the risk of death by starvation.

> The decisive stimulus for the motivation of economic activity under the conditions of a market economy is, for the have-nots, (a) the fact that they run the risk, both for themselves and their personal dependents, such as children, wives, sometimes parents, of not been provided for. . . (W.G., p. 60.)

Weber constantly defines *formal* rationality in contrast to *material*—in which the economic care of men is considered from the viewpoint of particular evaluative postulates (of whatever kind) (W.G., p. 44). Thus formal rationality is in conflict not only with traditional values and aims, but also with revolutionary ones. As an example, Weber mentions the opposition between formal

[1] *Wirtschaft und Gesellschaft* (Tübingen, 1922), p. 48 (cited hereafter as W.G.).

rationality on the one hand and the efforts to abolish the division of power on the other ('governments made up of councils, conventions, and welfare committees') (W.G., p. 167) i.e. with efforts to alter radically the existing form of government.

But is formal rationality as expressed in capitalist economy really so formal? Here is its definition once again:

> As the formal rationality of an economy we must here indicate the extent of accounting which is technically possible for it and actually applied by it.
>
> An economy can be called formally 'rational' to the extent to which the provision for needs, essential in any rational economy, can be expressed in numerical, calculable terms. (W.G., pp. 44–5.)

Obviously according to this definition, a total *planned economy*, i.e. a non-capitalist economy in the sense of formal rationality, would be more rational than the capitalist one, which is limited in calculability by the particular interests of private enterprise and the 'freedom' of the market (however regimented). When Weber declares that such a 'welfare-economy' is retrograde or even realistically impossible, he does so first of all for technological reasons: in modern industrialized society the separation of the worker from the means of production has become a technical necessity which demands individual and private guidance and control of the means of production, i.e. control by the entrepreneur who is personally responsible in the concern. The very material historical fact of private capitalist enterprise becomes (in Weber's sense of the word) a *formal* element of the structure of capitalism and of *rational* economy itself. But the rational social function of individual— control of production, based on the separation of the worker from the means of production, goes still further: it is the guarantor of the technically and economically necessary *discipline* of production which then becomes a model for the whole discipline required by modern industrial society. Even socialism, according to Weber, has its origin in factory discipline.

Modern socialism is born of this situation in life, i.e. out of factory discipline.[1]

The subordination of private economy to 'the discipline of labour' is on the one hand the rationality of a *personal hierarchy*; on

---

[1] *Gesammelte Aufsätze zur Soziologie und Sozialpolitik*, op. cit., p. 501 ('Der Sozialismus').

the other, rational control of *things* over men: 'that is to say, of the means over the end (the fulfilment of needs)'. Weber uses these words to quote a thesis of socialism;[1] he does not contest it, but believes that even socialist society will not alter the basic fact of the separation of the workers from the means of production, because this arises simply as a form of technical progress, which is industrialization. Socialism has to obey its own rationality, if it is to keep its own promise of meeting general needs and of satisfying the struggle for existence. The domination of men by things can only get rid of its irrationality in the rational control of *men by man*. The question for socialism is: 'Who shall take over and govern this new economy?'[2]

Industrialization is the fate of the modern world, and the fateful question for capitalist and socialist industrialization is only: what is the most rational form of *control* over industrialization, and thus over society?—'most rational' in the sense of that *formal rationality* determined by the accountable, calculable, regulated functioning of its own structure. But this rationality seems to have changed quite imperceptibly in the course of the development of the concept. In becoming a question of control, and thanks to its own inner rationality, it becomes subordinate to something else, i.e. governmental control. In so far as this formal rationality does not go beyond its own structure, and has only its own system as a norm of accounting and accountable activity, it is as a whole *dependent* and determined 'from without', by something other than itself—thus it becomes 'material' in Weber's own definition.

Industrialization as destiny, control as destiny—Weber's *concept of destiny* is an example of the material content of formal analysis. 'Destiny' is the legality of economy and society, far removed from dependence on individuals, and only to be defied under penalty of losing one's own power. But society is not nature —who decrees this destiny? Industrialization is a phase in the development of men's capabilities and needs—a phase in the struggle of man with nature and himself. This development can proceed in very different kinds of organization and planning: not only the forms of control, but also those of technology, and thus of 'needs' and their satisfaction are not at all 'fatal'—they only become so after being established in society; as the result of material, economic and psychological compulsion. Weber's

[1] Op. cit., p. 502.   [2] Op. cit., p. 511.

concept of destiny originates in such an exposition; he generalizes the blindness of a society whose process of reproduction is carried on behind the individual's back—a society in which the law of control appears as an objective technological legality. This legality is neither 'fateful' nor 'formal'. The context of Weber's analysis is the historical one, in which economic reason became the reason of control—control almost at any price. This fate is something which has come about, and as such can be destroyed. Scientific analysis which is not bound to this possibility of destruction is not devoted to 'the' reason, but to the reason of the 'establishment'. And capitalism, however mathematized and 'scientific', is still mathematized technological *control* over men, and socialism, however scientific and technological, is the erection of removal of control.

If in Weber's work the formal analysis of capitalism becomes the analysis of forms of control, this is not a break with the concept and the method: purity itself appears as impure—not because Weber was a bad or inconsistent sociologist, but because he was a true sociologist, possessed by the desire for knowledge about his own subject: truth becomes criticism, criticism becomes accusation, and accusation the function of science. If in his inaugural speech he provocatively subordinated the science of economies to politics, this *tour de force* appears in the light of his whole work as the inner logic of his method. Your science must stay 'pure': this is the only way you can keep faith with truth. But this truth compels you to recognize what external forces (over which you have no power) determine the subjects of your science. Your value-freedom is as necessary as it is illusory: neutrality is *real*, only if it has the power to ward off attacks: if not, it becomes the victim and the helper of the power which tries to utilize it—but let us get back to our subject!

The formal rationality of capitalism touches its inner limit at two points: one the fact of private enterprise and the private entrepreneur as the actual subject of the accountability of management, and the other the fact of the separation of the worker from the means of production, 'free' labour.

Weber thinks that these two facts belong to the specific rationality of capitalism (W.G., pp. 19–23), and are technological necessities. He does not ask whether these necessities are really and essentially 'technological' or whether they are the technological disguise of specific social interests. He thinks they are the basis of control as an integral element of capitalistic economic rationality in modern industrialized society. If this is so, control itself must be demonstrated as a form of modern economic rationality: Weber undertakes this demonstration in his analysis of *bureaucracy*.

Bureaucratic control is inseparable from the progress of industrialization: it transfers to society as a whole the productive capacity of industrial enterprise, when it has been developed to the utmost. It is formally the most rational kind of control thanks to its 'precision, constancy, discipline, tautness and reliability, i.e. calculability both for the masters and all those interested (W.G., p. 128), and it is all this because it is "control through knowledge", knowledge which can be established, calculated and calculating, in fact expert knowledge. Actually it is the apparatus in control here, for control based on expert knowledge is only control over the apparatus if it is fully adapted to its technical demands and possibilities; so command over the apparatus is possible only in a limited way for the non-specialist: the expert councillor is superior in the long run to the non-specialist minister' (W.G., p. 129).

And Weber stresses the point again that 'rational socialism' must simply 'take over and enhance' bureaucratic administration just because it is only material control, demanded by the matter in hand, valid equally in the case of the most diverse political, cultural and moral aims and institutions. And the matter itself is the actual apparatus, developing more and more productivity and more and more precisely calculable.

Expert scientific administration of apparatus as the most formally rational control: this is reification as reason—the *apotheosis* of reification. But the apotheosis becomes its own negation, *must* turn into its negation. For the apparatus which dictates its own practical administration is itself the *instrument*, the means—and there is no means 'by and of itself'. The most productive, most reified apparatus is the means to some end outside itself. As far as the economic apparatus of capitalism is concerned, it is not sufficient to quote the meeting of needs as this end. The concept is too general, too abstract, in the weaker sense of the word. For, as Weber himself saw, achieving ends is a by-product rather than a purpose of capitalist economy—or rather of the raw material of the economy which is moulded by the *form* of capitalist economy. Human need in this form is rational, as long as one is dependent on men as consumers (as producers they are to some extent redundant)

—consumers to whom one can sell destruction and atomic shelters, a subhuman subterranean existence. But if the bureaucratic administration of the capitalist apparatus remains in all its rationality, a means and therefore dependent, then it has its own limits as rationality: bureaucracy is subordinate to power outside and above itself—a force 'alien to industry'. And if rationality is embodied in administration, and only in that, this legislative force must be *irrational*. Weber's concept of reason ends up in irrational *charisma*.

Of all Weber's concepts, that of charisma is perhaps the most problematic: even as a term it contains the pre-judgment that endows every form of successful personal leadership with a re-ligious aura. The concept itself is not under discussion: it is only to be explored in so far as it throws light on the dialectic between rationality and irrationality in modern society. Charismatic domination appears as a stage in a two-fold process of develop-ment: on the one hand charisma tends to turn into the consolidated domination of particular interests and their bureaucratic organiza tion: on the other, bureaucratic organization is subordinate to a charismatic apex.

In his chapter 'The Transformation of Charisma' Weber describes how pure charismatic domination tends to be changed into 'permanent possession'; in the process it 'is delivered up to the conditions of everyday life, and the powers which govern it, above all economic interests' (W.G., p. 762). What begins as the charisma of an individual and his personal following is completed in the domination of a bureaucratic apparatus of acquired rights and functions, in which those who are controlled charismatically become law-abiding, tax-paying, duty-fulfilling 'subjects'.

But this rational administration of masses and things cannot dispense with its irrational charismatic apex. For administration would tend to supersede domination, to just the extent to which it is really rational and become an administration of things. But the apparatus of administration is built on domination and has been orientated to its maintenance and growth. Truly 'rational' administration would be the utilization of social wealth in the interests of the free development and satisfaction of human needs —and technical progress makes this rationality into an ever-more-real possibility. But this is contradicted by the reality of the appara-tus built on the repression of production. To the degree to which the contradiction is evident and irrational, it must be superseded by a new form of domination—if domination itself is to survive. Democratization, which is a consequence of technical progress—(egalitarian tendencies are the result of growing production) is thus thwarted by control and manipulation. Domination as the privilege of particular interests and self-determination as demanded by general interests are thus fused. This solution of the social contradiction has its classic manifestation in 'plebiscitary democracy' (W.G., pp. 156 ff., 174, 763 ff.) in which trained (and terrorized) masses install their own leaders, periodically ratify their position and even determine their policy—under prescribed conditions carefully controlled by the leaders. Thus, for Weber, universal franchise is not only a result of domination, but also an *instrument* of domination in the period of its technical perfection. Plebiscitary democracy is the political expression of irrationality turned to reason. How does this dialectic of reason (i.e. of formal 'ratio') manifest itself in the development of capitalism? Its prosaic power acts as a barrier against the idea of charisma, and Weber is reluctant to apply this term to present-day industrialized society, although his attitude and even his language during the war and against the revolution come near to charismatic decadence. But the *fact* is there: the formal reason of the technically perfected apparatus of administration is subject to the irrational. Weber's analysis of bureaucracy tears away the ideological veil: far ahead of his time he shows up the illusory character of modern mass-democracy with its pretended reconciliation and harmonization of class-conflicts. The bureaucratic administration of industrial capitalism is in fact a 'levelling', but 'the decisive thing here is exclusively the levelling of those dominated, as against the dominant bureaucratically organised group, which for its part can actually and often formally enjoy a position of autocracy' (W.G., p. 667).

He continually stresses the fact that the technically perfected apparatus of administration, thanks to its formal rationality, is a 'supreme instrument of power', 'for those who have the bureaucratic apparatus at their disposal'.

The dependence of the material fate of the masses on the constantly correct functioning of more and more bureaucratically organised private capitalist organisations is growing, and the idea of the possibility of eliminating them becomes more and more utopian. (W.G., p. 669.)

It is the total dependence on the functioning of an omnipresent apparatus which becomes the basis of all order, so that the apparatus itself is no longer questioned. 'Trained adjustment to obedient behaviour in these organisations' becomes the cement of a subordination, no longer aware of itself as such, because the organization itself is so terrifyingly rational, i.e. it administers and disposes so efficiently and calculably of the whole world of goods and production which the individual can no longer supervise or comprehend. Weber did not live to see how fully developed capitalism, in the efficiency of its rationality, creates greater and better prosperity out of the planned annihilations of millions of people and the planned destruction of their work: how obvious madness becomes the basis not only of progress, but of a more pleasant life. He did not live to see the 'affluent society' which in the face of inhuman misery and methodical cruelty dissipates and misuses its unmistakable technical, material and intellectual powers in the service of permanent mobilization. Even *before* this kind of reason grew in power, he pointed out the danger of a rational bureaucratic apparatus of administration that because of its own rationality is under alien domination.

Firstly Weber's conceptualization almost takes it for granted that administration in industrialized society needs a leadership which stands above and outside it. 'Every administration somehow needs control, for in order to guide it some power of command must be placed in someone's hand' (W.G., p. 607).

Bureaucratic control has inevitably at its apex an element which at least is not wholly bureaucratic. (W.G., p. 127.)

'Inevitably', because the value-free formal rationality of administration is dependent on values and aims imposed from without. In his 'Inaugural Speech' Weber had declared that the power-politics of the nation-state imposed values and aims on the economy: thus capitalism was defined as imperialism. In *Wirtschaft und Gesellschaft* he assembles some characteristic features of imperialist economy under the concept of 'politically orientated capitalism'. Then he says: 'It is clear from the beginning that those politically orientated phenomena, which offer (political) possibilities of profit, are economically *irrational*, from the point of view of a competitive market' (W.G., p. 96). Being irrational they can be replaced by others. Control over capital economy does not only require no expert qualifications, it is to a great extent replaceable.

Thus capitalism with all its rationality (or rather because of its specific rationality) ends up with an irrational accidental apex—not only in economics where specialist qualifications can be discouraged by those at the top, but also in the control of the bureaucratic administration itself, in the administration of the state. (It is hard not to be reminded of Hegel's philosophy of law, where the bourgeois state, a rational one, has its apex in the person of the monarch who owes his position to the accident of birth. Hegel and Weber both demonstrate the limits of bourgeois reason in their analysis of it: its completion is its own negation.)

Let us look back briefly at the stages of this conceptualization—and at the thing itself. Western capitalism arose under the particular social, political and economic conditions of the late Middle Ages and the Reformation; its 'spirit' was developed in that formal rationality which is accomplished by the psychological and economic attitude and activity of the bearer of the capitalist process (but not of its objects!). This formal rationality is the condition for the completion of industrialization, technical progress and the progressive meeting of human needs regardless of which need is concerned. We have seen that this formal rationality is developed on the basis of two very *material* historical facts, which still persist, and (according to Weber) are *conditions* of capitalism, namely: (1) private enterprise, and (2) 'free labour', the existence of a class compelled 'economically, under the threat of starvation', to sell its services (W.G., p. 240). As productive forces these conditions are part of formal reason: capitalism expands in the competitive struggle between dissimilar (but formally free) powers—the struggle for existence, persons, states, and international leagues. According to Weber capitalism's present stage is directed by national power-politics: it is imperialism. Its internal administration however remains formally rational: bureaucratic control. It administers the domination by things: rational value-free technology is the separation of man from the means of production, his subordination to technical efficiency and necessity—in the context of private enterprise. The machine determines, but the 'lifeless machine is an atrophied spirit. This is all that gives it power to force people into its service' (G.P.S., p. 151). And because it is 'atrophied spirit', it is also the domination of men by man: this kind of technical rationality reproduces slavery. Subjugation to technology becomes subjugation to control as such: formal technical rationality becomes material political rationality (or is it the other way round, since from the beginning technical reason was the domination of 'free labour' by private enterprise?) This destiny has been fulfilled, as Weber brilliantly foretold in one of his most compelling statements:

In conjunction with the lifeless machine, it (the bureaucratic organisation) is at work erecting the prison-house of that future bondage, into which men in their impotence will probably be forced, like the fellaheen of ancient Egypt, if they find that a rational official administration which is good purely from a technical point of view is the final and sole value determining the direction of their affairs. (G.P.S., p. 151.)

But it is precisely here at the most incisive point of Weber's analysis where it changes to self-criticism, that it becomes clear how profoundly Weber remained attached to his other identification, the equation of technical and bourgeois–capitalist reason. This prevented him from seeing that it was not 'pure' formal technical reason, but the reason of domination that was building the 'houses of bondage', and that the *perfection* of technical reason can very well become the instrument of man's liberation. To put it another way: Weber's analysis of capitalism was not value-free enough, in that it imported values and norms specific to capitalism into the 'pure' definitions of formal rationality. Thus the contradictions developed between formal and substantive rationality, and its obverse: the 'neutrality' of technical reason as against all external material values. This neutrality made it possible for Weber to accept the (reified) interests of the nation and its political power as the values determining technical reason.

The *concept of technical reason* is perhaps itself *ideology*. Not only its application but technique itself is domination (over nature and men), methodological, scientific, calculated and calculating control. Certain aims and interests of control are not 'additional' or externally dictated to technique—they are intrinsic to the construction of the technical apparatus itself: technique is a historical and social project: in it is projected what a society and its ruling interests decide to make of men and things. Such an 'aim' of domination is material to the form of technical reason itself.

Weber abstracted from this irreducible social material, and we

have stressed the correctness of this abstraction, in his analysis of
capitalist reason. Abstraction becomes criticism of this reason to
the extent that it shows the degree to which capitalist rationality
itself abstracts from man, and is indifferent to his needs: it becomes
more efficient, more calculating and methodical—and thus
builds and furnishes (very luxuriously!) houses of bondage
available to all. Thus far Weber's abstraction is justified by his
material: it passes a rational judgment on rational exchange-
society. But this society tends in its development to destroy its
own material foundations: the private entrepreneur is no longer
the responsible subject of economic rationality, 'free labour' is no
longer enslavement enforced by the threat of the 'scourge of
hunger'. Exchange-society in which everything is so free and
rational comes under the domination of economic and political
monopolies. The market and its freedoms, whose ideological
character Weber has described often enough, become subordinate
to a terrifyingly effective regulation in which general interests are
sharply limited and controlled by the dominant special interests.
Reification is thus thwarted. Separation from the means of production, which Weber rightly saw as a technical necessity, subordinated the whole of industry to a calculating manager. Capitalism's formal rationality celebrates its triumph in the electronic
computer, which serves any and every purpose, and is a powerful
instrument of manipulative politics, and calculates chances of loss
and gain with the utmost certitude—including the chance of total
annihilation, with the consent of the equally 'calculated' and
obedient population. Mass democracy becomes plebiscitary both
in economy and society, the masses themselves elect those who are
to lead them into the 'house of bondage'.

But if technical reason is thus revealed as political reason, this
is only because it was *this* technical reason and *this* political
reason, determined and limited by the specific interests of domination. Technical reason as political reason is *Historical*. If the
separation from the means of production is a technical necessity,
the *slavery* thus organized is not. On the basis of its own achievements—productive and calculable mechanization—it contains the
possibility of a qualitatively different rationality in which man's
separation from the *means of production* becomes separation from
socially necessary but dehumanizing *labour*. At the stage of auto-
mated production controlled by men thus freed from labour,

formal and substantive values would no longer necessarily be opposites—nor would formal reason assert itself impartially over men. For as an 'atrophied spirit' the machine *is not neutral*: technical reason is the contemporarily dominant social reason: it can undergo changes in its own structure. As technical reason it can be transformed into the technology of liberation.

For Weber this possibility was—*Utopia*. Today it seems as if he were right. But if contemporary industrialized society triumphs over its own explosive possibilities, it is no longer Weber's bourgeois reason which is the victor. It is difficult to see any reason, even mere 'technical' reason, in the 'house of bondage' as it closes in around us. Or was there *irony* in Weber's concept of reason, the irony of understanding and disavowal? Is he perhaps saying: is *that* what you call reason?

Industrialization and Capitalism

GEORG WEIPPERT

Professor Marcuse put forward the thesis that Weber's 'theory of the internal value-freedom of science' is shown in practice as the attempt to make science free to accept obligatory evaluations which are introduced from outside. In a discussion in depth it would be essential to show that for Weber the acceptance of an unavoidable process, as for instance of progressive rationalization or industrialization, is not on the side of evaluation, but on the side of accepting a firm datum, a necessary fact. The nation-state is of course one such historically necessary fact according to him. Yet we must admit that for someone convinced that historical–social situations could be decisively, i.e. basically, altered, the acceptance of a present social–historical constellation represents a value-decision.

What has this to do with Professor Marcuse's reference to Weber's hatred of the Socialists? Does Professor Marcuse not see the relationship with socialism and the socialists much too one-sidedly and from a quite definite extreme historical situation. First we must establish that Weber thought socialism historically possible, and that he made a decisive contribution to the theory of 'complete socialization' in *Wirtschaft und Gesellschaft* under the heading 'Rational Planned Economy'. But that is not all: immediately after the collapse he pressed for 'planned socialization'. Secondly, Weber was profoundly convinced that socialism cannot abolish or remove man's control of men. According to him the tendency to bureaucratization gains ground with socialization. For the sake of personal freedom he tried in the political arena to prevent socialism (in the sense of complete socialization). Thirdly, especially in the war years 1916–18 and the immediate post-war period, Weber declared that his viewpoint coincided with that of social democracy, to the point of being indistinguishable. Fourthly: the hate-filled phrases—who would deny that he was a great hater?—which Marcuse points out, were directed not mainly against socialism and the socialists, but the 'dilettanti' in economic matters, especially those in Berlin and Munich (Karl Liebknecht and Kurt Eisner). He does this primarily from concern that they might, by thoughtless measures, completely destroy the German economy, already tottering, and so give France and America the pretext of having to invade for the sake of order inside Germany.

Professor Marcuse places great hopes on automation and sees in it a means of abolishing man's control over men. I should like to ask Professor Marcuse whether the reference to the 'tertiary sector'—to use Fourastié's term—does not constitute a serious objection to it. In all industrialized countries the tendency is quite unmistakable (and not least by automation) towards a relative reduction of numbers employed in the industrial sector, and as a necessary consequence, towards a rise of those in management, transport and services. There is not much scope for automation in these sectors, so men still control other men.

Does Professor Marcuse not see Weber as a much firmer adherent of capitalism than he ever was? He not only always admitted the considerable modifiability of capitalism, but after entering upon a scientific career, he fought enthusiastically for such modifications against the prevailing opinion of the bourgeoisie. If he ascribed a relatively long life-span to capitalism, this was not least because of the high malleability of the free trade economy. Against contemporary capitalism he stood so far to the front, when he pressed unreservedly for the forming of free trade-unions and the collective work-contract, and when he spoke so impressively to the employers' conscience, as to be open to the workers' claims and their right to freedom. To use a current formulation Weber was concerned to give contemporary capitalism more social countenance, not least in order thus to let the workers become economically and practically at home in the nation-state.

A word about plebiscitary democracy: Weber saw a trend toward this in the Anglo-Saxon democracies long before the First World War. To a political sociological observer close to reality, the rejection of party plebiscitary democracy must seem very strange. Where party democracy is developed, plebiscitary democracy is necessarily established, even when the same party remains in control through several sessions of legislature. Even when we speak of a 'People's Chancellor' (*Volkskanzler*) do we think we have something different from plebiscitary democracy? And do not outstanding personalities in party leadership and charismatic power (charisma

L

in Weber's sense of the term) belong inseparably together? This would indicate that the working out of the concept of charisma in ideal types—together with the ideal types of traditional and rational (bureaucratic) control belongs to the most significant insights of Weber's political sociology, especially if one does not ignore the fact that the actual types of government sometimes represent combinations of all three.

It must be made clear that whereas Weber saw a completely rationalized official bureaucracy not only as a thing of horror, but also a serious political danger, he saw in the charismatic party leader or the charismatic statesman the most effective counter-agent against the dangers of this bureaucracy.

REINHARD BENDIX

Since in the following remarks I criticize sharply Professor Marcuse's interpretations, may I express in advance my very high personal esteem and respect for his shrewd analysis? The differences here are of a factual kind, since these analyses appear to me not to lead to Utopian thinking, but only to an empty Utopia, vanishing in negative criticism.

Absolute lack of presuppositions belongs to the realm of ideas in theology. All human interests are conditional. This also applies to Weber's concept of rationality. As a property of human action and thought rationality rests on historical pre-conditions and has historical consequences. Despite this I think it possible and purposeful to distinguish between rationality as a scientific proposition and the historical foundations and consequences of rationality.

If one denies the possibility of this distinction in principle, as Professor Marcuse does, then all scientific effort is conceived of and estimated as historical activity. This identification is of course provable by its premises and consequences. If Weber's concept of reason is 'bourgeois' what is the social status of 'a purposeful criticism of reification and de-humanisation'? Proletarian, or humanist–intellectual, or what? I do not know which adjective applies to this case, or would be accepted by Professor Marcuse. More important, however, would be the question about the greater scientific or moral power of persuasion which is supposed to result from the socio-historic status, whatever its name. I am also of the

opinion that many social-scientific concepts have a limited historical *application*, but I would distinguish this sharply from the
historical *conditioning* of the social scientist. In any case Marx
justified the relativization of intellectual perspectives to an appropriate social status by its basis in a theory of history dependent
on the Enlightenment (however questionable the values connected with it). But the corresponding intellectual basis for Marxists
or neo-Marxists in the sixties of the twentieth century is less
obvious, especially as Marcuse's critique of Weber is comparable
not only with that of Georg Lukács, but also with Leo Strauss,
Wolfgang Mommsen and Christoph Steding.[1] Further, if the
'scientifically pursued annihilation of man', even if not expressed
in so many words, is profoundly implicit in Weber's conceptualization, then the Stalinist terror can also be seen as an inherent
consequence of Marxist criticism of the bourgeois constitutional
state. In this case it is not exactly 'unexpressed', since Marx's
intellectual destruction of state legality and judicial forms results in
the idea that freedom is expressed in the complete subordination of
the state to society—and in the Soviet Union society is represented
by the party. I do not myself indulge in these reflections, however,
since I doubt whether there is any idea—whether positivism or the
above-mentioned value-based criticism of 'reification and de-
humanization'—which is actually proof against abuse. And,
correspondingly, I doubt whether one can draw from the genesis or
abuse of an idea any cogent conclusions about its value or usefulness. It seems to me that retrospective conclusions of this kind are
disposed of by the works of the great creators themselves. Their
multivalence, the multiplicity of strata and meanings allows them
to survive in altered forms. The dangerous germs are—pro-
visionally—contained in a purer, higher idea.[2]

With these remarks I simply wish to indicate why I am not in
a position to follow Professor Marcuse's shrewd exposition on the
basis he has chosen.

---

[1] Georg Lukács, *Die Zerstörung der Vernunft* (Berlin, 1955); Leo Strauss,
Naturrecht und Geschichte (Stuttgart, 1956); Wolfgang Mommsen, *Max Weber
und die Deutsche Politik 1890–1920* (Tübingen, 1959); and Christoph Steding,
Politik und Wissenschaft bei Max Weber (Breslau, 1932). The supporters of
absolute values, whether Marxists, scholastic philosophers, liberals, or National
Socialists are here all on the negative side.
[2] Robert Minder, *Kultur und Literatur in Deutschland und Frankreich* (Frankfurt, 1962), p. 37.

Weber's writings have as their main theme not abstract rationality as such, but its historical dependence and the possible irrationality of its consequences. The purpose of Weber's scientific approach is not 'to ignore everything human and historical', as Professor Marcuse thinks, but to define conceptually the phenomena he deals with, in order to analyse more clearly their pre-conditions and conditions. The possibility of such an analysis and scientific research depends, in any case, neither on the social status nor the good will and meticulousness of the researcher. It is relevant to ask whether researchers in the same field possess a common foundation. This is to be found not only in belief in the value of the science—despite everything questionable in this value. It is primarily created by the ability of the scholar in questions of formation of concepts and of methods of research to aim at a temporary unity from one case to another, which will make it possible to continue the work. These social presuppositions of scientific discussion and objectivity are what Marx had in view when in the preface to *Das Kapital* he compared his own analysis of England as a typical case with the physicist's methods of classifying types, although examples can also be found for Marx's use of the scientific character of his works as a polemic weapon. I shall presume in my following remarks that we here all have the same sociological concept of science.

At this point I should like to interpose an observation which summarizes my first impression of the discussions of the main proceedings. Earlier in the proceedings Professor Henrich spoke of an agreement among all concerned, orientated to science and its findings. We all know of the difficulty inherent in this orientation, of the discrepancy between theory and practice. But before these problems can become apparent, there must first be agreement among scientists. Professor Habermas called attention to the conditional nature of the various perspectives, particularly the fear that discussion of Weber in Germany cannot remain aloof from the historical and ideological burden of the country today, while American colleagues are in the more fortunate position of being able to appreciate Weber's work untrammelled by this burden. Our foreign colleagues will certainly recognize the intellectual significance of this burden for the appreciation of Weber in Germany today, and we can hardly expect the right sense of proportion always to be maintained. But there is food for thought in the fact that in Germany it is always the politician Max Weber who is mentioned, whereas, for example, during a study-journey to India various Indian colleagues spoke to me with admiration of Weber's studies of the sociology of religion in India. If one projects this state of affairs into the future, it could be that in Germany Weber's contributions will be seen only from a political aspect (on occasion his scientific ideas are already today simply put on one side because of this tendency to treat everything as political) while the appreciation of his scientific work is left to others abroad.

I turn now to the question which concerns Professor Marcuse, but shall treat it in my own way. In the time at my disposal, I will select two problems which form part of the analysis of Weber: the notorious basis of the capitalist spirit of Puritanism, and the problem of bureaucracy. In both cases I stress the conceptual side of the matter.

Critics of Weber's thesis of Protestantism are well known to overlook the limited intention of this thesis. In his own lifetime, Weber warned against this, but not always successfully. But Weber's own limitations of his theme, a limitation contained in the original text, throws light on the problems of social-scientific concept-structure to be discussed here. In this particular passage Weber says that his theme does not concern the officially taught, theoretical ethics of his time, however important this may have been in practice. He was more interested in the influence of those psychological drives which originate in religious belief and action and are now guide-posts for men's practical behaviour.[1] Let us suppose that this behaviour is to be called economically rational. Then Weber's central problem is how to trace rationality back to religious beliefs—and here I am supposing his train of thought to be familiar to you. In the passage referred to, Weber has had an interesting lapse, from the point of view of understanding

[1] 'We are of course not concerned with contemporary theoretical and official teaching of ethics—whatever its practical importance for the influence of the church in sermons and parochial welfare—but with something quite different: its spread through psychological impulses concerned with religious belief and practice, pointing out a way of life and sustaining the individual in this way. To a great extent these impulses originated in the character of religious beliefs. People at that time worried about apparently abstract dogmas to an extent which is only understandable when seen in connection with practical religious interests.' *Max Weber, Gesammelte Aufsätze zur Religionssoziologie* I (Tübingen, 1920), 86.

the matter. He speaks of psychological drives, which are contained in religious beliefs, whereas he should only have spoken of psychological stimuli. For the decisive problem in his research is how far the stimuli contained in belief can or have become drives. Weber's remark that people at that time took much more seriously than we do the theological matters he dealt with, is scarcely a satisfactory solution of this problem.

I mention this detail because I think it throws light on one decisive point, on the problem of the formation of the 'ideal type' concept. Weber always stressed that only with the help of simplifications and exaggeration would it be possible to control conceptually the infinitely complex nature of the historical world, and the fluidity of transitions typical of it. In his essay on Protestantism he says in particular that his exposition systematizes certain fundamental theological tenets and shows them as more logically coherent than they actually were originally. Such conceptualizations, or analogous ones, are in fact indispensable for social-scientific research, although one can have several opinions about the purpose of the expression 'ideal type'. On the other hand one should not forget that these analytically necessary simplifications and exaggerations exclude the multivalence of ideas and actions, and so the relevance of conceptually described phenomena for the understanding of human interests becomes problematic.

In the case we mentioned this means that the effect, hypothesized by Weber, of certain theological doctrines is only wholly applicable if imputed to a man completely devoted to his religious beliefs, for whom the most extreme logically conceived consequences of Calvinist doctrine have psychologically decisive significance. Weber emphasized that most men are not religious virtuosi in this sense, but it seems to me he has not clarified the relationship touched on here between unequivocal concept-structure and equivocal human existence, although he himself contributed relevant judgments. To anticipate this point: I think this discrepancy is an unavoidable problem in scientific research, for which there are only partial solutions, which probably can never be wholly satisfactory.

I would like to expound this problem by means of the concept of bureaucracy because I think this also sheds light on the questions dealt with by Professor Marcuse. Again I presume that you are familiar with Weber's definition of bureaucracy, but would point out that this definition was originally conceived in contrast to patriarchal administration. The literature, however, has always dealt with the concept independently of this connection and has thus made it absolute. If, for example, it is said in a bureaucracy that official duties are strictly shared, every newspaper reader knows that there are quarrels about competence at the ministries. Despite this, one would call the present-day ministerial administration bureaucratic in Weber's sense of the word, in so far as the settlement of such differences is 'determined in principle', subject to later revision. In patriarchal administration such a solution would only follow the merits of each case, as a result of the personal decisions of the governor. In contrast to patriarchal administration one can speak in this sense of a 'strict division of official duties'. Once one ignores this contrast and analyses bureaucracy as such, the significance of the principle of 'general settlement' emerges less clearly than before, since one has now to try to understand for oneself the quarrels about competence. This textbook example of discrepancy between unequivocal concept-formation and equivocal reality can be applied by analogy to all other criteria of Weber's concept. I would point out that both the contradictory concepts of patriarchal and bureaucratic administration and the empirical analysis of action (under the premise of one or the other concept) are elements of social-scientific research.

Weber made the connection between the fluidity of actual bureaucratic behaviour with his conceptualization in the following way:

Bureaucracy in its fullest state of development also comes in a specific sense under the principle of 'sine ira ac studio' (impartiality). Its specific character, welcomed by capitalism, develops all the more completely the more it is 'de-humanised'. By 'more completely' is meant, the more this specific character, which is seen as a virtue, succeeds in eliminating from all official business love, hate, all purely personal and all irrational elements of feeling, elements defying calculation. Instead of gentlemen of the old order, inspired by personal interest, favour, grace and gratitude, modern culture requires, for the external apparatus which supports it, the more complicated and specialised it becomes, the less humanly concerned, strictly 'practical *expert*'.[1]

This is certainly a very conditional formulation which starts

[1] Max Weber, *Wirtschaft und Gesellschaft*, II (Tübingen, 1920), 662.

from the patriarchal concept, and which, on the assumption of a full development of the opposite concept, deduces from it the logically connected elimination of elements of feeling. As such, this logical construction is quite justified, but it is based on simplifications and exaggerations, which first have to be referred to the equivocal nature of human existence. There is no bureaucracy which is fully developed and void of all feeling. In principle Weber recognized this, he repeatedly emphasized the 'unarticulated variety of the facts' which only goes to show 'that rigorous concepts must be correctly applied, not as schemes for the violation of historical data, but as tools with which to determine the character of a phenomenon, by assessing how far it approaches one or the other "ideal type" '.[1] In the same sense Weber also protested against the 'fashionable constructions of general schemes of development', and suggested in their stead the exposition of the nature of various developments as a research project.[2] In his *Rechtssoziologie* Weber has been guided by these points of view in his treatment of the various meanings of the rationality of law, and his emphasis in particular on the dialectics of absolute formalism and material rationality—the history of law.

On this basis one can make the concept of the constitutional state itself dependent on maintaining this dialectical tension, and this point of view can also be utilized for the empirical analysis of bureaucracy.[3]

Now Weber did not always pursue these perspectives which are contained in his works. In particular this is true of his political prognoses, in so far as they rest on 'ideal type' projections which can claim logical, not historical, validity.[4] Regarding the concept of bureaucracy only, Weber was, for example, inclined to apply his perspectives of universal history to the political problems of the day in Wilhelminian Germany, which is striking, but misleading,

[1] Max Weber, *Gesammelte Aufsätze zur Sozial- und Wirtschafts-geschichte* (Tübingen, 1924), p. 280.

[2] Op. cit., p. 288.

[3] Here I have to confine myself to this statement. Cf. further on the subject in my book *Herrschaft und Industriearbeit* (Frankfurt, 1960), pp. 319 ff.

[4] I would add to this that Weber often did keep to the exact formulation of such prognoses. Cf. e.g. the well-known passage in the essay on Russia beginning with the sentence 'The more the struggle for such "individualist" values in life has to contend with material conditions the less can its "realisation" be left to "economic development" ', Max Weber, *Gesammelte politische Schriften* (Tübingen, 1958), p. 60.

because ironically it takes insufficient notice precisely of the nature of the history of German officialdom. If you then outbid Weber's analysis by calling bureaucracy the 'apotheosis of reification', this is to produce an apocalypse of culture, a kind of apotheosis of 'ideal type' extrapolations, rather than scientific analysis. Weber often warned against such conceptual over-emphasis although he did not always avoid it himself.

A speaker in discussion must necessarily confine himself to a limited number of aspects. I have tried to demonstrate the problems of Weber's concept-structure in its relation to empirical analysis by two examples, precisely because I find both sides of the matter essential to an understanding of industrialization and capitalism. Weber himself always saw his analyses as provisional because the outstripping of previous results belongs to the nature of scientific research. That also means that successors must feel it their duty to make full use of previous experience.

BENJAMIN NELSON

It hardly seems possible or desirable to delay any longer in filing a claim on behalf of Max Weber's right to be ranked as a prophet of the twentieth century and a pioneer of contemporary social and political analysis.[1] The option of dawdling or being faint-hearted in this action is no longer open to us. Never since his death forty-four years ago have the issues been so sharply joined as now. Our successive meetings this week have illustrated this situation with particular poignancy. This will seem especially the case for those who remember the words which Karl Jaspers spoke in 1920 in his

---

[1] Fuller discussion of the themes touched upon here will be found in three of my previous papers: (1) 'The Future of Illusions', written in 1951. Abridged version in *Man and Contemporary Society*, ed. Contemporary Civilization Staff, Columbia College, 2 vols. (New York, Columbia University Press, 1956), 2, pp. 958–79. (2) 'Sociology and Psychoanalysis on Trial', in *Psychoanalysis and the Social-Cultural Sciences*, ed. B. Nelson (Special no. of *The Psa. Review*, Fall 1962) 49:2, pp. 144–60. (3) 'Dialogues Across the Centuries: Weber, Marx, Hegel, Luther', in John Weiss (ed.), *Origins of Modern Consciousness* (Detroit, Mich: Wayne State University Press, 1965, in press).

Those who wish to appreciate the full reach of Professor Marcuse's position must be sure to study his *Eros and Civilization* and his newly published *One-Dimensional Man* (Boston, 1964), chap. 10, passim, esp. pp. 251–2, notably the author's concept of 'an essentially new Historical Subject' which receives mention in the present pages.

memorial address on his departed friend to the Student Association at Heidelberg.

Professor Marcuse is not the first, nor will he be the last, to launch shafts at the shade of Max Weber. Weber has been attacked from every side in the name of every militant faith of the contemporary era. Stalinist Communism, non-Stalinist Marxism, German Nazism, International Neo-Thomism, Parisian Existentialism, American Neo-Anarchism, have all been relentlessly critical of Weber. German and European scholars do not need to be reminded at any length of the polemics against Weber by Georg Lukács, Christoph Steding,[1] Leo Strauss, Jean-Paul Sartre and their associates. In the United States, Weber has become a favourite butt of the so-called anti-Establishment opposition, which expresses what I have elsewhere described as a New Amalgam of neo-Marxian and post-Freudian motifs, rendered with anarchist and existentialist overtones.[2] Herbert Marcuse ranks among the leaders of the opposition, which includes the late C. Wright Mills, widely read literary men and cultural critics including Norman O. Brown, author of 'Life Against Death', and Paul Goodman, author of 'Growing up Absurd' and 'Utopian Essays and Practical Proposals'.

One is led to ask what men of such varied talents have in common or why they should be united in their opposition to Weber. Any attempt to answer this question must go to the root of Professor Marcuse's paper.

Everyone who finds himself encumbered or inconvenienced by what I am tempted to call the 'Social Reality Principle' will want to polemicize against Weber. Weber is both 'stumbling block' and 'scandal' to all who ardently quest for the total and the instant regeneration of self, society and culture; all Utopians and ideologists—whether of the left, right or centre—who are confirmed in their irrefutable assurances by every turn of history, however fateful.

Dare we here recall the name of Freud, for whose extremist disciples Weber had rightly so little regard?

As many of you know, Freud was several times tempted to speak of himself as one of those thinkers, along with Copernicus

---

[1] See, esp., his many references to Weber in his rarely cited work, *Das Reich und die Krankheit der europäischen Kultur* (Hamburg, 1938).

[2] 'Sociology and Psychoanalysis on Trial' (cf. note 1 above).

and Darwin, whose destiny it was to inflict mortal wounds upon the narcissism of man, by calling into question his autistic delusion of self-reference in respect to the special creation and central position of his earth, his species, his conscious ego. Man's ego, Freud contended, was far indeed from being master in its own house, captain of its own ship.

To the galaxy of names mentioned by Freud and others, we now need to add the names of those sociologists and social scientists who have gone beyond Freud or Marx in vindicating what I designated earlier as the social reality principle. Of this group I would especially nominate Max Weber now, holding in reserve for other more appropriate occasions the names of Emile Durkheim and Georg Simmel and a number of others who must now go unmentioned.

Max Weber and other pioneers of contemporary social science have been helping us to see the structure and workings of human society in a new light. We now know that wherever men in any number are involved in joint performance of complex functions, they elaborate social arrangements which pattern their relations, activities, feelings and outlooks. All organized systems of human social co-existence comprise shifting balances of rights and obligations, liberties and restraints, positive and negative inputs and outcomes, variously affecting individuals and groups. No social or cultural change, however revolutionary—not even collectivist planning or total sexual emancipation, for which so much is currently claimed by the spokesmen of the New Amalgam —will stamp out crime, vice, false consciousness, political domination, economic waste, group prejudice, status oppression, role conflict, religious fanaticism and other symptoms of individual and social malaise. They persist in varying proportions and with varying effects in all organized societies. They are the accompaniment and signs of strain among and within the several (but not concentric) systems which help to explain the characteristics of human action-systems we describe by the names of the personality, social–political–economic organization, and culture.

We owe gratitude to Weber and others who share his insights for a number of related understandings. Thanks to these men we are now better able to see beyond the illusions which have been the stock-in-trade of the traditional radicals of right and left. We are, so to speak, spared from endlessly becoming victims of 'repetition–

compulsion' in the social and political spheres. We learn to seek our desired relief by appropriate remedies, focusing on those features of knotted situations which can be changed for the better through the exercise of our productive powers. With greater ease and frequency we may engage in efforts at genuine social invention, seeking to expand the modes, measures and manner of individual and group fulfilments within our reach.

We now recognize that the tasks confronted by the facilitating systems of complex industrial societies are of staggering complexity and it is no wonder that structural strains are always in evidence. These can—and must—be held in check and mitigated, but they cannot be entirely eliminated for all time, neither by faith, dream, fiat or the proclamation of 'charismatic' communities of blood, love or goods.

The current representatives of the 'dialectic' tell us that what comes into being in time will pass away. But this is to miss the fact that whenever certain sets of fulfilments are to be achieved within a framework of determinate sets of resources and expectations, 'rational' allocation-schemes are likely to emerge. However such schemes be constituted they involve greater or lesser extents of 'rationalization' in one or another of Weber's senses. Such 'rationalization' will be present, indeed, even in those undertakings which are consciously dedicated to the maximum creation of the society. The explanation of this is simple but not widely enough understood. Rationality and rationalization of some sort arise in any activity involving (a) allocation of scarce resources to competing uses, (b) resort to a technology requiring a high division of labour.

So long, therefore, as large-scale differentiated society endures, reification, alienation and self-estrangement in some measure will occur. To think otherwise is to suffer from a tragic reluctance to accept the inevitable social–cultural imperatives of complex civil societies. Anarchist and totalitarian assurances of the transcendence of history through the emergence of 'an essentially new historical Subject' (in the striking idiom of current 'dialectic'), purified of all separateness of need, interest and will, are millenarian myths masquerading as political philosophies and programmes of social reconstruction. No other answer can be given to those who propose to make Max Weber and the industrial society scapegoats for the horrors of Hitler's totalitarianism and 'Final Solution'.

The alternatives to 'rationality' and 'rationalization' are not many; we may claim to solve our problems, as right–left solipsists and right–left totalitarianisms do by *dis-solving them*. We leap in one jump from the Kingdom of Necessity to the Realm of Freedom, where—by definition—all decisions are correctly made because—by definition—there is the free uncoerced consensus of all. This is what Marx meant by the phrase 'socialized Humanity'; this is what Professor Marcuse is now calling 'an essentially new historical Subject'. All those who compose the new historical *Subject* are assumed to be animated by a single spirit, moved by a single purpose, possessed of a single will.

In our everyday atmosphere, however, the alternatives to a 'rational calculus' are less edifying: ukase, bayonet, caste, the war of all against all, lawlessness, chaos. It does not matter that dialectical neo-anarchists regularly offer a communitarian Utopian mystique as proof of the superiority of their programme. Avowals of community which flatly deny the need for norms in the ordering of discrepant impulses and conflicting claims *dis-solve* the antinomies of organization by fiat. This is already done by the more ardent members of the community of Anticipation. Those who see themselves as the vanguard of the 'New Subject'—again to use Marcuse's idiom—abjure 'alienation' and 'self-estrangement' in any form, seeking to detach themselves from organized society, mass culture and non-Utopian undertakings.

Turning once more to Professor Marcuse's polemic against Weber's teachings, we are not surprised to learn that the Leaders of the New Amalgam have no place either in their world-views or their ways of life for scientific method or scientific neutrality in sociology or any other sphere of thought. Systematic sociology in the Weberian and Durkheimian manner are indicted on many counts:

1 The 'reality principle' both in Freud's version and the variant I have offered above under the name of the 'social reality principle' is groundless and pointless. Reality is *becoming*.
2 Science is irrelevant in the *becoming* and *making* of the truth.
3 Action is the true way to understanding.
4 Value-neutrality is a mask for conformist acceptance of the prevailing system of domination.
5 So-called structural-functional analysis and 'empirical research'

assume the irreversibility of existing social–political arrangements and cultural attitudes.

6   Scientific sociology fosters obliviousness to first order activity,
    namely incessant existential affirmation and creative acts of
    dissent, revolution and reconstruction.

Elsewhere I have explored these charges in some detail.[1]
Here I must be content to touch on two issues stressed in the
paper under discussion.

There is no basis for saying, as Utopian partisans regularly say,
that those who acknowledge Weber and Durkheim as sociological
forerunners are necessarily uncritical conformists, supporters of
any and every *status quo*. An increasing number of the world's
most prominent sociologists are disproving this daily both in word
and deed. Condemnation of contemporary sociology, both in the
Soviet Union and in Communist China, are an added proof that
Professor Marcuse and his friends have shot wide of the mark.

Our second observation addresses itself directly to the existentialist neo-Marxist strictures against scientific formalisms and the
alleged neutrality of scientific inquiry: Professor Marcuse and his
associates must surely know that wherever there is science there is
formal abstractive rationality; wherever there is science there is
the quest for logical precision, mathematical form and intersub-
jective validation. To equate mathematics and domination, as
Professor Marcuse does, is to do great violence to historical
tradition and fact.

Those who cannot endure the resort to scientific formalism are
irresistibly driven to engage in the fashioning of what Dugald
Stewart called by the telling name of 'conjectural history'.
Poetizing dialectic, whether of history or nature, may sometimes be
felt to put one in touch with a 'higher truth', but the time comes
when dialectic itself has to be translated into propositional form.
How else is it to be clearly formulated and reliably tested?
Dialectics, no less than science, has its day of reckoning.

Rarely, almost never, do the critics of Max Weber meet him
on his own ground; rarely, almost never, do they relate to him as
to an intellectual Titan who carried on a ceaseless dialogue
across decades and centuries with those whom he counted creative
spirits in the anguished search for truth and responsible existence.

[1] Ibid.

A heavy price is paid when this perspective is sacrificed on the twin altars of politics and topicality. To tie him without remainder to Wilhelminian Germany and National Liberal politics, as unfriendly critics are now doing, is in the end to rule out the import of his lifelong strivings for universal vision and ultimate relevance, to turn him into what he was not—a mere creature of his time, a spokesman for reactionary imperialist interests, a quixotic mediocrity in the self-assumed role of a Macchiavelli, an irresponsible adventurer ready to underwrite military dictatorship—indeed, a forerunner of 1933. Surely his own time knew him and the future will remember him under other guises than these.

Who else in his day struggled so hard to defend (and decide between) the social–structure and existential options which the entire course of development had offered to the human imagination? Who brooded so restlessly as he over problems posed by central traditions and paradigmatic figures and groups in the history of thought: Kant, Hegel, Marx, Overbeck, Kierkegaard, Nietzsche, Tolstoy, Luther, St. Paul, Jesus of the Sermon on the Mount, the Hebrew prophets, the Hindu Brahmins, the Chinese mandarins? Even in the last year of his life, as his unforgettable addresses on the vocations of science and politics so vividly show, he fought to compose the wars raging within him among his own inner demons.

Professor Marcuse's insistent forthrightness in blaming so many of the ills of recent times on the 'rationalism' which Weber, in his view, espoused in so undialectical a fashion, underscores a little known fact: Weber's renowned comparative studies from his *Protestant Ethic* (1904–5)[1] to his *Wirtschaft und Gesellschaft* have yet to be understood in their true light. They are much more than they seem or are generally understood to be, comparative sociological investigations against the background of the history of Western civilization and culture. In a sense which many overlook, they are prophecies and warnings—prophecies about the menacing shape of things to come, warnings against the further expansion of the domain of conscienceless reason, even in the name of the most noble ideals. Whoever regarded history intently, Weber meant to say, might expect to verify for himself one of its least attractive paradoxes. The noblest impulse only too often gave rise to the

[1] For my forthcoming rejoinder to Herbert Luethy's recent critique of Weber's *Protestant Ethic*, see *Encounter* (London, 1964, in press).

most baleful consequences. Thus, the disenchanted world order of contemporary industrial 'capitalist' society had been spurred on its fateful course by the pronouncements on the part of the Reformers, especially Calvin, of new theological doctrines of a deeply ascetic cast. In short, high-minded altruistic religious impulses rather than amoral indifference of hardened cynicism had been the ultimate source of the power on the present age of unthinking mechanism and the cult of competitive 'gamesmanship'.

A second point needs to be made before we can fully grasp the deeper purposes of Weber's works. Seen in their proper religious and philosophical settings, they compose a unique twentieth-century report of the ambiguous turnings of the spirit of rationalization in both Orient and Occident. Each of his successive studies breaks new sociological and historical ground calling into question established images of the 'phenomenology', 'alienation', and 'progress' of Reason and Mind in world history. More precisely, Weber demythologizes and reassembles two of the central schemas of the century of his birth: Marx's Promethean saga of the lapses from and restorations of the primal state of undividedness of society, self and culture; and Hegel's intricate thematics from his *Phenomenology of Spirit* to his *Philosophy of History* and *Philosophy of Right*.

During the past few days we have been deluged with proofs that Weber was no flawless paragon. Weber could and did become crude and gauche in some of his forays into *Machtpolitik*. Surely we have not been gathered here in his beloved Heidelberg to hear this one side of the story. Nor is this in any profound sense how his life and work demand to be understood.

In my view, Weber comes into clearest focus when he is seen to be one of those self-appointed mentors who seeks to prepare his own generation and those yet to come for the sterner trials ahead. He was surely the greatest sociologist–historian of his age, but he was much more than that. In the interim of the post-Christian post-rationalist twilight he was a pathfinder and a herald. Sensing that his country and, indeed, his posterity would soon be passing through the Dark Night of their souls, he sought to warn them against the seductions which would numb them—their senses and spirits alike—to the ultimate convulsions and petrifications which were in progress. In an era of galloping anomie he steadfastly came to the defence of treasured historic values, but he just as steadfastly refused to engage in any 'sacrifice of the intellect' to the Gods and myths of his forefathers. For heaven-stormers of the right or left he had little regard. He was convinced that Utopias meant to be heavens-on-earth regularly became totalitarian hells.

The nature and extent of Weber's break with the century of his birth are sharply rendered in the themes which sound ever more clearly as he nears the zenith of his life:

1. Western man must somehow learn at the eleventh hour to curb his suicidal drive to rationalize all corners of his life. He must come to see that personal freedom loses ground as conscienceless reason extends its inhuman sway into every last corner of the world of human affairs and existence.

2. All programmes to reorganize the world by adopting acosmic injunctions, whether Christian or socialist, are attended by radical paradox. The everyday world of passions and interest cannot escape the burden of organization, force and hierarchy, if public order and wider civil interests are to prevail.

3. The appeal to prophecy with a view to the abolition of all traces of 'outer bondage' involves a maximum threat to the spiritual man's 'inner freedom'.

4. A grim fate stalks the career of acosmic ideals. Their pristine purity is almost certain to be modified, even perverted. Bureaucratization seems to be the fate of every revolutionary impulse; standardization, the destiny of every new vision; uniformity, the outcome of every form-bursting work of the spirit. Behind the prophet stands the bureaucrat. The spirit of inner-worldly asceticism, above all, Calvin's summons to establish God's sovereign will in every one of men's earthly relations, had issued in a triumph of mechanism, of technique, of routine—in a word, the dominion of conscienceless reason. (How different all this was from the promise of Hegel's *Philosophy of History* and Marx's *Manifesto*, the two images of destiny which continued to haunt the imaginations of men in Weber's day and which, as I have implied above, comprise the almost invisible background of his mighty monographs on the social psychology and economic ethic of the world religions!)

5. The age on which we are now embarked, Weber sensed, is one of drift and hovering doom. The churches remain open but there

M

is no return to their abandoned altars. Nor can one pin one's faith on 'prophetic' creeds fabricated by professional or professorial visionaries.

6. In the interim we are all obliged to live, we must struggle to preserve our human dignity. We must find nurture for our best selves in intimate communions and we must tend the flickering light of freedom in our various callings.

In sum, the more we meditate on Weber from the angle of his compelling—albeit neglected—religious and philosophical concerns, the more we must come to see him as a wracked but heroic spirit of an age of Trial.

From the perspective of our own time, Weber stands forth as a thinker of cosmic cast who felt called upon to explore men's predicaments and possibilities in what some are now describing as 'the first post-Christian generation on the European continent', the generation after Nietzsche's fateful proclamation. There is hardly a theme celebrated by modern existentialists from Kierkegaard to Sartre, which is not sounded in a distinctive way by Weber. Where Weber remains unique, however, is in his desperate (not despairing) efforts to discover sense and promote sensibility and scientific understanding in the face of the absurd.

All the current charges against Weber—those of Professor Marcuse included—crumble before two irreducible facts. Weber was a pioneer in the twentieth-century struggle against bureaucratic and technocratic totalitarianism. While many of his contemporaries were continuing to acclaim the beneficent course of Reason, History and Progress, he struck out against the profanations of the human spirit which a new class of nullities, as he called them—'specialists without spirit, sensualists without heart' —was shamelessly hailing as the 'highest level of civilization ever before attained'. Indeed, his announcements of threats of a mechanized and robotized society anticipate the eerie insights of Eugene Zamiatin's *We*, Aldous Huxley's *Brave New World* and George Orwell's *1984*.

Who, indeed, has explored the dilemmas of action in the twentieth century so deeply and honestly as did Weber? Not Tolstoy, not Freud, not Schweitzer; not Camus or Sartre, not even Kafka—none of the acclaimed moralists of our century— matched Weber in the range of his moral imagination or in his courage to reject simple solutions. Successive utterances from his early letters to his two majestic swan songs, *Wissenschaft als Beruf* and *Politik als Beruf* are the stations on his way, his unveilings of the ambiguities of the twentieth-century existence. Say what one will of his politics, he has no peer as an examiner of the central options of historic cultures, the tangled problems of a world of nations, and the moral quandaries at every level of existence and decision—the individual self, the social group, the political community.

The mis-steps he made in all good faith in responding to the awesome challenges of his day do not weigh heavily in the balance against the immense services he rendered to mankind. In the end, indeed, it is at the moment when his weaknesses and strengths are fused that he appears in his truest light—a paradigm of a tormented Titan and a prophet of our distraught era.

To hold him responsible for the advent of 1933 or the nightmare of Auschwitz, as a number of his aroused countrymen are now doing, is to commit error and wrong at one and the same time. One may be allowed to hope that posterity will make amends for this misguided gesture. His countrymen should not wish to do less for one who struggled so valiantly, albeit so vainly, to guard them against the disasters which lay ahead.

Prophets need not always be without honour in their own country.

GEORGES FRIEDMANN

I will confine myself to a few reflections on Professor Marcuse's report in which I underline the points which concern Weber as theoretician of the rationality of modern capitalism, and which were either confirmed by the development of industrial society or have taken another course.

1. Weber studied the specific characteristics of Western capitalism with admirable clear-sightedness and variety of perspective. The concept of *rationality* which he makes central to his thinking, allows him to throw light on the most diverse aspects, reaching at times a positively prophetic power of reflection. His analysis of the role of science in the development of capitalist economy (particularly the dependence of industry on natural science, which is based on mathematics and rational experiment) explains one of the essential aspects of capitalist rationality; that of the correct

estimation of the most important technical factors. They allow us today to understand the peculiarity of Western technical civilization on a plane which is, on the whole, even if in different stages, subordinated to the *fate* of industrialization. In a world conditioned by technique and science, industry, permeated by electronic techniques and automation, tends to become itself a gigantic field of rationalized experimental methodology.

Concerned with the multi-stratified research into the origins of development, Weber links Western industrialization with, on the one hand, the 'rational organization of formally free labour' in bourgeois profiteering capitalism and, on the other, with the calculations of traditional book-keeping (confrontation of a result expressed in money with an investment estimated in money). Here one could make a comparison (which has not been specially dealt with in discussion) between the mission Marx ascribed to the bourgeoisie in its 'progressive' period, and the 'fascination', as Professor Marcuse put it, which the historic mission of the bourgeoisie exercised on Weber.

From his research into agrarian conditions in the ancient world (*Die römische Agrargeschichte in ihrer Bedentung fur das Staats- Und Privatrecht*) and his comparative history of capitalism there emerges a *relativity* in the 'rationality' of culture and a kind of privilege of the Western bourgeoisie who alone were capable of successfully developing industrialization. Apart from that, he strongly emphasized the fact that socialism, embarking in the same direction, must be equally subject to the claims of rationalization and the organization of specialized and competent bureaucrats.

Weber himself was a pioneer in sociological observation of the great capitalist industry of his times. His essay 'On the psychophysics of industrial labour' was one of the first studies to call special attention forcefully and precisely to the relationships between, on the one hand, the mentality of the worker (what we call his attitude to directors and management and the trade union movement) and on the other, production output, and particularly the important phenomenon of 'go-slow'—work to rule which has been much discussed in the last thirty years. His study of social selection, of career choice and adaptation to work is similarly prophetic.

2. To estimate correctly the present-day repercussions of Weber's ideas, we must spotlight the concept of bureaucratic control,

which in his view was inseparable from the progress of capitalist industrialization, and bound up with the development of the modern state. This form of control has had, more than forty years after his death, a spectacular reincarnation in *technical bureaucracy*, which was created and extensively developed by the so-called 'scientific organization of labour'. In forms which change with the progress of the means of production—and in various national guises—this has, since Taylor, caused the radical separation of two spheres: the sphere of planning, decision and power (which becomes scientific and technical) from the sphere of productive labour, in which, apart from a few individual cases, the whole labour force is trapped without any possibility of escape. The gap between these two spheres and their qualities is partly characterized by the present form of capitalist industrialization. But we have definite information that this split or dichotomy in organization is repeated *mutatis mutandis* in those so-called socialist countries that are economically most developed. The considerable level of development of technical bureaucracy displays, greatly enlarged, many traits which Weber used in his classic theory to describe the bureaucratic organization of Western capitalism.

3. To some extent, Weber had a presentiment of the dangers entailed by rationality in controlling all activity of the state and of the modern world. Man suffers under capitalist conditions of production: (let us remember the well-known formulation: The Puritans *wanted* to be professional men: we *have* to be).

Professor Marcuse's paper was often brilliant, but I would criticize him for not investigating sufficiently the relations between Weber's rationality and the different aspects of the rationalization of industrial society, as he observed it.

Rationalization in Weber's sense permeates not only industry, but also administration, agriculture, trade, banking: not only working life, but with the development of technical means of information, mass-communication and life outside working hours. The only chance of salvation from these dangers which Weber sees is activity in political as well as the moral sphere, choosing the highest values and forms of expression of freedom. We may assume that Weber's reactions to the greatest personalities among the 'charismatic demagogues' since the Second World War in the West would have been favourable, if not entirely enthusiastic.

We could dream here for a moment about Weber's vision of a 'charismatic demagogue', today especially close to us in France.

But Weber identified himself too much with the bourgeois–capitalist mission of rationalization to be able to foresee what irrationalities it would lead to, even in his time, and in this sense too, how it would develop in the future. In this context I think an earlier scholar, Cournot (with his theory of development 'from the vital to the rational') understood more profoundly the dangers of rationalization for moral values, dignity, and even man's psychological equilibrium in technicalized civilization.

The dichotomy of organization which seems inevitable in capitalist industrialization has provoked many irrational phenomena. Following the logic of rationality (simplification of labour, increased production, cutting overheads), it has gone as far as the physiological and psychological stupidity of the division of labour, economic losses, 'diminishing returns' the creation of dozens, hundreds and millions of split tasks (even in socialist countries and those of the 'Third World', which have been infected by this rationality), which are contrary to the ideas of workers' happiness and participation.

Automation will not solve this problem so easily and completely as its optimistic theoreticians (e.g. Diebold and Drucker in the U.S.) had assumed. As for the speculation of cybernetics in this sphere, they detract from human, social and psychological reality and are to some extent stupendously naïve.

The rationality of capitalist industry led to all the irrationalities of the so-called 'surplus' society, especially to the multiplication of the more or less artificial 'necessities', the unrestrained production of 'gadgets'; the consumer caught by advertisements is less lacking in money to buy them than in time to enjoy them, and above all in the necessary education to be able to make a sensible *choice* among material and cultural products (mass-culture). In the country which is the most highly developed example of this, i.e. the U.S., capitalist rationalization has created a margin ('liberated margin') of chronic unemployment, which accounts for 6 per cent or—if one also reckons women, all forms of partial unemployment and under-employment in industry, administration and agriculture—about 25 per cent of the active population. The efforts of the 'surplus' societies to bring aid to the developing countries of the 'Third World', whose population amounts to three-quarters of the total population of the world, have up till now been dilatory and of little effect—for a variety of reasons which lie outside the context of my objections.

It would be easy to oppose Weber's trust in the historic mission of bourgeois capitalism by present-day outbreaks of irrationality in industry, and still more generally, in the mass-society of technological civilization. But one could just as easily draw up in its favour an impressive list of achievements, of progress in the spheres of hygiene, economics, culture and even personal freedom. Weber, a dramatic thinker by nature, was not unaware of the irrationality of the world and the fact that the results of human effort often go counter to its intentions. It would be unfair to imagine (and perhaps Professor Marcuse did not sufficiently stress this) that if Weber were still alive in today's mass society, and could follow the developments of industrialization since 1920, he would not revise some of his conceptions. His work is too clear-sighted, too concerned about differentiations, too conscious of the responsibilities of the learned, for us to permit ourselves such cheap criticism of one of the greatest thinkers of this century.

RICHARD F. BEHRENDT

I am glad my two American colleagues have already said what I thought should basically be said about Professor Marcuse's paper. Leaving the question of principles, I should like to take up a point which has not been dealt with expressly in Professor Marcuse's paper—indeed not at all during this congress, i.e. the relations between industry and capitalism in the foreseeable future, and especially the question of whether and how far industrialization is still supported today, and will be further supported in the future, by elements of capitalism, in so far as there is to be such a thing as industrialization at all.

This question appears to me of decisive importance with regard especially to those territories that never belonged to the realm of active capitalism in countries which produced no capitalist impulses of their own, which would have determined the character of their economy and society—but were partially and passively exposed to capitalism as a largely exogenous factor. This obviously refers to today's so-called communist regions and developing countries. What can be learnt from Weber relevant to the socio-economic problems of present-day developing countries?

The foreword to the *Gesammelte Aufsätzen zur Religionssozio-logie*[1] begins with the question: 'What chain of circumstances has led to the appearance in the West, and only here, of cultural phenomena whose direction of development was of *universal* significance and validity?'

This question plays a great part in present efforts to help the so-called developing countries. And yet we stand today in the middle of a process (at first sight contradictory) of the dissolution of an oligarchic world-order which was made possible by the effects of those cultural phenomena (some of which appeared for the first time in the West and some of which appeared only in the West) together with a universalization of these same cultural phenomena. The formation of human syncretism of practical evaluations occurs on the basis of the 'modernism' which arose in the West—to use first of all a neutral concept.

A considerable part of Weber's work consists in the exposition of the characteristics of Western economic and social development, which precisely by its originality and its material military and socio-organizational supremacy, revolutionalized all non-Western social orders and has itself become a model for more and more people belonging to cultures until now non-Western.

Industrialization and capitalism are elements of this revolutionizing process, which arises from much deeper strata and affects far wider spheres. As a comprehensive concept I prefer *dynamics*; it denotes a social form of life in which cultural growth is predominant, in which, correspondingly, a noticeable change in value-orders, in modes of thought and behaviour, technical equipment, methods of production and organization constantly goes on, over long periods and over several generations, predominantly in the direction of expansion and multiplication of human and material energies of social groups, relationships and structures considered most important for life. In contradistinction to mere change and sporadic growth of culture, dynamics is an original phenomenon of modern times, of the third phase of culture (to use Ralph Linton's terminology).[2] It found its first concretization in modern capitalism—which according to Weber, and in contradistinction to the numerous sporadic and fragmentary acts

[1] Tübingen, 1920, p. 1.
[2] *The Tree of Culture* (New York, 1955), pp. 661 ff.

that were also called 'capitalist', was an exclusively Western phenomenon. It finds its concretization also in industrialization, in the influence of machines on technique economy, driven by mechanized energy, served by free labour-forces in overwhelmingly large, spatially concentrated and rationally organized enterprises. 'Industrialization' in this context means the organizational and institutional concretization of those rational methods of production and distribution, which, in the last two centuries, have become possible by the dynamic development of the natural sciences, technology, and the economic sciences which until now have proved to be the indispensable preconditions for every decisive rise in productivity and with it the standard of living.

This socio-economic dynamics is historically the product of modern capitalism in Weber's sense of the word. It arose in a few countries of Western and Central European culture, where the psychological, intellectual and socio–structural predispositions were favourable, and was then carried to those regions of North America, Australia and New Zealand colonized by people from these cultures: these regions in turn entered the sphere of active socio-economic dynamics and thus of capitalism, and became co-supporters of the system.

The logic of this new dynamic system required that, for the first time in human experience, it draw all the rest of the world into its sphere of influence as fringe-spheres of the dynamic centre. Since in these fringe-spheres there existed no adequate independent drives and predispositions of social structure for dynamic development, these countries ended up in unilateral economic—and often also political—dependence on the nucleus of dynamic countries.

The hegemony of this nucleus established in this way over the whole of mankind was always unstable and of necessity transient. It was unstable on account of the disunity of cultural changes inside this nucleus of dynamic countries and the struggles of power-politics which, arising from socio-structural residues, occurred between them. It proved transitory by the inner logic of dynamics, which tends to a levelling of individual and collective chances of mobility and advance for all participants in the system, while the antiquated *political* structures and modes of behaviour of the original dynamic countries—among each other as well as in their relation to the fringe-spheres—tried to hinder such a levelling and democratization in international and inter-racial relations. In Weber's position this immobility of political mentality was obvious.

From this there resulted in the course of our century

1   basic socio-structural changes inside the central countries, in the sense of a progressive 'socialisation' of the original capitalistic motives and forms of order;

2   the shifting of the geographical centre of the socio-economic dynamics of West and Central Europe to North America;

3   the expansion of the circle of central dynamic countries to European and Asiatic Russia and at the same time the differentiation of the supporters of socio-economic dynamics between the direct and indirect heirs of capitalism, who continue its essential achievements in state-socialist form; and finally

4   the forced entry of the rest of the countries at the fringe into a process—which they at least demand, and which is partly also systematically promoted—of socio-economic development, by which they want to share as quickly as possible in those results of capitalism which increase general well-being.

So we are concerned with

1   a tendency to the universalization of socio-economic dynamics;

2   a tendency to a *selective* taking-over of the only socio-economic system which till now has made possible a distinct improvement in men's living conditions—not only in material ways, but also in physical and mental—i.e. capitalism.

This taking-over is said to be selective in so far as in the so-called developing countries one might anticipate and thus avoid the radical differences of income, possessions and power and the socially and psychologically disadvantageous effects of inharmonious cultural change, that were typical of early capitalist development in the West.

The pluralistic forces of the dynamic system itself have thus produced structural changes not only in the dynamic core countries but also in the fringe territories, and thus cause it to appear doubtful whether in any country on earth *capitalism* can be called the determining element of economic and social order. On the other hand socio-economic *dynamics*—at least as a guiding idea and socio-political demand—has become a universal sign of our times and with particular force in the great majority of men who have never lived in the active sphere of capitalism nor shared directly and decisively in its symptoms and effects—which include increased productivity.

It follows therefore

(a) that capitalism must be seen systematically—as a partial phenomenon and historically as a pioneer episode of more comprehensive and permanent dynamics;

(b) that dynamics, introduced by and concretized by capitalism, outlives it;

(c) that we must distinguish between forms and effects of dynamics, which are specifically capitalistic and as such not essential for dynamics *in general*, but ephemeral and variable, and others which in any case on the basis of our previous experience are *generally* valid for dynamics, essential and therefore relatively constant.

Every attempt at a concrete distinction between such variables and constants is of course risky and at most provisional, especially in this context. Even so it may be assumed that this-worldly asceticism, profit motives concentrated in private enterprise, property bound up with enterprise and management, exclusive orientation to the lottery of the markets, are variable, non-essential elements of dynamics: on the other hand, the dynamic orientation of life to a better future, imagined as humanly shapable, purposefulness in economics, law, and public administration, systematic adaptation and utilization of scientific knowledge for technology and economics, high-grade rationally operated division of labour—and thereby more extensive industrialization and interdependence in larger and larger social structures—all represent essential and constant elements of dynamics and unalterable requirements for socio-economic development.

At a more profound level of analysis we come upon entirely new phenomenon in social structure—the equivalents of cultural items that appeared for the first time in capitalism—for instance the trends towards secularization, the weakening of primary social structures, the widening of individual autonomy and reification and bureaucratization. Here in the whole realm of capitalism's progeny we find such striking analogies that we come close to supposing that, viewed from the analysis of structure, they are constant characteristics, not only of capitalism, but of dynamics, at least with the proviso that these too will change dynamically.

Whether the 'absolute unavoidable imprisonment of our whole

existence in the cage of a specialist organization of officialdom'[1]
first announced by Weber, and then by Professor Marcuse, really
represents the last word of fate, I would doubt without being able
to give detailed reasons for my doubt. I would like to give a warning against the widespread tendency (already very strong in
Weber) to celebrate orgies of determinist feeling for life by
demoniac hypostasizing of rationality in technology and administration, and their supporters—presumed or real—the bureaucrats.
Professor Bahrdt and Bendix, yesterday and earlier, in different
contexts have both indicated certain tendencies towards the
relaxation of bureaucratic massing of power in today's society,
often falsely presented as wholly unified and monolithic. It seems
to me that long-term irreconcilability of generally valid bureaucracy with dynamics becomes more and more clear, in all countries
which inherited capitalism, under whatever ideological banner
they stand, and the necessity of decentralization and democratization of methods of discussion, decision-taking and execution arises
from the hard experience of our times, especially of those societies
under authoritarian control.[2]

Capitalism has brought very different descendants into the
world (to take this phrase quite literally): all supporters and even
all challengers of socio-economic dynamics follow in its wake,
though not as Marx presumably imagined, for their inheritance is
not limited to technical and organizational modes of production,
but is reinforced also in broad spheres of psycho-social motiva-
tions, guiding ideas and modes of behaviour, etc. and in problems
of bureaucratization for its own sake, whose particular force in
socialism Weber had already pointed out.[3]

It must of course be admitted that there remains a considerable
range of variables concerning the structure of power, for instance
the division of managerial and executive functions and the results
of dynamics, both (a) socio-structural, related to their usufruc-
tuaries, and (b) in the cultural sector, referring to concrete targets
and objects of development (which combine elements of (a) and
(b)). The problems usually concern the forms of social order, the
social substructure, socio-political framework, for the beginning or

[1] *Gesammelte Aufsätze zur Religionssoziologie*, p. 3.
[2] For more detail cf. my article 'Dynamische Gesellschaft: Über die Gestalt-
barkeit der Zukunft' (Berne–Stuttgart), 1963, and 'Gesellschaftliche Dynamik—
demokratisches Wachstum', in: *Offene Welt*, no. 83 (March 1964), pp. 12–28.
[3] *Gesammelte politische Schriften* (Munich, 1921), pp. 150-1.

continuance of economic development in the second half of the twentieth century, where the goal of maintenance and growth of dynamic energies and productivity is accepted as a constant and universal factor.

The following questions can be put more concretely (and clearly we can only *ask* them here):

(*a*) how far are originally specifically 'capitalist' modes of procedure and behaviour indispensable for all socio-economic dynamics?;

(*b*) how far are the experiences of the West in respect of methods —originally but not exclusively capitalist—of socio-economic development usable as criteria and copyable;

(*c*) how far are the sociological categories which Weber uses to describe the development of capitalist dynamics—till recently the *only* form—also valid for understanding the problems of making the hitherto non-capitalist countries dynamic?;

(*d*) how far do we know dynamic social techniques 'conforming to development' outside Western experience or Weber's scheme of ideas?

Professor Marcuse has endeavoured to expound sociologically some of Weber's basic categories as conditioned and restricted by his 'bourgeois' status. If we agreed with Professor Marcuse, Weber's categories would prove outmoded as an aid to understanding present-day problems of development.

I think on the contrary that particularly the concept of formal rationality, which Professor Marcuse finds so important for his purposes, signified a necessary generally valid method of effective management, and one which is applicable not only to capitalism as known hitherto, but also to its rebel or critical sons in present-day 'communism' and the developing countries. This is already shown to be so by Weber's distinction between formal and substantive rationality, and by his reference[1] to the fact that the criteria of orientation of substantive rationality can be completely pluralist, and of course socialist too. Rationality according to Max Weber— in its purest form of expression the calculation of capital—is an indispensable mode of procedure for any dynamic economic development, an essential steering instrument in any society which is technically progressive, differentiated in division of

[1] *Grundriss der Socialökonomik*, vol. III, *Wirtschaft und Gesellschaft*, 2nd enlarged edition, 1st half-volume (Tübingen, 1925), pp. 44–5 and § 9.

labour, complex in social organization, geographically extensive
and at the same time basically independent of any system of
sharing and any political ideology of social order.

Since Weber's death we have had almost fifty years' experience
of the first non-capitalist yet dynamic social system, the Soviet
Union, and have learnt how strongly what I call the essential
elements of dynamics are effected there, and how the necessity
for rationality and calculability asserts itself, at least as a demand.
And we have no reason to believe that the present-day so-called
developing countries will not also be exposed to the validity of
all these categories, and all the more so since developing is a
genuine desire on their part and influences their modes of behaviour, whether simply as a desire or as effective advancement.

There, too, and in the socialist countries it is proved (as Professor Marcuse has expressed it) that 'technique is sometimes a
historical and social project'; there, too, the problems of utilization
of technical and organizational rationality by political will—the
dualism of formal and material rationality—is not eliminated or
automatically solved as a piece of social justice, however longed
for, but it becomes a task of socio-political organization, a task
which is further from its solution there than with us, who have
developed more effective techniques for its formulation and discussion. Rationality remains; the problem of control, i.e. the
question of social methods of deciding aims, choosing means and
enjoying the profits of dynamics—that also remains.

A lasting merit of Max Weber seems to me to be that he was the
first to demonstrate the premises of socio-economic dynamics with
the help of the genesis of modern capitalism. It remains for us to
make the distinction between the generally valid dynamic constants
and the specifically capitalist variables and to draw the moral from
it for its practical application to present-day problems in the
developing countries. On the one hand, we see the necessity for
adopting certain modes of behaviour and social structures which
took shape for the first time in the West, but are not confined to the
West. On the other hand, there is a considerable 'sphere of freedom' a sphere of autonomous independent structuring, in which
every developing society must find its own way and prove its own
creativity.

In analysing experiences, hitherto mainly negative, in the
progress of development in the West in the last twenty years, we

constantly get the impression that mistakes can usually be traced back to a neglect of the essential elements of dynamics, particularly in so far as they concern the socio-structural and behavioural premises of dynamics and rational modes of behaviour in economics, the state, and the communities. Even the 'communist' countries have till now found no effective alternative for certain motives and modes of behaviour, which up to now have been part of society only since capitalism, and without which no dynamics could be produced.

On the other hand this distinction should help us overcome the idea of a unified economic development passing through similar stages—this is how it is represented by some authors who one-sidedly only consider its material aspects.[1]

Finally comes understanding of the whole of the *decisive* practical problems (decisive because valid for dynamic society) and scientific questioning for the future: for us, the direct heirs of capitalism and for its indirect heirs in the so-called communist sphere and in the developing countries. We are all heirs of capitalism, and experiment with its structural elements in technology, economics, and society to different degrees, and in partial disguise, in combination with new factors and reacting to new data, which are in fact products of the dynamics we owe to capitalism.

The predominant attitudes behind this experimentation are revisionist in the West, polemical under 'communism' and eclectic in the developing countries—but the half-way and long-term problems, possibilities and trends which arise from them seem to me surprisingly similar.[2]

WOLFGANG J. MOMMSEN

Please allow me to make a brief personal observation. Yesterday I was called 'public prosecutor' in my attitude to Weber, a reproach which hurt me very deeply, for I have an intense admiration for this last great liberal of modern times. Today I find myself in the strange position of appearing in his defence, in connection with one point in Professor Marcuse's discourse. Referring to the documents collected in my book about Weber's attitude to the 1918–19

[1] Particularly Walt W. Rostow, *Stadien wirtschaftlichen Wachstums* (Göttingen, 1960).

[2] Cf. a more detailed treatment in my book *Soziale Strategie für Entwicklungsländer: Entwurf einer Entwicklungssoziologie* (Frankfurt, 1965).

revolution, he said that Weber had formed an alliance with the Right against the socialist Left. From this, in a rather generalized formulation, he drew a line straight to the crimes committed by National Socialism against the Jews and other peoples. I want therefore to affirm quite concretely that Weber was against the 1918–19 revolution for three reasons. The first was that he thought the revolution had destroyed any chance of a reasonable and tolerable peace settlement for Germany—in this he came near to the 'stab in the back' legend. The second was that he thought socialization would endanger future economic development. And the third—the imperative one for me—is the following: that he believed a temporary, dilettante regime of the extreme left must provoke an equally dilettante brutal regime of extreme right. I think therefore that we must correct the statement that Weber sided with the extreme right. In his basic views Weber was an aristocratic liberal, even if on occasion he resorted to means which one would not call liberal in the strict sense of the word: but he never considered a direct alliance with the right wing. He fought all his life *against* an alliance of the German bourgeoisie with the aristocracy and for co-operation in moderation with the socialist left. If we gave a different impression, this would sorely damage Weber's authority.

Conclusion

HERBERT MARCUSE

First of all in answer to Professor Weippert's question: It is correct that Weber considered socialism as theoretically possible. I did not go into that. I was only concerned to show that even if he thought it theoretically possible, he still considered it as a historical crime against western reason. The second question (the front against contemporary capitalism): here I agree with Professor Weippert. I thought I had stressed in my paper the extent of Weber's criticism of capitalism.

To Professor Mommsen's 'rectification', I can unfortunately say nothing, since I cannot see in what way it is a rectification. In my paper I said nothing about the personal reasons which led Weber to his attitude. The rest was based exclusively on material which I took from Professor Mommsen's own book.

I am absolutely of the same opinion as Professor Friedmann.

Regarding Professor Behrendt's paper I should like to clear up two misunderstandings. Determinism—Weber's determinism, which sees the prison-cage of bondage as an absolute necessity—is the determinism which I criticized. I said that one *cannot* understand how there can be any fateful necessity in this development. Secondly the concept of rationality: this question will take me a little longer. Professor Behrendt said rationality is always with us. I wish it were. I intended precisely to emphasize that what we now term rationality is either not yet rationality or so closely bound up with irrational impulses that the task of re-establishing rationality seems to be one of priority.

I should now like to deal, although briefly, with the two papers by Professor Bendix and Professor Nelson, and here I must ask to be excused. I have been accused of so many fantastic and dreadful crimes against good-mannered and orderly thought that I will now allow myself to become somewhat personal and really commit a tiny one of these crimes.

It seems to me that something quite strong was expressed in both these contributions: an enormous distrust, a resentment, a fear of any conceptualization going beyond what already exists: beyond it, not into a transcendental world, but into history, so far as history is already heralded in the present. All comprehensible thinking—and I stress 'comprehensible thinking' because I claim to know what rational thinking is, and to be able to distinguish rational thinking from magic, and from wishful thinking—all rational thinking which regards only the idea of another kind of reason, another society as historic possibility, is immediately denounced. Denounced as poetic thinking—that is honourable and good: then as Utopia—I think that an honour too—and then as the most dreadful of all, as dialectics. What dialectics must have on its conscience does not bear thinking about. I would really like to confess to Utopia for the simple reason that nowadays the concept of Utopia has become meaningless. If we look at present-day intellectual and material wealth, if we look at ourselves, what we know and can do, there is actually nothing which rationally and with a good conscience we should despise and denounce as Utopian. We could actually do anything today. We could certainly have a rational society, and just *because* that is such a near possibility its actual realization is more 'Utopian' than ever before; the whole force of the *status quo* is mobilized against it.

N

The transcending critical conceptualization is suspected of dispensing with science and rational thought. But critical conceptualization must be just as rational and just as scientific as present-day rationality and present-day science. It must go beyond this, and on the basis of this science and rationality it must liberate science and rationality from their remaining irrational elements.

I should like to close with a quotation from Professor Nelson's paper, which seems to me the most incredible and yet most courteous denunciation of critical thought: 'Any thought that structural necessities and strains of large scale complex industrial societies and organisations can be dissolved by fiat or wished away by dreams or transcended by the collective permanent overcoming of reification, alienation and self-estrangement or eliminated by the establishment of the collective ownership of the means of production results from a tragic reluctance to acknowledge the inevitable features of the social cultural realities of our time.'

If it is 'tragic reluctance' to regard the 'features' of present-day social–cultural reality as 'inevitable', then this 'tragic reluctance' is mine. I could only wish that more had it, and probably Professor Nelson had it once. It is the reasonable willingness, not to see facts as inevitable, but to draw the conclusions of one's own capabilities. If we have gone so far as to call it 'tragic reluctance', if one does not recognize this 'inevitability', all thought has become meaningless; for thought which decides beforehand that facts are inevitable is not really thought at all.

PART IV

1. The Sociology of Religion

The topicality of Max Weber in the modern sociology of religion

PROFESSOR TAUBES concentrated on some ideologically critical remarks in Weber's essay 'The Origin of the Jewish Pariahs'. Volume III of the collected essays on the sociology of religion[1] was one of the first attempts at an objective historical analysis of the Israelite religion. The key to the whole work, the first part of which deals with the 'Israelite confederacy and Yahweh', the second with 'The Origins of the Jewish Pariahs', is found in the comparison between the Jews as a guest people separated from the society around them, and the lower castes of Indian society. Professor Taubes continued:

Weber tried to derive from their particular status all essential characteristics of the Jews' attitude to other peoples, 'above all their voluntary ghetto-existence long before they were forcibly interned' (pp. 4 ff.). Weber himself indicated three important differences between the Indian pariah and the Jews:

1. They became pariahs in a caste-less society.

2. Eschatology: 'for the Indian pariahs the reward for behaving according to ritual and caste is reincarnation at a higher level within the world's caste-order, otherwise thought of as eternal and unchanging' (p. 5). An eminently conservative social behaviour was the pre-requisite of all salvation, for the rotation of the world was supposed to be eternal and it therefore had no history. But according to the Jews the promise was exactly the contrary: the world was neither eternal nor unchanging, but was created, and its present order was a product of human action, 'a historical product therefore, intended to make room again for a God-willed condition' (p. 6). The whole attitude of the ancient Jews towards life was determined by this notion of a future political and social revolution led by God.

---

[1] Max Weber, *Gesammelte Aufsätze zur Religionssoziologie* (Tübingen, 1921); (subsequently quoted as R.S.).

187

3. On the basis of a ritual born of a conditioned separation from surrounding society, there is a religious ethic of this-worldly behaviour, 'highly rational, free from magic and all forms of irrational search for salvation . . . this ethic is to a great extent at the basis of present-day European and Near-Eastern religious ethics' (p. 6).

The problem overshadowing Weber's analysis is therefore: how did the Jews become pariahs with this highly specific characteristic? His whole analysis stands or falls on the concept of pariah. The differentiation which Weber himself introduced into this concept leads us to conclude that the comparison is not unforced. Yet Weber attributes the utmost importance to it, and sets it at the beginning of his analysis in order to determine the specifically 'plebeian' character of Jewish morality (the basis for universal historical interest in Judaism).

In fact this comparison has been attacked by critics. In the *Monatschrift für Geschichte und Wissenschaft des Judentums.* Julius Guttman (1925; pp. 195, 223, esp. pp. 219–20) described this comparison as scientifically misleading and warns us not to give this term a place in the vocabulary of sociology. In his *Social and Religious History of the Jews* both in the first edition (1937) and in the second, greatly enlarged (1952), Salo W. Baron polemicized against the totally misleading analogy.

What is Weber's source for this formulation? Why this comparison between the Indian pariah-caste and ancient Jewry? Weber's comparison between the Jewish people and the Indian pariah-caste has its origin in Nietzsche's critique of Christendom and its pre-history. Nietzsche was the first to apply the word *Tschandala* from Indian vocabulary to the pre-history and history of Christianity, and tried to explain the origin of Christianity from the rebellion of the lowest instincts of the lowest classes against privilege. A pariah-group which is not tied to a caste-order conceived of as eternal and unalterable, but which in its eschatological views turns the social order of the world into the contrary of what is promised for the future, prepares the ground for 'God-guided' political and social revolution. *Tschandala* plus eschatology determined the Jewish–Christian reversal of values and led to the victory of plebeian morality in Europe.

The slaves' uprising in morality begins when resentment itself becomes creative and engendered values: the resentment of such beings to whom the proper reaction, that of the deed, is denied, and who only indemnify themselves by an imaginary revenge. (*Genealogie der Moral*, Aph. 10.)

Resentment becomes creative, when it produces a concept contrary to the 'natural conditions' of life. The post-exilic community reversed one after the other the religions, cults, morality, history of early Israel in 'contradiction of their natural values'. The same reversal of values meets us once again, and 'in unutterably greater proportions, although only as a copy: the Christian church compared with the "chosen people", lacks any claim to originality' (*Antichrist*, Aph. 24).

Nietzsche called the history of Israel 'a typical history of all denaturalisation of natural values'. With this thesis he merely drew conclusions from the premises of modern Protestant Bible-criticism since Wellhausen. For Wellhausen, in his *Prolegomena zur Geschichte Israels* (first published in 1878) had already turned against the falsification, executed by the later prophets and post-exilic historiography, which edited and censored a great portion of Old Testament literature.

What have the Chronicles made of David! The founder of the empire has become founder of the temple and divine service, the king and hero at the head of his comrades in arms, a cantor and mouthpiece of a swarm of priests and Levites, his sharply-drawn figure a dull picture of a saint wreathed in a cloud of incense! (*Prolegomena*, 1899, p. 181.)

The motives and criteria of Protestant Bible criticism have rarely been brought to light. It is not by accident that outsiders like Nietzsche and Weber show a finer feeling than scholars of the faith for the ideological premises of historical construction of Protestant Bible criticism. Nietzsche also draws conclusions from Wellhausen's essay for the history of Christianity, which Wellhausen opposes from his Christian standpoint. Wellhausen does call attention to the congruity between the Christian church and the theocracy of the post-exilic community but thinks he can exempt the Apostle Paul from those involved in the decline or reversal of natural values. Overbeck has pointed out this contradiction in Wellhausen; 'One of Wellhausen's judgements diametrically opposed in Nietzsche. However antipathetic I find its invective character, I prefer it' (*Christentum und Kultur*, 1919, pp. 55–6). Nietzsche quotes I Corinthians 1, 20 ff. as first-rate evidence for the psychology of any *Tschandala* morality.

Nietzsche and Weber, the one tacitly, the other explicitly, take over Tolstoy's views on Christianity ('Resist not evil', Matthew V, 39); they both recognize the absolute ethic of the Sermon on the mount as a possibility for one's private life, but reject it as a guide for social existence.

Christianity is possible as the most private form of existence; it presumes a narrow, withdrawn, absolutely unpolitical society—it belongs to the conventicle. . . . Christianity is still possible at any moment. . . . Christianity, is a practice, not a doctrine of belief. It tells us how we are to act, not what we are to believe. . . . Whoever would now say, 'I do not want to be a soldier', 'I don't care about the law-courts', 'I will make no claim on the services of the police', 'I will do nothing to disturb my inner peace; and if I have to suffer, nothing will sustain my peace more than suffering'—he would be a Christian. (*Witte zur Macht*, Aph. 211–12.)

Weber similarly stated the alternatives of Christian and political existence:

In the Sermon on the Mount (I mean the absolute ethic of the Gospel) things are more serious than is believed by those who like to quote the commandments nowadays. It is no joking matter. The same applied to it as was said of causality in science: it is not a cab to be stopped at one's pleasure, to get in and out where one likes. It is a matter of all or nothing, if anything other than trivialities are to come of it. . . . An ethic of loss of dignity, except for a saint. That is it—one must be a saint in *everything*, at least one must *want* to live like Jesus, the apostles, Saint Francis and his companions, then this ethic is meaningful and expressive of dignity. *Not otherwise*: for if the conclusion of the ethic of love is 'do not resist evil with force'—the sentence has to be reversed for the politician—you *shall* resist evil with force, otherwise you are responsible for its increase. (G.P.S., p. 440.)

As Weber did with the concept 'pariah', Nietzsche transferred the concept *Tschandala* to late Judaic and early Christian society. Nietzsche saw in the priests the élite of the *Tschandala*, while Weber points to the 'prophets' who as 'demagogues and publicists' (pp. 288 f.) prepared this reversal of values.

The prophets did not all come from the same social class. There is no question of their being predominantly proletarian or under-privileged or uncultured. Certainly their socio-ethical position was not deter-mined by their personal ancestry. For they were unified despite very different social origins. Throughout they pleaded passionately for the socio-ethical commandments of charity in the Levite exhortation on behalf of 'humble people' and preferred to sling their angry curses against the great and the wealthy. (R.S., III, p. 291.)

While Nietzsche took up an unequivocal position against the ascetic ideals of the *Tschandala* morality, Weber remained equivocal in his judgment. In one breath he both accepts and rejects the fateful process, of rationalization; the ascetic rationalism of the bourgeois–capitalist world (which Weber, like Nietzsche traces to its origins in the history of Israel) changed the world into a 'steel cage'. The history of the Western mind, which reached its terminus in the spirit of capitalism, is not for Weber (unlike Hegel and Marx) a story with a happy end. Our whole existence, the basic political technical and economic conditions of our existence, remain imprisoned in the 'steel cage' of the bourgeois–capitalist world.

Nobody yet knows who will live in this cage in the future and whether at the end of this enormous development there will be completely new prophets or a mighty rebirth of old ideas and ideals, or—if neither of these—mechanized petrifaction in a framework of convulsive self-importance. Then this development could become the word for truth for the last men, experts without a mind, pleasure-seekers without a heart; this nonentity imagines it has reached a stage mankind has never before attained! (R.S., p. 104.)

The Marxist prophecy of salvation of a 'classless society' is darkened for Weber into a prognosis of the coming mechanized 'petrifaction' of society, for which he quoted Nietzsche's vision of the last man. Like Nietzsche, Weber considers whether at the end of this decline, in the counterthrust, there will be 'completely new prophets or a mighty rebirth of old ideas or ideals'. Against Nietzsche's idiosyncrasies, particularly against his contemporary Nietzscheans, Weber stands opposed in his abhorrence of 'monumental' writing of history and opinions on art, in his aversion to a sterile religious neo-culture, 'without any new, genuine prophesy', which can only produce 'lamentable miscreations'. Like Spengler, he merely thought one should bear this destiny of our times 'manfully'. And the only virtue which, like Nietzsche, he can see in his nihilist interim is

simple intellectual honesty. It only orders us to establish the fact that for all those many people who are waiting for new prophets and saviours the situation is the same, as we hear in the Edomite's watchman's song repeated by Isaiah in exile. . . . 'There comes a call from Seir in Edom— watchman, what of the night? the watchman speaks: the morning is coming, but it is still night. If you want to know, come another time.' The people to whom that was said asked and and waited for more than 2000 years, and we know their moving fate. We must learn a lesson from this; that longing and waiting are not enough and we must do otherwise —humanly and professionally. That is simple and easy, if everyone can find and obey the demon who holds the thread of his life. (W.L. p. 597.)

PROFESSOR JOSEPH MAIER

A comment on Weber's Ancient Judaism[1]

Unlike Werner Sombart's *The Jews and Modern Capitalism*, which dealt with a limited aspect of Judaism only, namely as one of the allegedly necessary and sufficient conditions for the emergence of modern capitalism, Max Weber aimed at an all-round sociological analysis of Judaism. His writings on ancient Judaism formed volume three of his *Gesammelte Aufsätze zur Religionssociologie*, published in 1921, shortly after his death. After more than forty years they are still as rich and suggestive as when they first saw the light of day. This is all the more remarkable in view of the fact that Weber knew most sources only in translation and relied heavily on secondary literature. His chief interest was in the emergence of post-exilic Judaism, or in his own words: 'How did Jewry develop into a pariah people with highly specific peculiarities?'

It was Weber's aim to proceed from an analysis of ancient Judaism to an investigation of Diaspora Judaism. Alas, his sociology of the Jews remained incomplete. As with his attempts on early Christianity and Islamism, death prevented him from rounding off his studies of Judaism with an analysis of the Psalms, the Book of Job and Talmudic Jewry. What we possess are two essays, 'The Israelite Confederacy and Yahweh' and 'The Emergence of the Jewish Pariah People', supplemented by a short piece on, 'The Pharisees', which make up the present volume. To be sure, there are various references to Jewry and Judaism in Weber's other works, especially in *Wirtschaft und Gesellschaft*, to

[1] The following quotations are from the English translation by Hans H. Gert and Don Martindale, *Ancient Judaism* (Glencoe, Illinois, 1952).

permit at least an inkling of his thinking on Diaspora Jewry. They are not, however, an adequate substitute for what is missing in his sociology of the Jews.

To Max Weber, the post-exilic Jews are 'sociologically speaking a pariah people'. That means, he says, 'as we know from India, a guest people separated ritually, formally or *de facto*, from their social surroundings'. But he proceeds at once to point out the differences between the Jewish and Indian pariah tribes. As the first difference he lists the fact that 'Jewry was, or rather became, a pariah people in a surrounding free of castes'. That alone would suffice to make the use of the term in its technical sense a highly dubious one.

More important than the basic qualifications made by Max Weber himself is Salo W. Baron's reminder of the religious disparity between the Jews and their Gentile rulers: That in India it was within the same religion that the position of an inferior, unchangeable caste was determined by the dominant religious doctrine and, on the whole, accepted by the pariahs themselves; that Judaism had remained a religion with its own values and counter-values and that it had always regarded the passing of a member to another camp as a serious loss to the person concerned, rather than as a reward.[1] The reply that 'religious differences may sharpen the distinction between guest and host', that they 'help to maximize the social distance or mutual strangeness', completely fails to meet Baron's point.[2]

Socially, the Diaspora Jews were limited neither in their occupational choice nor in their class membership, as indeed we find them in all layers of society. Psychologically, there is a great difference between the pariah's acquiescence in and the Jew's rejection of his degradation. Jewish separateness was interpreted in antiquity preponderantly in norms of Jewish pride and arrogance. In short, in its precise scientific meaning, the term 'pariah people' is not applicable to the Jews. As Max Weber uses it, it is at least equivocal What is unequivocal about it is its connotation of detraction and contempt, a connotation that is not entirely absent from Weber's presentation. (I am, of course, in general agreement with the assurance that 'Weber was neither an anti-

[1] Salo W. Baron, *A Social and Religious History of the Jews*, III (New York, 1937), 5.
[2] Hans Gerth and Don Martindale, op. cit., XXIV.

semite nor an equally dangerous philo-semite',[1] although I cannot quite understand how a *Schrulle*-like philo-semitism can be compared with anti-semitism and considered 'equally dangerous', especially after the historical experiences of the last thirty years.)

Max Weber is at his best when trying to show how the 'confessional' elements in prophecy blend with the separatistic ritualism of priesthood in creating the climate for an internationally settled 'guest people'. 'The new religious association,' says Weber, 'by ritualistic incapsulation, could consider itself as the direct continuation of the old ritualistic fold community precisely because the prophets had offered no means for the formation of a new religious community, and because, in practice, the substance of the eschatological message consisted solely in sublimation of the traditional religion into ethical absolutism.

In this connection Max Weber speaks of the peculiarly 'plebeian' character of the prophetic ethic. These 'demagogues', the prophets, advocated the ethic of humility and obedience. If Weber is suggesting that the prophets argued their 'social–ethical charity-commandments of the Levite exhortation' primarily for the benefit of 'the little people', the suggestion is plausible. He is also right in disputing the notion, frequently made in modern times, that the prophets were champions of democratic social ideals. The prophets were intellectuals. They demanded justice and humanity for the powerless, but their message was primarily religiously motivated. At any rate they were not democrats in the sense that they demanded the rule of the people, pronounced any sort of religious 'natural law', or advocated a right to revolution or self-help of the masses suppressed by the mighty.

It is equally plausible that the prophetic ethic of obedience and humility was peculiarly suited to the position of impotence of post-exilic Jewry. There was then little room for an aristocratic ethic of proud self-confidence, trust in one's own abilities and self-renown. The prophetic ethic of humility 'fitted' better. However, by subsuming it under the concept of a 'plebeian' or 'pariah people's' ethic, Max Weber brings the prophetic ethic into the neighbourhood of phenomena with which it has little in common. For 'plebeian' in Weber's sense are all those forms of ethics which satisfy the needs of socially oppressed groups or arise as the consequence of social oppression.

[1] Op. cit., XIV.

But does this not apply to quite different sorts of ethics? Weber refers to the figure of the suffering Servant of God as a glorification of the Jewish pariah situation. Granted the type of religiosity represented in that figure was a result of suffering, was not its function to derive religious meaning from that experience? Does not this type of religiosity and ethic differ in nature from the forms invented by oppressed groups to make the worse appear the better?

Certainly the prophetic ethic is not plebeian in the sense that it extols the poor *per se* as the pious, or enforced subservience as virtue, or craftiness and slyness as the legitimate weapons of the powerless. Not even in its glorification of humility does it come close to that kind of ethic, as Weber often appears to suggest. On the contrary, there is an element of heroism in the prophetic ethic—a heroism that has nothing to do with 'whistling in the dark'. The conviction that they are fighting for the cause of the Lord is the source of the prophet's courage in their passionate struggle against the Israelite rulers. That conviction was alive in the struggles of the Maccabees and the wars of Bar Kochba. And may one not say with equal justice that something of that conviction was also alive in the twentieth century in the struggle for the establishment of the State of Israel, where everything else now appears to be alive—except the specific pariah ethic of humility and subservience in the face of misery, ugliness and suffering?

In times of oppression and deprivation decreed by the Lord, the prophetic ethic yields a sense of dignity and honour that is completely alien to the vulgar 'plebeian' ethic. There is, to be sure, always the danger of the former declining into the latter, of a petit-bourgeois workaday morality accruing to and contaminating the religious ethic of Judaism. The particularity of the spiritual development of Judaism, however, is characterized by the tension between the powerful inwardness of its religious ethic and its emasculation in the workaday morality of a 'non-resident foreign trading people'.[1]

The messianic hope of Judaism renders the world that is into something tentative and transitional. It holds that the social and political order ordained by the Lord is only to come. At times, such a view fostered an attitude of utter indifference towards the

[1] Max Weber, *General Economic History*, transl. by Frank H. Knight (Glencoe, Illinois, The Free Press, 1950), p. 217.

present. In the main, however, it resulted in Jewry's acquiescing in and adjusting to a world in which, in the last analysis, it was not at home. It lived in a permanent state of transition, as it were, seeking a niche in a world that shows little resemblance to the Heavenly City. The norms of legality were, therefore, its principal guides in this world.'

PROFESSOR BENJAMIN NELSON

(Professor Nelson's remarks started from the point that he did not know of any research into the relationships between Jews and Christians in the Middle Ages.)

There are numerous studies of Jewish communities in the West, some done by noted Christian scholars, most done by very able Jewish scholars. But characteristically studies done of Jewish communities are about Jewish communities and almost never relate to any of the problems which I am certain Max Weber would have wanted to analyse. I do not recall whether either of the features of the subject referred to his very useful sociological notions which he derived from the Roman Law, that is to say, the notions of *connexium* and *connubium*. No sociological analysis of a historical nature which dealt with the Jews and Christians in the Western World would be satisfactory which did not put them into stable encounters with one another. May I say why I think this issue is of such importance now: The story of post-exilic Jewry cannot be written except by those who know what Christianity is— medieval Christianity and Reformation Christianity. I think all of you must be aware of the fact that that sense is disappearing in our world. It is so rapidly declining that it is to be hoped that those who are truly related to Christianity will at the earliest opportunity come into contact with this subject. I would say additionally that it is hardly likely that anyone will be able to write of this era who is not in some profound way connected with what Judaism is about. May I add that the sense of this is also rapidly disappearing.

Two of my colleagues have referred to the notable volumes of Professor S. W. Baron. His book was written against what he described as the tragic view of Jewish history, and he wished to show that one could only hope to understand it by seeing Jewish history in relation to the general history of society. The idea was a very good one, but it cannot be accomplished if one's assumptions are altogether of a secular and, in my view, somewhat non-historical nature. I absolutely deny that it is possible to understand the relations of post-exilic Jewry with the Western world by pointing simply to the fact that they were a minority and underwent many of the deprivations of ordinary minorities. May I also add that it is totally and absolutely false to say that any occupation was open to them. May I remind whoever believes that, that almost all occupations of any consequence in the Middle Ages were so thoroughly connected with the Christian religion, that the entire guild structure was so completely religious through and through that it is totally inconceivable.

I would also like to speak of a research of my own which is connected with this issue. I had occasion some years ago to study the development of the idea of usury, and as you perhaps know Weber refers to this in his *General Economic History* in a most powerful passage, in which he refers to Deuteronomy 23, 19–20: 'Thou shalt not take usury from thy brother'. And the suggestion is then that you may take it from a hostile alien enemy, but not from a brother. Now, as we know, Weber did not himself believe that the understanding of the Protestant Ethic was really to be derived by studying the history of the idea of usury. Nor do I believe this. But it is of great importance that there was this double notion in Deuteronomy; and as you know, Christianity was committed if anything to universalism and this encounter between brother-other-ethics and universalism was one of the most impressive in the whole history of the Western world. It is simply not to be imagined for a second that either Jew or Christian throughout the medieval period related to this issue purely in economic terms. This is a completely false sense of the matter in my view!

PROFESSOR TALCOTT PARSONS

(Professor Parsons, in his contribution, drew attention to one aspect of Weber's pariah-concept not hitherto mentioned in the discussion.)

One of the principal criteria of the pariah group is its separation by ritual barrier. This distinguishes it from a class in the ordinary sense, which is not separated. I myself do not think that Baron fully refuted Weber on this whole point. Very far from it! I think there is a valid comparison with the Indian caste. It does not concern higher or lower status as such, it concerns ritual exclusion. This is independent of whether the exclusion is willed more on one side or on the other. Weber was quite right that the Jewish case was one to a very large extent of self-exclusion rather than imposed exclusion by Gentile. The Book of Daniel for example is an excellent testimony to that. Daniel was a hero to the Jews because he refused the opportunity to become a Babylonian under the most advantageous circumstances. This phenomenon is by no means gone from the world. We find it at many points. You are of course aware of the extent to which the colour problem has become very acute indeed in the United States. We have a long history—I think on the whole an extraordinarily successful history—of the absorption of disadvantaged groups who have gone through periods of being discriminated against. This includes the Jews to a large extent. And there is a particular resistance to the absorption of the Negroes which generates high emotional excitement. I think in the next year or two we are likely to see more rather than less disturbance over this. This has ritual roots in part, which to be sure have become secularized and are now terribly visible at many points. But they relate to those aspects of religiously grounded ritual which tie in with unconscious psychological factors (i.e. unconscious in the Freudian sense). They relate to several different themes—sexuality is very much involved—the imputation of inferiority, of incapacity to perform the role of full citizen; whether this imputation be justified or not is another matter. I think it is partly because of the vicious circle. The consequences of exclusion in fact incapacitate a very non-rational, partly religious, partly psycho-factual attitude, and it is correct to call the American Negro a pariah group very much in Weber's sense.

PROFESSOR FÜRSTENBERG stressed the fact that we must regard it as an enduring merit of Weber that he brought the two spheres of existence, religion and economics, into direct relationship by means of his historical–sociological research. This approach to the problem could just as easily be ideologized by explaining the relationship by an unequivocally determined causal link as by its inclusion in a scheme of social change, determined by philosophical–historical premises. It would appear as if these possibilities, or even their avoidance, had strongly influenced research, at least that which has been published, by Weber's successors. In face of this we must ask what is the significance of Weber's research for present-day sociology of religion. Starting with this question, Professor Fürstenberg continued:

Wherever the sociology of religion has become emancipated both from a traditional historical–systematic procedure and from the biased ecclesiastical sociological interest of the great churches, there is special significance in the question of forms of modern religiosity not sanctioned by the church, possibly even religiosity only concerned with this world, and in the question of the relationship between these behavioural determinants and certain social phenomena.

In this connection Weber's question about the evaluative bases of purely secular, e.g. economic, modes of behaviour can be extremely instructive. If the mentality of those working under early capitalism was stamped by basic religious ideas, it is quite meaningful to ask what, in late capitalism (to retain this nomenclature) stamps the mentality of the economic subject and how far evaluating notions play a role here. The results of economic science, building on premises of pure objectivity, in view of optical profit-earning behaviour in economic life, do not rest on an analysis of actual economic behaviour, but on observation of models which give guidance for correct action. The results of analyses of pure economic theory tell us little about the motives of economic man: the social doctrines of the great churches are equally inadequate as standards for actual economic behaviour. So the task remains of establishing empirically whether there are any basic convictions embodying the nature of a creed in the sense of unquestioning acceptance and the possibility of non-empirical justification, which affect economic behaviour. The following basic notions, important for economic behaviour, offer a starting point:

1 any interpretation of work and vocation where the kind and intensity of ethical convictions are remarkable by their absence;
2 the recognized criteria for evaluating economic activity: to these belong all ideas of aim, which influence the utilization of economic means;
3 the basic attitudes to the question of justifying economic behaviour.

By what objective norms and what subjective convictions is it sanctioned? An investigation of this kind could come to the conclusion that in their economic decisions men are usually guided by the immanent practical logic of their respective spheres of activity, and evaluative ideas play a subsidiary role. Then the question would still remain open, whether there are institutionalized evaluative maxims of behaviour on a supra-individual level, which make it possible to co-ordinate the activities in various spheres. One could here consider such complexes of evaluative notions as 'priority of competition', 'raising the standard of living', 'priority of the general welfare', 'stabilizing the standard of living by subsidies', etc.

Weber's legacy to us is the fact that in the breadth of his enquiry into the relationship between Protestantism and capitalism he showed the importance of research into the sociology of religion for a theory of society as a whole. It is time to reflect more seriously about this legacy, in order to strengthen the links between the sociology of religion and general sociology, but more especially to contribute to a better knowledge of the evaluative bases of our society.

2. The Sociology of Organization

Bureaucracy and rationality in organizations

In many basic works on the sociology of organization Weber is named as the most important predecessor and earliest theoretician in this field, mainly by virtue of his concept and theory of bureaucracy. The sociology of organization did not develop immediately from Weber, inspired by him and continuing his analysis of bureaucratic organization, yet on looking back, we think we have found a fairly complete list of definitive criteria for organizations in his concept of bureaucracy. Actually, in his treatment of it, Weber mentioned nearly all the social forms which are included today under the term 'organization'. This supposed coincidence turned out on closer examination to be wrong: the result was that organizational sociologists criticized from many points of view the 'ideal type' of bureaucracy. So finally Weber's ideas were productive for the sociology of organization not by the adoption of his categories but by a critical discussion of them. Whether this criticism be shown to rest often on misunderstandings or on a full acceptance of his works, the result was in any case a clarification of the special tasks of the sociology of organization, and the solution of a number of special problems and the research needed to answer them. This connection, here only briefly indicated, should be kept in mind as background to the reports of the four papers read to the sub-committee.

These papers were not concerned with a scientific–historical analysis of Weber's influence on the sociology of organization, but to give examples of present-day work in a sphere in whose development the discussion by Weber played a considerable part, and which in the meantime has progressed to a fruitful posing of its own questions.

In the first paper, read by DR. WIGARD SIEBEL (Dortmund) on 'Rationality and Norm-Orientation in Organisation',[1] rationality

[1] Published in *Zeitschrift für die gesamte Staatswissenschaft*, vol. 120, 1964, pp. 678–85.

was discussed as the generally acclaimed characteristic—even definitive characteristic—of organizations. The elucidation of this characteristic is important since despite its central significance, its utilization in the sociology of organization is often rather un-critical, and compared without any discussion to the conscious objectivity of organizational activity. According to this, rationality of organization was already decisively orientated to its (*ex defini-tione*) specific goal.

Dr. Siebel referred to the concept of rationality which he finds treated by Weber on the level of sociological content firstly as a special type of legal control with administrative personnel which is rational (bureaucratic); secondly as a social process of rationaliza-tion; and thirdly as a definite kind of setting of norms for social activity. He then asks what is common to these different aspects of rationality; what unifies them. He finds a way to an answer in the limited concept of rationality as used in economic theory, i.e. activity is rational if it follows the economic principle of aiming at the greatest utilization of (scarce) available means. Transaction orientated to the scarcity of means and their price determined by supply and demand is defined as a sub-form of the general category of transaction which always implies a relationship between means and end. He derived two basic forms of social transaction from this distinction: 'In the first basic form the transaction is so arranged as to choose those means which together cost the lowest price and yet allow the goal to be realized. Only this way of transact-ing is economical and deserves in the narrower sense the designa-tion "rational transaction". In the second form activity is directed towards deciding on "correct" (fitting, appropriate, in accordance with rank, becoming, or even—in the original sense of the word— "fair") means. . . . This form of transaction may be called by the rather old-fashioned term "bargaining" or—if one does not strain the expression—"political transaction". A transaction which "bargains" of course contains rationality, but only in a quite general sense, in that it weighs the means that are at stake in relation to the lawful aim.' ('Bargaining must not be confused with objective action, as Weber sees it. For the latter is defined by the lack of consideration of prospective consequences. . . .')

Bargaining constitutes a 'property' of the objects being con-sidered as means: 'Bargaining documents the connection between certain means (objects) and certain ends. Thus the reference is connected with the objects, even when they are not used, i.e. they possess a symbolic function. This is supported by more or less strongly sanctioned limitations of action. Thus the object must not be used without further notice for *any* aim, but as a rule only for certain defined aims. But the intrinsic value is not completely constituted by the known aims to which it can be attached. Uses which are not yet fully experienced are co-determinants. Bargaining thus completes the interpretation of norms and so is evaluative for the objects which are suitable for fulfilling norms. Rational activity as required by economic activity does not constitute an intrinsic value of the means, and in fact must be viewed separately. If the intrinsic value of the means is not being considered, the value of the aim (e.g. target of production) and of aims in general must be considered. Thus the means themselves take on the character of ends: this becomes clearer, the more they are utilised in various connections. Rational activity leads to profit and to the conservation and engendering of means for all sorts of ends.'

At the root of all the various aspects of rationality mentioned previously lies 'the lack of specific norm-orientation for action, i.e. of such norms as are not immediately derivable from the aim of the activity. If an object—whether thing or person—is not regarded as possessing an intrinsic value, it demands no specific form of activity, the activity is no longer limited, and the norms are less compelling and relevant as requirements. If every means has its own value, the aim of activity cannot be constructed linearly, but only as a hierarchy of norms which are mutually determinant. That is the strongly characteristic mark of activity in a pre-rational period, orientated by a multiplicity of norms each requiring certain forms of demonstration or representation in social activity. Rational activity on the contrary is characterised by being orientated by a few norms only, or even by one single norm.'

Organization is characterized by this rationality in a narrower sense, in contrast to the orientation of 'bargaining', i.e. it contains only a few objects of intrinsic value: most are 'mere material, which is defencelessly open to any kind of utilisation. . . . Narrow limitation of aims to be reached and the elimination of as many as possible of the norms to be considered (subsidiary aims) yields increased striking power and particularly the power of a control unthinkable in a pre-rational system of norms, orientated multi-dimensionally (i.e. hierarchically). Any fixing of uncontrolled subsidiary aims can be stopped from the viewpoint of the main aim. This increase of power is the decisive reason for the adoption of a rational way of life in all societies. . . . In an extreme case of organisation there is only one variable for constituting the value of all relevant factors, and this takes its value from the one aim in the given situation. If the circumstances change, so does the value of the factors, and they themselves become variable, i.e. objects without intrinsic value.'

This describes a tendency rather than a state of affairs as Dr. Siebel says: 'Norms which are not immediately derivable from the aims of the action are by no means eliminated in rational society. Even if the element of compulsion is diminished, they still play a substantial role: one has only to think of norms as expressed in human and civil rights. In this view, man is considered as bearing a value, and thus as a norm in any sphere of action. One may only treat him in *this* way, not in *that*. To a certain extent this also applies to other spheres: protection of animals, protection of the countryside, sometimes of works of art (protection of monuments) etc. . . . rationality is therefore a relative concept: one has constantly to think of a form of society or of control, which is more rational than the existing one, because it no longer respects certain norms.'

Returning to the initial question of the specifically rational, co-defined with organization, Dr. Siebel said in conclusion: 'The specific nature of the object of the sociology of organisation seems to me to consist in the fact that organisation possesses the tendency to judge its components (whether things or persons) exclusively according to its aims, i.e. to abolish the values contained in the components. Its rationality consists in this relative advantage over other groups. Linked with this is the relative absence of symbols, the relatively easy interchangeability of its component parts (capacity for re-organisation). Rationality as an essential mark of organisation signifies the formulation of a task, or perhaps *the* task of the sociology of organisation, namely to make plain the conclusions to be drawn from the most varied conditions.'

The paper by DR. H. KLAGES (Dortmund), 'Research as an Industry—Bureaucracy and Rationality in Research Organisations', also relates to the discussion of Weber's sociology of organization, especially to the 'ideal type' of bureaucracy. Various objections have been made to Weber's concept of bureaucracy. Either he has been understood or rather misunderstood as descriptive, and then criticized as inadequate, which led to the investigation of the 'defective' aspects of the reality of organization, i.e. of informal phenomena or the unforeseen consequences of planned measures. Or the 'ideal type' of bureaucracy has been conceived as theory. Even this misunderstanding has inspired research, e.g. into the empirically provable correlations between the individual characteristics which make up the 'ideal type' of bureaucracy. A third question arises from the correct understanding of the 'ideal type' of bureaucracy as an objective type of correctness and thus a model answer to the question of the most suitable form of organization (or more precisely—form of administrative staff in legal control). Taken as a hypothesis, this assertion of suitability has become the object of empirical research, which has already succeeded in establishing the concrete conditions under which the bureaucratic structure pattern is actually particularly suitable, and in developing alternative structure patterns for deviants. Dr. Klages's paper can be classed with the group of special subjects which deal particularly with the effects of various forms of research organization on the results of the research.

Dr. Klages dealt first with the view, first expounded at the end of the nineteenth century, and formulated clearly by Weber in 1918, according to which research in the course of the development of modern society becomes more and more like an industrial enterprise by a process determined both by chance and individual talent for research. According to this thesis, social organization grows up in the course of research, just as in other spheres of the modern professional world, which could be described as a differentiated system of roles; these roles are structured on a basis of rational ends and means, and their functional character assured by the rules of the profession, the prescribed routes of communication and a hierarchy of authority in the scale of management. Research organized as an enterprise and turned into a professional undertaking can become a system of integrated parts, on the same obvious principle as any other sphere of effort fittingly organized. In view of the fact that consumer research has won a firm place in universities and colleges, and that research has gone beyond the colleges straight into various practical spheres, particularly those of

economics and the armed forces, Dr. Klages sees this attitude as
realistic. Research organized with a single aim is apparently
becoming one of the cardinal conditions of economic growth and
military defence preparation.

It is precisely the enormously increased importance of research
which lends weight to those voices who speak of the danger of
diminishing productivity of research, and who connect this danger
with the bureaucratic research organization described above.
Among the various arguments for this connection—as for instance
losses through friction because of the size of the research instituted,
or frequent cases of duplication because of the difficulty of super-
vising extensive investigations—there is an important objection
that 'the highly organised research projects of the present day
only afford very inadequate scope for the creative unfolding of a
researcher's talent'.

Dr. Klages remarks that the discussion of the diminishing
productivity of research coincides with another much discussed
topic, i.e. the allegedly ubiquitous tension leading to crisis and
conflict between researchers and those groups with whom they
have to deal in the course of developing research into socially
established, highly organized big business. The current assimilation of the research industry and economic or military organizations is, as Dr. Klages maintains, not the result of simultaneous
and similar trends of development in the various spheres, but at
least for the greater part the result of an extraneously caused
transformation of research by means of organizational principles
akin to research. Those engaged in research apparently rebel
against the discipline considered necessary by leaders of industry
or the armed services, the precision of timing and costing, security
measures, strict division of labour, etc. The question arises of
relaxing the tension either for the benefit of research workers or for
the benefit of officials and managers. 'Is "freedom" or "planning"
the right motto for research?' Both alternatives find their advocates.
Dr. Klages dealt with each in turn.

The advocates of planning represent the opinion that '. . . the
libertine sub-culture of scientists is nothing but the product of
their own basically ideological stereotype. Viewed objectively,
research can be organised without further ado like labour and
industry and made into an efficient and flexibly functioning instrument of external purposes. The only hindrance is an out-dated

value-system in the minds of research workers.' Representatives of this view suggest gradually changing this value-system by first of all establishing research laboratories with an 'academic atmosphere', but then, by using the workshop climate this creates gradually, bringing the target-setting of the sponsoring organization nearer to the research workers, until accepted by them.

This idea is found both in the U.S. and in Europe: it is opposed by the supporters of freedom. '. . . The research worker who is indoctrinated and manipulated into "fitting in" is at the same time inefficient and creatively unproductive.' The value-system of the rational big-business organization destroys the conditions of creative achievement so to speak at the source. 'Various writers have pointed out that enforced "team-spirit" impairs the readiness and capacity for unconventional solutions of a pioneering nature, that the "adapted" researcher thinks more of his career in big business than of his work, that his willingness to take risks declines, and particularly to take productive risks, still a prime source of progress in science.' So a research organization is required, autonomous from within, informal in its internal activity, and based on the principle of personality.

Referring to the first results of an investigation entrusted by him to the social research department of Münster University, Dr. Klages claimed that the partial correctness of both positions, with regard to any special research situation, must be demonstrated. He finds the decisive factor in a situation for the purposes of bureaucratically or non-bureaucratically organized research to be the operationally conceivable measure of the research's capacity. 'Generally the availability and need for organisation falls as quotas of serendipity rise, i.e. with increasing readiness to take chances. The reverse is also true. Readiness to take chances is not a constant requirement in this case but one which varies in importance in different spheres of research . . . in the context of modern research, irrevocably confronted with the needs of society, both research which is wide open to change, and has its own dynamics, and research low in both these qualities, have a firm position.' The first refers to basic and pioneering research, the second to research which extends, develops and is directed to practical application. This dimension of the research organization must be differentiated, and the relationship of communication and co-operation in both spheres assured. Following up these ideas,

Dr. Klages mentioned comparable projects in the States, and traditional conceptions in, for example, the German chemical industry. At the same time he discussed a whole series of special problems in research organizations, e.g. the need for a quantitative scheme of voting and agreement, and practical communication between the various types of function in research, or the problematic fact that extent of application (= nature of the basis) and the non-terminability of the research are correlated. The whole process of innovation seems to develop at its peak an irrational 'law unto itself', which can only be fitted into the results of research by the utmost expansion of the chances of selection. In fact the inevitable search for planning substitutes in the sphere of the 'research peak' seems to be in full flood; apart from the selection of results, the pre-selection of research workers who are interested and whose activities are foreseeably productive for the organization represents a possibility already put into practice.

In his summary Dr. Klages declared himself in favour of de-ideologizing the vital question of ensuring the productivity of the research, and considered it a step in the right direction if research nowadays is seen more and more as a system of transactions based in principle on division of function, and organized according to roles, differing in their readiness to take chances, their internal dynamics, goal-definition and applicability of the research activity, and thus requiring differentiated forms of organization.

3. Scientific Theory in
Max Weber's Methodology

I

Max Weber's methodology, which constitutes a historically orientated sociology of 'Verstehen', is particularly opposed to the postulates and categories of the analytical theory of science. In the introductory paper, 'Ideal Type and Model', DR. HERMANN VETTER (Mannheim) tried to modify one of Weber's central methodological concepts to bring it into line with the concept of 'Model'. Vetter maintains that the concept of 'ideal type' can still be used today if it is extended to coincide with the concept of the 'model'.

Dr. Vetter first pointed out that his remarks do not introduce anything substantially new, but are already to be found in, for instance, the work of Carl G. Hempel:

I take Weber's concept of the 'ideal type' from his methodological treatises, and do not here attempt to analyse, from the rest of his work, how Weber actually used 'ideal types' in research. Weber's basic definition of the ideal type from his essay on objectivity is as follows:

[The ideal type] is achieved by enhancing unilaterally one or more points of view, and by bringing together a mass of single phenomena, some extensive, some hidden, some more so, some less, some not at all, which combine with those unilaterally accentuated points of view in a uniform set of ideas.[1] It is not a representation of the real, but it attempts to lend significant means of expression to its representation (p. 190). It is meant to point the way for the formation of hypotheses (p. 190). It is a structure of ideas which has the significance of a purely ideal delimiting concept, by which reality is measured for the clarification of certain significant elements in its empirical content, and with which it is compared (p. 194). . . . [the ideal type concepts] are not represented, or only singly, in full conceptual purity (pp. 194–5). [The ideal type concept] . . .

[1] *Gesammelte Aufsätze zur Wissenschaftslehre* (Tübingen, 1951), p. 191. The quotations on the subsequent pages are from this work unless otherwise identified.

is a Utopia, and for the historian there is an increasing task to establish in each single case how near or how far apart reality and the idea stand (p. 191). [The ideal type] will guide research in a way which leads to a sharper comprehension of those elements [in the observed phenomena] [which do not correspond to it]. If it leads to this result, it has fulfilled its logical purpose in manifesting its own unreality. (p. 203.)

The following quotations are taken partly from 'Roscher and Knies', the essay on categories and value-freedom: 'In contrast to scientific hypotheses, the fact that [ideal-typical schemes of interpretation] lack validity in concrete cases does not effect their cognitive value, any more than, for example, the empirical invalidity of pseudo-spherical space affect the "correctness" of its construction. Interpretation by means of rational schema was not possible in this case, because the aims assumed in the schema did not exist as motives in the concrete case—which does not, however, exclude the possibility of their utilisation for any other case. A hypothetical "law of nature" which definitely fails in one case collapses once and for all as a hypothesis. The ideal-type constructions of political economy on the other hand do not claim—if rightly understood—general validity, while a "law of nature" must make this claim, if it does not wish to lose its significance' (p. 131).

The comparison with non-euclidean space seems to indicate that Weber conceived of ideal-type constructions in the arts as mathematical; it seems to suggest that he thought it was sufficient for them to be constructed essentially free of contradictions. Whether there was to be any empirical sphere of objects for which they were valid was a matter of indifference. This would be an over-hasty judgment, however, for Weber says elsewhere: 'It is a matter of constructing connections which present themselves to our imagination as accessibly motivated, and so objectively possible and to our nomological knowledge'. (W.L., p. 192). The 'ideal type' therefore is required not only to conform to the rules of logic, but also to the empirical laws of the sphere of objects under observation. We know Weber was of the opinion that one could not deduce a real situation from laws alone, but that one needed empirical data—limiting conditions—to which the laws could be applied. This is of course also true of the natural sciences. For example one cannot deduce from Newtonian mechanics how many planets there are, at what distance they orbit the sun, and what their positions are in relation to each other. These data must be known for a given point in time: then prior and subsequent circumstances must be taken into account together with the laws.

So far the distinction which Weber tries to make here between the arts and sciences seems to me unfounded: when he says that the laws of hypothesis in the natural sciences are always valid, but not the ideal-type constructions in the arts he is not comparing appropriate items with each other. He should compare the natural–scientific laws with cultural–scientific laws (which obviously exist, in his opinion): he speaks of our nominological cognition, for which the ideal-type construction must be adequate). . . . Between these laws there exists of course in principle no distinction of general validity. Again he would have to compare the ideal-type construction in the arts with those in the sciences, which seemed to him to exist (and which, as we shall see, actually do exist: 'logically there is no difference: whether an ideal type is formed from syntheses that are understandable through the senses or specifically not so. . . . [In this case] an empirical facticity, sublimated to "pure type", forms the ideal type' (W.L., p. 438). We shall remember that for Weber not all scientific processes are sensuously comprehensible. We will return later to his statement '. . . Developments can also be construed as ideal types'.

Finally we will state what, according to Weber, the ideal type is *not*. From the foregoing it is clear that the 'ideal type' is

not in any way formed as a mean or average [of all observed phenomena]. Further, nothing would be [more dangerous than the belief] that the 'essence' of historical reality has been fixed in these theoretical conceptual images . . . or that 'ideas' are hypostasised as 'actual' reality, 'real' forces, behind fleeting appearances . . . (W.L., p. 195). Finally conceptions of 'the ideal' in the sense of 'what should be', are to be carefully excluded from this model, which is 'ideal' in the sense of pure logic. [It is] an elementary duty of scientific discipline, and the only way to guard against accidental errors, to distinguish sharply between the logically comparative relevance of reality to ideal types in the logical sense, and the evaluative judgment of reality from ideals. An 'ideal type' in our sense of the word is something completely indifferent to evaluative judgment. There are ideal types of brothels as well as of religions . . . (W.L., p. 200). There could also be deliberately chosen ideal types of errors (W.L., p. 438) of false conclusions, of unsuitable behaviour (W.L., p. 521).

That is all I am going to quote from Weber's own statements

about the 'ideal type'. Next I should like to give a critical estimate and some proposals for extending the ideal-type concept to the concept of the model.

I shall start with the fact that the 'ideal type' does not coincide with reality. Weber considered this as an essential irremovable trait of the ideal type, which made it useful. I would oppose that with the idea that it is desirable and possible for an ideal type to approximate progressively to reality, so that it can describe and predict empirical phenomena in a constantly improving way. If we rely on Weber's previously quoted statement that the ideal type should help to express clearly the representation of reality, we shall not undertake a biased promotion of certain elements of reality into a uniform set of ideas, but introduce a language with the following qualities: every mark of the variable is observed, not only the pure and the extreme. Further, any and every combination of marks of variables is observed, not only a certain typical combination. Whether certain combinations of characteristic marks are particularly frequent, and whether one can accordingly speak of the existence of certain types has to be decided by an empirical analysis of correlations.

After this concept-structure has been set up, hypotheses are introduced according to whose rules the variables are interconnected and become altered: these are laws. For application in certain cases we need to suppose which values the variables assume in these cases. These are the marginal conditions. A description of the observed empirical relationship is given in the language of the variables used, and we get predictions of the future values of these variables. Weber himself applies the dynamic or progressive aspect when as we know he speaks of ideal types of development.

First the coincidence between these predictions and reality will be imperfect, since one does not generally grasp all relevant variables, and one will have estimated the relations between them too simply. We shall not rest content with the first *rapprochement*, however, but attempt to lessen progressively the discrepancy between the empirical and theoretical data by re-defining the variables or by introducing new variables and by refining the relationship between them and their temporal alteration, until the deviations are merely attributed to errors of calculation, or are not worth considering. We do not rest content with the noncoincidence between the ideal type and the empirical data, but introduce so to speak an ideal-type contradiction for the deviations and so on, until the theory satisfactorily reproduces the data.

The difference between working with models, as I have just outlined it, and the ideal-type procedure, is as follows: the nature of the type, the commitment to a certain rigid combination of data, is abandoned. The impulse of idealization remains, yet we constantly attempt to reduce it.

Allow me to exemplify working with a model by a particularly lucid example from science—the kinetic theory of gas. The first stage of approximating the behaviour of gases by a mechanical model is named appositely ideal gas, and so provokes comparison with the ideal type. At this stage we imagine gas as consisting of a great number of small, quickly moving, perfectly elastic balls, the gas molecules, whose own volume is negligibly small, and which exercise no influence on each other except for the elastic movement. At first the gas molecules could not be tested directly. It was a hypothetical idea introduced into theory and could only be tested according to the success of its consequences.

Starting from this notion we get to the well-known ideal gas equation, a very simple relationship between pressure, volume and temperature. This equation describes very well the behaviour of many gases in a great range of conditions, yet there are strong deviations in high pressure and low temperatures.

May I be allowed an imaginative comparison: If Max Weber had been a physicist he would have said something like the following: we have an ideal marginal concept of gas, which is particularly simple, lucid and understandable. It is true that it describes the behaviour of real gases only very imperfectly, but this does not mean it is not useful. On the contrary it is useful because it is not valid: if I use it, I recognize in which cases the behaviour of real gases deviates from it. In these cases this ideal notion of gas molecules is not appropriate, but there are evidently some disturbing influences. And that would have been the end of the matter.

For the physicists however it was just getting interesting. They set themselves the task of making certain precise corrections to the model, which increase its conformity with the empirical data. So a not inconsiderable volume was ascribed to the gas molecules and it was assumed that these exercise certain powers of attraction upon each other according to a certain law. Thus a modification was reached of the ideal equation for gas, the Van der Waals equation, which describes the behaviour of real gases substantially better than the ideal equation for gas. In it appear two specific constants characteristic for the respective gases, and which must be measured empirically each time.

A further refinement of the model was undertaken to explain the various specific heats of gases. The molecules of gas were now imagined differently: either of one atom, spherical, or of two atoms, dumbell-shaped, or of three atoms, where the three atoms can be arranged in a straight line or a triangle, and so on for gases of four or more atoms. From these notions the observed values for the specific heats of the various gases can be quite well deduced, but with some deviations. These could be mostly removed by simple ideas from quantum mechanics, assuming that the molecules can only absorb slight amounts of vibratory and rotatory energy.

I hope that the procedure of progressive rapprochement of the model to the empirical data has become clear. Please do not object that such a procedure is only possible in the natural sciences. It can be exemplified just as well in a human science, e.g. economics. I would choose micro-economics, as related to psychology and sociology in the form of the theory of use and decision.

A simple hypothesis about so-called rational behaviour proves that people try to maximize the expected profits, i.e. the sum of the product of financial gain and the probability of its appearance. Experience shows however that this rule is often violated, for example, when one takes out an insurance or gambles in a lottery. The model is modified by replacing the amount of money by which its subjective usefulness increases at a diminishing rate the more the sum of money grows. This can explain why people take out insurances, for example, but there are still deviations from the pattern. One can explain these partly by the introduction of pleasure in a game of chance. As we see, we are already in the sphere of the psychological theory of personality. A whole series of further modifications of the original pattern, some of them basic, is necessary to reproduce human behaviour at all adequately under differing conditions. It ought to be clear that theories of human behaviour can go no other way than other scientific theories. The difference is simply that human–scientific data consist for the great part of verbal and other symbolic material, and further that the researcher can derive certain stimuli for forming hypotheses from the introspective observation of his own consciousness. These are always to be considered as heuristic references, and to be tested strictly on other individuals, since individual and cultural differences are great.

Perhaps a few remarks are in order as to why we should form models or theories at all. It seems to me that theoretical notions are fairly indispensable as guides for setting up strategically good observations and experiments. Without theoretical principles and hypotheses one would never hit upon many complex arrangements for experiments and data for observation. Further, with the help of a well-substantiated theory one can describe clearly a quantity of observation-data, and make predictions for such schemes as are not yet directly and empirically tested, but can be expressed by the variables of the model. One is often dependent on the introduction of intervening variables which cannot be tested directly, but hold good because they enable us to make predictions which would otherwise be impossible. We have seen previously in our reference to the example of the atom-theory of gases that 'intervening variables' are not limited to the human sciences.

A characteristic of the model *vis-à-vis* the ideal type was the observation of any degree of distinction of the variables, i.e. the use of quantitative variables. Since there are still many misunderstandings about quantification I should like to posit a few theses about it:

1. Qualitative–quantitative is not a simple choice of alternatives, but gives many degrees of transition between extremes.

From the theory of gradation we know that there are the following main types of variable, of which the first deals with qualities and classifications, e.g. a person's sex or religion. A quantitative moment is introduced here, since one can count the individuals who fall into qualitative classes. So statistical operations like four-field coefficients of correlation and χ^2-tests can be applied.

There are also variables in order in rank, as when someone arranges a row of photographs of people in the order in which he likes them. Here there is comparison—a 'more or a less', but one cannot say by how much one photo is more likeable than another.

Finally there is the scale of intervals in which the differences between positions can be specified quantitatively. One makes the distinction here as to whether a meaningful zero and therefore a scale of relationships is present or not. For temperature one had for a long time only scales of intervals, like Celsius and Fahrenheit. Their zero points are arbitrary and different. Similar differences of temperature in Celsius are also similar in Fahrenheit, but there would be for instance no point in saying 20° C is twice as warm as 10° C: in the Fahrenheit scale the corresponding values do not stand in the ratio 2:1. Later, temperatures were introduced with a meaningful zero point: at 20° abs. certain molecular energies are double what they are at 10° abs.

Between these three main types of scales one can think of transitional forms. For instance between the classificatory and the hierarchical (order of preference) variables, we can imagine variables whose elements are divided into classes which also have an order or status: e.g. essays can be divided into the categories very good, good, satisfactory, adequate, unsatisfactory. Or there can be an order of rank between that scale and the scale of intervals where the differences are not measured quantitatively, but also in order or rank. People can be classed according to size, their sizes estimated, and then one can say: the interval from the biggest to the second biggest is greater than the interval from the second to the third, but without being able to say exactly by how much he is bigger.

There is also a quasi-continuous transition from purely qualitative to purely quantitative statements. Parallel to this, there is in mathematics a transition from quantitative to purely qualitative disciplines. It would be biased and old-fashioned to define mathematics as the science of quantities, numbers and geometrical figures. In reality, mathematics contains as a basis the purely qualitative–classificatory logical calculus of statements as well as a multiplicity of forms of abstract algebra like set-theory, from which a few axioms are given here:

We imagine a set of elements. Two elements can always be combined by a linking operation and thus produce a third element which belongs to the set.

There is one outstanding element, the integer, which, when combined with any other, produces this other element—to every element there is an inverse element, such that the two combined produce the integer.

So there is no question here of figures and sizes. By 'elements' we can imagine anything we like, so long as it fulfils the axioms.

Similarly there is a branch of geometry, topology, in which

there is no mention of lines and angles: here one observes only such properties as remain unchanged if one draws the figures on a rubber sheet and stretches this at will.

The common factor, the mathematical nature of all these disciplines, is not that they deal with numbers and sizes, that quantitative statements are made, but that quite exact concepts and axioms are introduced and conclusions are drawn only according to explicit logical rules. In other words the disciplines are formalized and axiomatized.

From these observations I derive my second thesis:

2. There is no need to quantify unconditionally: it is more important to mathematize, i.e. to use a precise language with precise rules of usage for all expressions.

3. Quantitative statements do however have their advantages. They are not, as we sometimes hear, poorer than qualitative ones, but richer. They contain all that a qualitative statement must, and refinement besides: i.e. referring to the 'how much' of quality. This refinement has the advantage that the information-content of the statement is increased. This increases its falsifiability, which determines whether it can be tested empirically. The falsifiability of a statement is great if the statement offers many possibilities, and thus asserts something as definitely as possible. If a statement is not falsifiable, i.e. if no possible facts contradict it, the statement is empirically empty of content. Not every kind of statement is at all quantifiable: for example, statements about the religion to which a person belongs.

4. The question whether one ought to quantify or not, is not a dilemma where one has to decide whether to proceed in the one or the other way, but how far one can and will proceed on one and the same way.

II

The discussion began with a question to Dr. Vetter as to how much he thinks actually remains of Weber's 'ideal type'. The differences between the logical structures of the 'ideal type' and the 'model' had not been very clearly brought out: Dr. Vetter had tried instead to reduce the 'ideal type' to a 'model'. The ideal type had developed historically in the cultural sciences, and could be traced back to Herder. With its help 'profiles' of culture could be diagnosed. These are concerned with the systematic comprehension and

P

typological experience of manifold cultural phenomena. The 'ideal type' does not start from an initial idea which proceeds by the analytical separation of variables. Ideal types would be significant in cases where one intended interpretations close to history. One should not want to modernize the ideal type while trying to reduce it logically to models.

One can perhaps state four kinds of ideal type in Weber's work relevant in different ways to the notion of reality:

1   Simple analytical assumptions about human action. This form represents a descriptive concept of classes of activity, e.g. 'purposeful type of activity'.

2   Economic 'Robinson Crusoe', models according to the 'Homo oeconomicus'. In its cognitive function this is the type most nearly relevant to 'models'.

3   Types of historic–empirical structure, as e.g. medieval town-economy. They were distilled from the reality of the traditional, in that single variables were chosen and combined to form a conceptual image.

4   Ideal types of historical development. They concern regular occurrences in the course of history.

All four ideal types tended towards a meaningful understanding of social phenomena. The criterion of empirical validity was not only immediately applicable to them. The assertion made by Dr. Vetter that with ideal types, after their transformation into models, one can determine historical phenomena quantitatively in their nearness to or distance from the concept, is not tenable, since they are qualitative concepts which constitute the 'ideal type'.

For the problem of the *rapprochement* of ideal types to experience, our attention was drawn to the relationship between catalectics and statistics in political economy. To reconcile models and empiricism seems an almost insoluble problem. The econometricians constructed models which could not be elucidated immediately by collection of statistical data. The problems thus set remain insoluble as long as the models, without reflecting the possibilities of collecting the data, are deduced from a theory. The *'rapprochement'* of models and reality was interpreted by Dr. Vetter somewhat unproblematically.

The discussion turned to the possibilities and limits and rational imitative construction of ideal types. This construction is aimed at imitating the logical structure of ideal types in the model in such a way that its dimensions are made explicit, and the variables in their mutual dependence, are made understandable and even accessible to empirical interpretation. The intention of the rational construction is thus the development of an empirically testable theory. This procedure takes account of only one aspect of the ideal type. Even in the modern theory-formation of positivistic persuasion there are aspects which cannot simply be transposed into the empirical field without more ado; we have only to think of the role which constructs play in modern theory-formation. But this shows that we can no longer work *ad hoc* with the old principles of verification; logical theory has already gone further than this. In Germany the newer developments are not yet appreciated, and outmoded arguments of this theory of science were used in the discussion.

Today there is a 'post-positivist' re-appearance in the newer scientific theoretical literature in English of the problem of explaining and understanding, which once occupied German philosophy and Max Weber 'pre-positivistically'. We have only to think of the work of Gilbert Ryle and Peter Winch. It is symptomatic that Rickert is now being translated and studied in America. We shall dishonour Weber's motives if, for the sake of the rational reconstruction, we see the 'ideal type' solely as a hypothetical system of rules. For example his ideal types of church and sect showed how much he was concerned to explain structures of meaning hermeneutically.

The different cognitive function of ideal type and model led to the question: how can one make models productive for empirical research, since the model, because it consisted only of tautological transformations, admitted the possibility of understanding all the theoretical concepts appearing in it as implicitly defined, and thus immunizing the researcher against experience? To this it was objected that this was an obvious misunderstanding.

It appeared particularly in discussion that model and theory were to a great extent identified. The difference between model and theory would have to be made clear, as evidenced by the fact that certain theoretical concepts were understood as gaps in theory, which in the model appear as clearly defined. The theoretical concepts which were conceived of as lacunae had a vagueness of intention, which they would lose in the course of the research.

Next Dr. Vetter dealt with the difference between understanding and explanation in Weber's work. He maintained that the concept of 'Verstehen' was based in a certain sense on introspection as a method, while explanation represents nothing other than the subsumption under laws with special marginal conditions. This interpretation was criticized. Weber did not understand sociology as introspection but as a science which enquires into the significance of social activity in order to explain its course and its effects.

The discussion dealt finally with the problems of quantitative and qualitative concepts in connection with ideal types and the formation of models. In representing the causes of any empirical phenomenon it is inevitable that one should have recourse to qualitative estimation. In interpreting empirical facts one was driven to assumptions of a qualitative nature. For an adequate interpretation of quantitatively chosen material there was always the necessity of returning to the historical connections. The historical interpretation of quantitatively selected data is usual with qualitative concepts. In particular interpretations of correlations needed statements about the presence and the direction of the functional or causal connections of qualitative estimations. Dr. Vetter explained that qualitative estimations could only transmit heuristic principles, but themselves allowed of no causal explanation. In this view, he added that causal explanations were only possible if the variables entering into the explanation were describable by means of continuous scales. To this it was objected that the interpretation of variables by means of scales of rank and order was itself enough to make causal explanations possible, as Zeisel had already shown.

Max Weber's Contribution to the
Sociology of Culture

URSULA JAERISCH (Frankfurt-am-Main): Weber refers to cultural and educational institutions only in his sociology of religion and the sociology of government in *Wirtschaft und Gesellschaft*. 'The direction of education' is determined by the type of administration manifested by each government, and by the classes and social strata which supply any particular administrative hierarchy.[1] Education and culture are here defined principally as a qualification for government, and their content is seen as conditioned by one of three specific types of government. To state this connection and to take up Weber's incidental remarks is not sufficient to establish a sociology of culture. To treat this issue *only* from the aspect of government is typical of the whole of Weber's sociology: because of his individualist approach, Weber, who tends to derive society and its institutions from the social behaviour of individuals, hits upon the problem of just what 'motives' meaningfully determine the individual's social behaviour. Apart from customary usage, and subjective interests of direct external compulsion, a criterion for it is the belief in the 'legitimacy' of orders which are each linked with the types of government. Central to this analysis is the functioning of the government's apparatus of force, and its self-maintenance. In the functional analyses in *Wirtschaft und Gesellschaft* there is little mention of the individual and his actions, and so not much about how far this action is conditioned by the processes and content of education and culture.

The difference between the individualistic approach of his sociology and the functional and historical analyses which reveal the objective coercive tendency of social institutions is reflected in Weber's ambivalent attitude to the 'specialist'. In the name of the freedom of the individual he protests against the universal bureaucratization (while describing it as unavoidable) which creates a

---

[1] Max Weber, *Wirtschaft und Gesellschaft*, 4th ed. (Tübingen, 1956), p. 155 (subsequently referred to as W.G.).

'prison-house of bondage'.[1] The decline of culture, noted everywhere today, into professional and vocational training, which prepares the individual to fit into established organizations, is a product of the historical process of rationalization and bureaucratization. This process of rationalization, the history of the control of nature, is at one and the same time the social history of the individual, that of his development and of his collapse.

The attempt to follow up aspects of the sociology of culture in Weber has to ensure the relevance of culture and vocational training to authority, and then the connection of this with some elements of Weber's analysis of the economic and political structure of 'rational' capitalist society. Also in this context are the practical political implications of the doctrine of value-freedom and Weber's programmatic lectures on science and politics as vocations.

In *Wirtschaft und Gesellschaft* culture and education are said always to qualify for participation in authority, and the structure of authority, for its part, influences the 'ideal of culture' and educational institutions (W.G., p. 586). Weber here means not so much the possible conception of the aims of education, but what institutions of education and culture actually produce by way of an existing order of government. If in the case of the typology of authority he sets himself against three-stage theory of development that passes from charismatic via traditional to rational authority (W.G., p. 678) it is not possible to conceal a certain affinity with such a historical sequence in the case of types of law and education conceived analogously to the types of government and most closely associated with it.

The polarity of charisma and 'ratio', characteristic of Weber's sociology, is repeated in the types of education, even if the two are not opposed 'without relevance or transition'. 'The two most extreme historical poles in the sphere of the aims of education are: the awakening of charisma (heroic qualities and magical gifts) on the one hand—and the provision of specialist training on the other'.[2]

In so far as education plays any part in the 'awakening of charisma', it always includes technico-rational elements, since

[1] Max Weber, *Gesammelte politische Schriften*, 2nd ed. (Tübingen, 1958), pp. 320 ff. (subsequently referred to as G.P.S.).
[2] Max Weber, *Gesammelte Aufsätze zur Religionssoziologie*, I (Tübingen, 1920/21), 408 (subsequently referred to as R.S.).

magic too is aimed at the practical mastery of nature and men.

This empirical specialist element, apprenticeship, often treated as a 'trade secret' in the interest of prestige and monopoly, increases with the growing differentiation of professions, and the expansion of specialized knowledge, quantitatively as well as in its rational quality; the familiar phenomena (fagging, flogging, etc.) of military and student life are left within what has become a predominantly specialist training as the *caput mortuum* of the old ascetic ways of arousing and testing charismatic ability! (W.G., p. 685.)

Thorstein Veblen sees the 'source of all higher learning' precisely in this element of the secret which—originally an element of magical knowledge—still attaches to knowledge, and grants privileges to those who possess it.[1] Weber too points out that the rational bureaucratic organization, 'authority by virtue of knowledge', still contains elements of secret knowledge, through which it secures its position of power.

Between charismatic and specialized rational education are the educational systems corresponding to the traditional type of government, which have as a common purpose education towards a class-biased way of life. Culture as 'stylisation of life' (W.G., p. 537) and objective education have their origin here. Only this 'pedagogy of culturalization' aims at producing a cultivated man according to the ideals of the class which participates in government (R.S., p. 408).

The cultivated personality, either knightly or ascetic or (as in China) literary, or (as in Greece) gymnastic and artistic, or like the conventional Anglo-Saxon gentleman, was the cultural ideal influenced by the structure of government and the social conditions of membership of the upper class. The qualification of the upper class as such rested on a greater share of 'cultural quality' (in the variable value-free sense here ascribed to the concept), not on specialist knowledge. (W.G., p. 586.)

As long as government is incorporated in exclusive classes, culture is a prestige-quality of those who govern. What Veblen discussed in detail, Weber hints at: that the objectivity of culture and the 'higher learning' provides the requisite for privileged classes, free from the economic necessity of work. Culture and art in conjunction with feudal possessions or merely by their

[1] Cf. Veblen, *The Theory of the Leisure Class*, Mentor edition (New York, 1953), pp. 236 f.

exclusivity are the 'innermost and most in superable of all class differences' (R.S., p. 568). Even where, as in patriarchal systems, a literary education qualifies clerics or humanists for office in the hierarchy, economic uselessness has its social function.

The need for ostentation, for outer show and impressive splendour, for providing life with objects which have no *raison d'être*, in usefulness in the Wildean sense of 'beautiful', arises primarily from the class need for prestige, as an obvious instrument of power for asserting the master-position by mass-suggestion. 'Luxury' in the sense of rejection of purposeful orientation to use is for the feudal upper classes not something 'superfluous', but one of the means of their social self-assertion. (W.G., p. 659.)

If government cannot be unequivocally localized as far as the governed are concerned, purpose-free education loses its meaning as a qualification for government, without forfeiting that for prestige. In his paper on politics as a vocation, Weber deals with the history of the professional official and politician in the European state and the relevant changes in schooling, whose centre of gravity shifted with the entry of different classes into the service of the state—clergy, humanist men of letters, court nobility, university-trained lawyers. The technical needs of absolutist administration, its tax- and finance-policies, and the centralization of jurisdiction in the interest of capitalism finally required the development of a professional civil service with specialist training. The apparatus of bureaucracy, by means of which government is achieved in the modern state and in a capitalist economy, no longer needed a purpose-free culture; in its place specialist training was required, which applies science as technology. Anything beyond the practically applicable is superfluous as a requirement for a post in the bureaucratic apparatus of government.

Behind all present-day discussions of the bases of education there is in a definitive position the struggle of the 'expert' against the former 'cultivated man'—caused by the continual encroachment of the bureaucratisation of all public and private relations of authority and by the ever-increasing importance of specialisation, involved in all the most intimate problems of culture. (W.G., p. 586.)

In the mere opposition to limited specialist knowledge the 'cultivated man's' ideal of culture becomes rigidified in its inherited content, which is handed down as a cultural possession. Attempts to set up new guiding patterns for education, like those undertaken by Ernst Troeltsch in combining ancient, Christian and 'nordic German' cultural elements in a national ideal of culture,[1] belong, according to Weber to the irrational reactions against the control of the 'specialist' and the rationalism which is after all the father of it (W.G., p. 512). Individuality can only be realized by devotion to the specialization which provides the individual with an inner freedom within the rationalized and rationally governed world.

The revolutionary bourgeois concept of culture, aimed at social freedom and autonomy, is left behind by Weber. It must have appeared irrelevant to his sociology which indeed views the forms of authority as changing, but authority itself as a constant. The sociology of authority emphasizes particularly the integrating power of the double meaning of culture—being an attribute of authority, and yet effective as a means of emancipation. Bourgeois individualist freedom, for Weber the essence and the maximum of possible freedom, is according to him already past and gone as a real possibility in European history. That specialist training may be effective in itself and not only in the interest of the existing authority structure occurs in Weber's work only in the case of the lawyer, whose role without the rise of the absolute state is as unthinkable as the (bourgeois) revolution' (G.P.S., p. 511, cf. W.G., pp. 502 ff.).

Weber sees bourgeois emancipation as the beginning of new forms of control, because

those claims of formal equality in law and economic freedom of move-ment indirectly pave the way for bureaucratisation, and on the other hand come up against the expansion of capitalism. Like the this-worldly asceticism adopted by the different sects, who disciplined capitalist thinking and the rationally acting 'professional man' needed by capitalism, human basic laws offered the pre-conditions for the free equation of capitalist effort with goods and men. (W.G., p. 734.)

The development towards bureaucratization and professional and specialist training as a practical cultural ideal is a part of that process of rationalization, the increasing controllability of 'all things by calculation'.[2] It culminates in capitalism where calcula-

---

[1] Cf. E. Troeltsch, 'Deutsche Bildung, Vortrag 1918', in E. Troeltsch, *Deutscher Geist und Westeuropa* (Tübingen, 1925), p. 169 ff.

[2] Max Weber, *Soziologie—Weltgeschichtliche Analysen—Politik*, Kröners pocket edition (Stuttgart, 1956), p. 317 (subsequently quoted as Kröner).

bility is established as a universal principle. With the capitalist economic system a purposefulness develops, whose essence, rational exchange, is seen by Weber—as it was by Marx—as an antagonistic relationship between men, which has come about through unequal economic power and compulsion (W.G., p. 37). Formal rationality by which things and men are calculated and used as means to an end is not limited to economics. Weber deduces the formal rationalization of state and law historically from the powerful interests of the juridical and political classes whose effects are felt alongside those of capitalists operating the market: the calculable rationality of the law and the state are at the same time the necessary precondition for the 'economic control of capital' and its 'impersonal character' in contrast to all other forms of authority' (W.G., p. 716). In spite of Weber's attempt to separate them categorically, formal rationality and social authority appear as mutually conditioned: the formal rationality of economics needs the political authority ensured by property and the freedom of contract, and the 'subordination of workers to the control of employers' (W.G., p. 78). Conversely authority is reproduced by formal rationality, whose main aim, the calculation of capital, is orientated to profit.

The rationality of 'means and end', which not only determines the economic activity of isolated individuals but also the bureaucratic organization of public and private authority, has a bearing on the education of the individuals who experience such rationality and are subordinated to it. The category of 'vocation' is in Weber's sociology the only one which can effect mediation between individual and society. This reminds us of Durkheim's concept, in which, together with the progressive division of labour, vocation becomes an essential connecting link between society and individuals.[1] Rational continuous vocational work is a condition of the structure of capitalism, and an objective necessity for individuals. Once set in motion, the formal rationality of the capitalist system requires asceticism in professional work, without needing the 'psychological prizes' of votes by favour and a subjective anchoring in religion.

The Puritans wanted to be professional men, we *have* to be. For while asceticism was continued from the monk's cell into professional

[1] Cf. E. Durkheim, *De la Division du Travail Social*, 7th ed. (Paris, 1960), pp. 395 ff.

life, and this-worldly morality began to predominate, it shared in helping to build that mighty cosmos of a modern economic order bound to the technical and economic requirements of mechanised production, which overwhelmingly determines the way of life of *every* individual born into this mechanical travail—not only those actively employed in it. The idea of 'professional duty' goes around in our lives like a ghost of former religious beliefs. (R.S., p. 203.)

Thus education, in so far as it is socially necessary, becomes training for the imparting of technical knowledge for the vocations of capitalist bureaucratized society whose formal rationality determines not only the function but also the form and content of specialized knowledge, schooling and training. Training in the sense of specialized knowledge arises with the expansion of the market and rational division of labour. While progressive association by means of the market, the increase of standing orders and the scientific systematization of technology in its domination of nature complicate these divided spheres, and on the other hand capitalist industry under the dictatorship of profit is as dependent on a calculable natural science as on the principled calculability of law and administration, the training of those who exercise 'white-collar professions' becomes necessary. It imparts a relevant generalizing method of controlling and ordering spheres of society and corresponds to the formal rationality of the calculus. Historically this specialist training is inseparable from the development of the principle of exchange. This is exemplified by training in law, with which Weber deals in most detail.

A 'construction of formalistic character' in law can only apply to an exchange 'developing the function of metals as money'[1] if the purchase allows of the abstraction needed by formally rational justice. At the same time exchange as 'financial contract' is the 'definitive means of the profanation of law'[2] and contradicts the content of juristic training, while the identity of law and morality is severed in order to settle the conflicts of primarily economic interests. The increasing market trade in consumer goods requires a calculable legal order, which can be developed and applied only by a class of 'professionally trained practitioners of the law'.[3]

Modern forms of enterprise with their static capital and exact calculation are far too susceptible to irrationalities of the law and

[1] Max Weber, *Rechtssoziologie* (Neuwied, 1960), p. 113.
[2] Ibid.   [3] Op. cit., p. 196.

administration. They could only arise where either, (1) as in England, the practical structuring of the law lay actually in the hands of lawyers, who thought up the appropriate forms of business for their clientèle, who had capitalist interests, and from whose midst came judges strictly concerned with 'cases of precedence' and calculable schemes; or where (2) the judge, as in the bureaucratic state with its rational laws, is more or less an automaton quoting chapter and verse, acts plus costs and taxes are put in at the top, so that he can spit out the judgment below, together with more or less valid reasons—whose functioning therefore is by and large calculable. (G.P.S., p. 311, cf. W.G., p. 507.)

The imparting of knowledge and the content of training in law are mutually conditioned by their removal from practice.[1] While in England a formal rational body of law in the sense of a logical tightly closed system cannot be born of the activity of a legal class bound absolutely to practice, on the continent a form of university education has arisen which obeys the 'autonomy' of legal thought, capable of creating a formally rational system of law increasingly isolated from practice. The content of this formal legal training is dictated, on the one hand, by the demands of the market, not in the sense that it has to satisfy these needs immediately but that it contains the principle of calculability: on the other hand, by the systematization of the law which produces an autonomy freed from the sphere of production and the market.[2] The content of specialist training which has arisen in this way conflicts with the rationality of the market: this not only expresses society's antagonism strengthened by the formal rationality of divided spheres, but it also characterizes the objectivized content of education, offered to the individual as juristic theory. However closely calculability in principle connects law, technology and science with the economic basis, their progressive rationalization leads by virtue of the autonomy of their immanent logic to their secession from the process of production of society, allows them to appear as ends in themselves and turns them into the domain of specialists.

As a labour-dividing organization of specialist knowledge, bureaucracy (by which Weber means more than merely the administration in state and economics) corresponds to the division and co-ordination of labour in mechanized industry. The basis of the structure of control is in both cases the concentration of the whole

[1] Cf. Max Weber, *Rechtssoziologie*, pp. 197 ff.
[2] Cf. op. cit., p. 280 and p. 201.

enterprise, the separation of the industrial worker from the means of production, the separation of the official or employee from the means of administration, research and finance (G.P.S., p. 310). The arrangement of things and people in the rationality of means and ends, and impersonal matter-of-factness characterizes the organized specialist training of bureaucracy as a child of that same rationalism which Weber considers as the specific quality of modern capitalism. Bureaucratic division of labour is orientated in principle to 'impartial' points of view, i.e. 'calculable rules' (W.G., p. 570) which trace out every individual's activity and make it repeatable. The individual must fit in to the system claimed by the bureaucratic machine if his behaviour and the functioning of the apparatus are to remain calculable (cf. W.G., p. 578). A necessity for the exercise of a function is a specialist training from which all individual spontaneity must be banned in the interest of technical usefulness. Knowledge becomes stereotyped and applied as fixed and immutable.

A lifeless machine is an atrophied spirit . . . and so too is that living machine represented by bureaucratic organisation with its specialisation of trained expertise, its demarcations of competence, its rules and regulations and hierarchically graded relationships of obedience. (G.P.S., p. 320.)

If specialist knowledge has become indispensable for satisfying society's material needs by its complex technique and administration, it serves at the same time private profit and the power of the state. The same technically rational knowledge, which guarantees a better satisfaction of our needs, contributes within these social relationships of control to their perpetuation and establishment. Both functions of specialist knowledge, to guarantee that the productive processes of society will be maintained and to serve in controlling them, are, according to Weber, indissolubly linked. Where Weber makes clearest the historical interweaving of rationality and authority, that is in his analysis of the process of bureaucratization, this interweaving is itself reified, and progressive bureaucratization, inseparably linked with authority over men, is mythologized as an inevitable destiny.

Specialist knowledge is not only a means in the service of private and public authority; the possession of this knowledge gives one an economic advantage and a claim to share in authority. Like all education, specialist training creates class differences:

the privilege of sharing in authority, which in feudal society was linked with inheritance, has been taken over by the certificate of education acquired by examination.

The provision of degrees by universities, colleges of technology and commerce, the call to create certificates of education in all spheres serve to form a privileged class in office and counting-house. . . . If we hear in all spheres a loud demand for the introduction of regulated courses of instruction and specialist examination, the reason is not of course the sudden awakening of an urge for culture, but an effort to limit the candidature for positions and their monopolisation in favour of those who possess these certificates of education. (W.G., p. 585.)

The privileges won through specialist knowledge are supported by 'trade secrets'. The 'official secret' of bureaucracy is 'in its relation to specialist knowledge comparable to the relation of commercial secrets of the trade to technical ones' (W.G., p. 129). This secret knowledge is not gained as a general rule but in service as individual knowledge, removed from public control. As a component part of public and private organizations secret knowledge indicates that bureaucracy's controlling position does not rely on expert rational knowledge.

The fact that those privileged by knowledge consider obvious practicality a duty, and take pride in fulfilling conscientiously the individual tasks entrusted to them is to the benefit of the ruling class (W.G., p. 566). Matter-of-factness already tailored to fit the interests of the ruling class becomes an ideology into the bargain.

Since Weber reveals the affinity of stolid specialization and specialist training as an instrument of authority, it is all the more striking that in *Wissenschaft als Beruf* he does not deal with the social function of labour-dividing science, directed only at training specialized research workers and experts for the apparatus of public and private authority. As 'both member and driving force' (Kröner, p. 318) science belongs to the Western process of rationalization, which places the natural sciences methodologically at the service of economics, and the expert knowledge of law and administration—finally involving social science as well—at the service of bureaucracy.

Rationalization in this sense is identical with scientification. The 'disenchantment of the world' is defined by Weber in the very words which describe what science achieves in practice; it provides 'knowledge about the technique which helps man control life and external things as well as men's actions by calculation' (Kröner, p. 332).

The immanent development of the exact sciences is determined by economic returns, which depend upon the practical application of the sciences, i.e. 'indirectly but positively upon capitalist economic conditions'.[1] With increasing investment in the realm of applied science the organization of research changes. The independent scholar, like the craftsman using his own means of production becomes a marginal phenomenon.

The great institutes of medicine or the natural sciences are state-capitalist undertakings. They cannot be administered without a considerable amount of industrial means. The same applies here as everywhere in capitalist industry—the 'separation of the worker from the means of production'. The worker, therefore the assistant, is directed to the means of work which the state places at his disposal, therefore he is just as dependent on the principal of the institute as an employee on the manager of a factory.[2]

Weber saw that this development would not remain confined to the natural sciences, and that, with the organization of the university, the nature of science and of teaching would shift. Organized like a factory, the university offers outdated knowledge as goods. The *ex cathedra* pronouncements in German lecture-rooms and German students' behaviour, ruled by a belief in authority, are contested by Weber with the purely consumer attitude, hostile to authority, of the American student. 'He has this idea of the teacher who stands in front of him: he sells me his knowledge and methods in return for my father's money, just as the greengrocer sells my mother a cabbage' (Kröner, p. 331).

Weber's liberalism tries to interpret the fact that science has become consumer-goods as meaning that the relationship of authority between university teachers and students has become an anachronism. The university should not misuse its authority to preach an ideology, but confine itself to imparting specialist training.

At the same time Weber maintains the claim that science is

[1] Max Weber, *Gesammelte Aufsätze zur Soziologie und Socialpolitik* (Tübingen, 1924), p. 455; cf. R.S., p. 10.
[2] Max Weber, *Gesammelte Aufsätze zur Wissenschaftslehre*, 2nd ed. (Tübingen, 1951), p. 568; cf. W.G., p. 575.

morally bound to objective truth, pursued as a vocation it should be excluded from the process of rationalization, which locks both labour and knowledge into the 'means- and-ends relationship'.

Why does one indulge in an activity which in reality does not and cannot come to anything? . . . firstly for purely practical, and in the wider sense of the word, technical, purposes: to be able to orientate our practical activity to what others expect of us because of our scientific experience. Good. But that only means something to the practical man. But what is the inner attitude of the scientist himself to his vocation? To practise science for its own sake, and not simply because others use it for technical or commercial success, and to be able to feed, clothe, light, and govern themselves better. (Kröner, p. 316.)

After the optimism of science that hopes, by the search for truth, to find the way to correct behaviour, to the true God, to real nature or happiness, has proved illusory, science sees itself thrown back on the knowledge of 'objective' facts (cf. Kröner, p. 322). To keep science from being used as a mere tool in a rationalized world, Weber thinks its claim to objectivity can only be saved if it does not presume to decide about the reasonableness (or lack of reasonableness) of goals, and confines itself to the value-neutral cognition of mere facts. An education which imparts these is premised as clear and responsible. The idea that knowledge, although its pursuit must be stimulated by interest, is not involved with that interest, results in the separation of values and objectivity.

Only in science as a vocation does that part of a cultural process seem to be realized, in which the relationship between the subject of culture and the individual is not reduced to the external adoption of knowledge which is ready-made.

Personality in the scientific sphere is only possessed by the one who serves the cause whole-heartedly. It is certainly not the one who goes on stage with the matter he is presenting, like an impresario. (Kröner, p. 314 f.)

This educational process is destined to specialist fragmentation: internalisation of specialism now approaches in significance devotion to the subject.

Not only externally but internally, the state of things is such that the individual can only be quite sure of achieving something really perfect in the scientific sphere if he specialises as strictly as possible. (Kröner, p. 311.)

The duty of the scientist to be matter-of-fact, 'intellectually honest', becomes a bar to thought, in so far as the social division of labour in science is blindly passed off as being appropriate. With reference to the ascetic traits of vocational work, to which the individual must subscribe under the objective pressure of economic relationships, Weber makes the statement in the *Protestant Ethic* 'that the limitation of specialised work at the present time is a pre-requisite for value-based action, therefore "action" and "abstinence" are mutually and unalterably conditioned' (R.S., p. 203). The ambiguity of 'value-based' is also applicable to specialized science. Capitalism, as a system designed for a specific end, and its bureaucratic organization, require a science whose results can be valued as technical means and can be calculated like other wares according to an economic principle. This is also what Weber's 'value-free' social science amounts to: it is to provide the estimation of means and consequences for a given purpose. Only its 'value-freedom' guarantees that it can be utilized and turns it into an information-office which places its store of rules at the disposal of anybody interested. The limitation to specialist research, if it leaves the individual evaluating irrationally to reflect on purposes himself, degrades science to a mere tool, and Weber wants to safeguard it from this. The self-comprehension of the scientist seeking for truth goes hand in hand with the objective function of social science, conceived in the image of the natural sciences. This social science, as a tool for the calculated domination of men's actions, is according to Weber's own analysis an instrument of authority.

Weber's constant insistence on the value-freedom of social science repeats Humboldt's aim of emancipating the university as an institution, and particularly of freeing scientific research from the immediate pressure of particular interests. Politically this claim opposes the preaching of state-sponsored ideals, particularly on the part of 'pulpit socialists', who saw the existing state as an instrument for resolving class contradictions.[1] Weber stressed again and again that the value-freedom of science does not imply

[1] Cf. Max Weber, *Gesammelte Aufsätze zur Wissenschaftslehre*, note 40, p. 482, and Max Weber, 'Die sogenannte Lehrfreiheit an den deutschen Universitäten', in *Frankfurter Zeitung*, No. 262 (20.9.1908, 5th morning edition); Max Weber 'Der Fall Bernhard' in *Frankfurter Zeitung* no. 168 (18.6.1908, 1st morning edition); Max Weber, 'Über das System Althoff' in *Frankfurter Zeitung*, no. 298 (27.10.1911, evening edition).

Q

the political abstinence of the scientist, and put this into practice with his own publications. But the relationship of his scientific writings to his political ones shows that his scientific analysis and political aims are not so closely aligned.

Social Darwinism and ideas of power fall into the categories of Weber's interpretative sociology (W.G., p. 21), and the value-free concept of charisma promises to justify the dominance of a political élite in the interest of the national imperialist state: democracy is harnessed to legitimizing this élite. On the other hand the most controversial of Webers' essays on voting rights and democracy in Germany, and on parliamentarianism and government in the reformed Germany—essays based on detailed social analysis, which contain some passages almost word for word identical with the historical parts of his sociology of authority—treat as necessary the introduction of a certain political practice, democratic franchise and parliamentary government for Germany. The changed relationship of education and political authority corresponds to the social development which replaces culture by specialist training: where possessions and culture constituted a public of free citizens confronting the state, culture was the means and the expression of civil emancipation. Weber was one of the first to see that the development of parliamentarianism from the party of the upper class to the democratic mass-party destroys the political importance of the cultured individual. With the bureaucratization of the parties, for which the pacemakers were the democratic parties which arose in opposition to the honorific authority by those with possessions and culture (W.G., p. 576), the struggle against authority changed to a struggle for authority between the organizations (W.G., p. 548). Politics becomes the business of experts, high-ranking officials, whose material interests are directed to the extrusion and establishment of their bureaucratic privileges. Culture which does not end in specialist knowledge is impotent against such authority and reduced to being a decorative attribute of non-political intimacy.

Weber seems to interpret the concept of democracy according to its content when he views as its 'implicit postulates' the 'prevention of the development of a closed official class' in the interest of the general accessibility of offices and the minimizing of the power authority in the interest of the utmost expansion of the sphere of influence of 'public opinion' (W.G., p. 576). The bureaucratization of state and parties removes the transparency of political procedure and deprives a critical public of suppositions. Weber had already remarked that 'so-called "public opinion" under the conditions of mass-democracy is a communal activity born of irrational "feelings" and normally stage-directed by party leaders and press' (W.G., p. 574). But he blurs over the discrepancy between the claims of a critical public opinion and the reality of a manipulated public in democracy, by differentiating the type of plebiscitary leader-democracy from that of leaderless democracy 'which is characterised by striving to minimise man's dominance over man' (W.G., p. 157). This leaderless democracy is only capable of realization in small states, which require a minimum of relatively stable administration, not dependent on specialist training, while 'the concept of democracy in the case of mass-administration [changes] its sociological meaning so that it is absurd to look for something similar behind the same collective name' (W.G., p. 548). Since the rise of mass parties plebiscitary democracy is the only possibility and that means control by party leaders, supported by the party machine which obeys them 'blindly' 'as long as they are successful' (G.P.S., p. 336), installed by the acclamation of the masses. Weber does also speak about political education: in his Freiburg inaugural speech the 'political education of our nation' is defined as the 'ultimate goal' of a policy of political economy designed in the interest of the German nation-state (G.P.S., p. 24). The essay on politics as a vocation deals with the qualifications of a political élite. This was neither the German bourgeoisie as a whole, whose defection in the time of the Kaiser showed that economic power and capacity for political leadership are in no way identical (G.P.S., p. 18) nor the working-class, nor an 'aristocracy of workers' who, said Weber, lacked the 'instincts for power', which he thought a class must possess for political leadership. The notion of a political élite is to be connected with the concept of vocation, and leads to the isolation of politics from generality and its own establishment as a vocation. Parliamentary democracy is intended less to serve to represent particular interests than to win for the charismatic leader 'the trust and faith of the masses in him, and his power, by mass-demagogic means' (G.P.S., p. 381). The autonomy of politics is bought with the irrationality of the belief in a leader, who is to crown the nation's power-interests with success.

Knowledge and action, which were interdependent in the revolutionary bourgeois concept of education, have drifted apart: within a rationalized and bureaucratized world, knowledge has become the privilege of science practised as a profession, autonomous action has become that of the professional politician, and finally that of the charismatic leader.

Weber's essays on science as a vocation and politics as a vocation emphasize this radical separation of theory and practice. This schism has not left the separate parts unchanged. Like the professional scientist, the professional politician is distinguished by his 'passionate' devotion to the matter in hand. For the scientist this means restriction to objective knowledge. As the price of its autonomy, science renounces criticism of the social conditions in which it is applied. Weber does not yet see that, with the hardening of bureaucratic apparatus, the qualitative differences in actual specialist knowledge, and so the concept of specialist knowledge itself, are eliminated in favour of the application of mere methods. 'The appearance of the matter, in whose service the politician strives for power and uses power, is a matter of faith' (G.P.S., p. 535). The renunciation of reason in theory provides the warrant for the continuance of social irrationality, man's domination over man.

KURT WOLFF

In the introduction to his paper, PROFESSOR KURT WOLFF (Brandeis-Waltham, U.S.A.) remarked that Fräulein Jaerisch had the great merit of having collected whatever there was on the topic of the sociology of education which was only too widely dispersed in Weber's writings. The next step was the interpretation of what had been collected.

For this purpose, I will try to present the preliminaries briefly, and to begin with I would suggest that it both helps clarification and heightens the relevance if we distinguish three approaches to interpretation: systematic, sociological–historical, and existential. By the systematic approach I mean the question of what we can learn from Weber about the order of things—in this case mainly about the relationships between society, or more precisely authority, and education and culture. By the sociological–historical approach I mean the question of how it happens that Weber says what he says, sees what he sees, and does not see what he does not see—and these questions are asked in the hope that a look at his times and society will help us answer them. Finally I mean by the existential approach the question of the meaning for us today of the problems, and where possible the answers, produced by the first two approaches: what they mean for us in general, and for us as sociologists, and as sociologists of different nations and schools. This last approach may therefore also be called practical. I will deal with them in this order but must confine myself to examples.

Weber develops the idea that education and culture serve authority and the type of prevailing authority determines their institutions and ideals. With particular relevance to modern bureaucratized capitalist society, the typical forms are specialist education and training, and what remains from earlier times has become prestige and ornament. Fräulein Jaerisch rightly says that in view of his conception of authority which he saw as a constant in society Weber only hinted at the fact that even specialist training does not necessarily have to work in the interests of the existing relationships of control. Here I would intervene to ask whether Weber's main thesis about the relationship of authority and culture or education is unrestrictedly tenable. On the one hand we can generalize the allusion just mentioned and point out that the products of specialist knowledge, of science, often influence and therefore change social and authority relationships. On the other hand, I think, and more importantly since it throws light on Weber's approach and goes beyond our special topic, one could say that Weber, for reasons which cannot be discussed here, did not do sufficient justice to the irreducibility of certain classes of pheno-mena, which can become objects of research for the social scientist. I quote the following passage from Fräulein Jaerisch's paper:

> However close the connection of the calculability in principle of law, technology and the economic basis, it is their progressive rationalisation which leads by virtue of the autonomy of their immanent logic to their isolation from society's productive processes, lets them appear as ends in themselves, and turns them into the domain of specialists.

The question which arises here is whether law, technology, and science do only appear as ends in themselves, or are such partly by nature: more precisely whether they follow partly their own laws, and only partly the conditions of authority, and the same question is also valid for education. The answer is unequivocally positive, for example with reference to language, otherwise there would only be a sociology of language, and no philology, or history of literature or style. In a similarly positive answer Talcott Parsons differentiated systematically the analysis of the social system from that of the system of culture and personality, and phenomenology talks quite differently—here I am thinking particularly of Alfred Schutz's application of it to social science—of several worlds not mutually reducible (multiple realities).

I come next to the sociological–historical, for as soon as we reflect further on Weber's questionable thesis about the relationship between authority and culture, we recognize that one of his main problems was the relationship between society and culture in general. To be sure that was only partly the expression of what, if I remember rightly, Albert Salomon called his lifelong dialogue with the ghost of Karl Marx: I will only remind you of *The Protestant Ethic and the Spirit of Capitalism* as the most emphatic example of this. Partly, too, it was due to his disagreement with his times and society, as Fräulein Jaerisch has so strikingly shown in her analysis of his attitude to specialist knowledge and particularly to the bureaucratization of science. If, as she says, knowledge has become merchandise, Weber finally reduces the university, once the stronghold of culture, to the producer of what one could call specialist or quality goods; for in view of the value-freedom to which it is sworn, it has as little power as science in general to decide which goods shall be produced, and for what reasons: or less metaphorically, why anyone strives to know anything. This science spoke of ends, and not only of means: Weber had expressly forbidden this, both for science and for himself. And since he 'privatizes' or randomizes ends (he usually calls them values) both in science and in politics, it is not clear on the basis of what theoretical or systematic arguments the 'clarity and responsibility', the aim of scientific education, is a virtue, i.e. more than a matter of Weber's private taste. His influence most probably contributes to the fact that even in university education in the social sciences the 'how', the methodology, is so strongly emphasized and the 'what' and the 'why' so little, if at all: and to the fact that it is a private idiosyncratic affair of the individual scholar or student, if he does not want his knowledge to become anybody's and everybody's tool. Here lies one of the approaches to the problem of the contradiction between certain of Weber's writings on methodology in the social sciences on the one hand, and his essential works on the other, which, as particularly Leo Strauss has tried to show, he could not have written if he had followed his own instructions. And this conflict between a spontaneous approach to historic material—and to an incomparable amount of historic material!—and a methodological asceticism, which would have made this approach impossible, is first of all simply overpowering and heartbreaking. Here I shall refer to the third approach to Weber, the existential or practical. This conflict in so enormously great a mind is only a variant of several others, like our own and those of our times. What is our attitude to specialist knowledge? To bureaucratization, rationalization, science, politics, society, the individual, culture? In his passionate search for an answer to these questions, Weber sometimes ended in a blind alley, and if we will only take him seriously and read him carefully, we shall be more able to distinguish clearly and plainly between blind alleys and clear paths. He can help us to accept ourselves and our blundering, and to do something about it, for it may be that we have nothing else. What we perhaps need most of all is a picture and critique of society as a basis for recognizing when knowledge becomes 'atrophied spirit', when the prophet becomes a charlatan, when the ethics of principle becomes fanaticism, and the ethics of responsibility opportunism. From Weber's pronouncements on these subjects we can hardly find an answer to these questions, but perhaps we can form a better understanding of the man, whose writings fail us here.

5. The Problem of 'Pariahs'

CHRISTIAN SIGRIST

Pariah-groups were by no means of mere peripheral interest to Max Weber. Apart from the many external sources he used he was himself connected, not only by name, but also by recent generations of his family, with a previously outlawed occupational group (his grandfather was a pedlar) and it is a striking fact that the subject of one of his first scientific studies was the Polish itinerant workers, and that many years later, when he had been using the pariah-concept scientifically, he used it emotively in a time of crisis: in 1919 Weber said in a lecture in Munich: 'We are all under foreign domination. Like the Jews, we have been turned into outcasts.'[1]

In my paper we shall be concerned with Weber's general pronouncements rather than with the descriptive analysis of the Jewish outsiders and Indian pariahs, dealt with in his essays on the sociology of religion. In one passage Weber defines a 'pariah' people as

a group which has become an individual inheriting community, without an autonomous political link, bound together on the one hand by (originally) magical, taboo and ritual bonds of commensality and connubial community vis-à-vis others, by political and socially negative privilege with extensive special economic treatment, on the other.[2]

He writes also of pariahs as

communities who have acquired specific vocational traditions of a craft or other nature, who practise a belief peculiar to their community, and now live in the Diaspora, in a very precarious situation strictly segregated from all intercourse with outsiders which is not unavoidable, but tolerated because they are economically indispensable, and often even privileged political groups: the Jews are the most sublime historical example.

The essay on Hinduism introduces a further criterion: ritual

[1] Marianne Weber, *Max Weber—ein Lebensbild* (Tübingen, 1926), p. 673.
[2] *Wirtschaft und Gesellschaft*, 1st half-volume (Tübingen, 1956), p. 300 (subsequently quoted as W.G.), and p. 536.

240

uncleanness.[1] At the same time the application of the word 'pariah' is confined to the setting of ritual limitations on a minority group. In the essay on ancient Judaism, Weber defines a pariah people as a minority group, segregated ritually, in form or fact, from surrounding society (R.S., III, p. 3).

The weakness of Weber's conceptualization seems to me to be that it is not confined to a few characteristics, but leaves the concept vague; thus according to the application he sometimes takes a characteristic as essential, at other times as dispensable. Such inconsistently utilised characteristics are vocational specialisation and ritual uncleanness. Weber saw no inconsistency in this, since the sum of characteristics applied to different cases produces the 'ideal type'. The flexibility of application of single characteristics corresponds to the incongruity Weber identified between concept and reality. It does however make possible a conventionalist strategy—in always pointing out the incomplete congruity in contrary cases, and the defective 'fulfilment' of the ideal type by reality. I support Hemel and Oppenheim's opposition to this ideal–typological methodology. They object particularly to the confusion of definition, description and hypothesis, and the lack of distinction between tautological propositions and statements of fact.

Ideal types . . . are usually introduced without even an attempt at specifying appropriate criteria of order, and they are not used for the kind of generalisation characteristic of ordering types: instead they are involved as a specific device for the explanation of social and historical phenomena. . . . In intent at least, ideal types represent not concepts properly speaking, but rather theories.[2]

It remains unclear whether statements about pariah groups are valid generally or only where all the characteristics are present. The tendency to look only for conforming cases, which are asymptomatic with regard to extreme values, and to neglect the contrary, is particularly problematic. In this sense Thurwald's otherwise invalid attacks on Weber's ideal types are justified.

The ideal–typological concept was followed by Mühlmann in his work *Chiliasmus und Nativismus*.[3] He refers to the 'socially

---

[1] *Gesammelte Aufsätze zur Religionssoziologie*, II (Tübingen, 1921), 12 (subsequently quoted as R.S.).

[2] Carl G. Hempel, 'Problems of Concept and Theory Formation in the Social Sciences', in *Science, Language and Human Rights* (Philadelphia, 1952), pp. 71 ff.

[3] Wilhelm E. Muhlmann, *Chiliasmus und Nativismus* (Berlin, 1961).

despised wandering craftsmen' who are assigned to the 'context of
the caste belt', extending roughly from Bengal in the East to the
Sudanese mandated territory in the West. He uses the term
'pariahs' technically for any despised underprivileged occupational
castes (not only the Hindus!); but he does not exclude minority
groups from the definition. As conceptual traits Mühlmann
instances: denial of marriage and commensality; ritual apartheid;
contempt on the part of the higher caste; diminished rights before
the law. In this case the difficulty arises of finding operational
definitions for ritual apartheid. It is possible that the refusal of
commensality might not be found in a whole series of cases which
Mühlmann would include: the criterion of diminished legal rights
and social underprivilege would also apply to class-based societies.

To meet these objections, I suggest a simpler definition, which
refers nonetheless to Weber's characteristics: I call 'pariah group'
a group living endogamously within a symbiotic society and having
a precarious situation before the law.

Ascriptive roles are a characteristic not explicitly contained in
the definition. While affinity is ascriptive by definition, the ascription of other roles such as occupational roles, remains still to be
investigated by forming hypotheses. It is part of the said confusion
in ideal-type thinking that hypotheses about determinants and
resultants are included in this ideal type. My definition contains
no hypothesis of origin and no hypothesis about the general
correlation of endogamy and a precarious legal situation. I do not
assert any general simultaneity of the two variables.

The usefulness of my definition is shown by the fact that it
makes the topic of our session 'Pariahs and Outcast Proletariat'
more precise. The developing countries which Mühlmann,
influenced by Toynbee, defined as 'outcast proletariat' do not in
general come under my heading of 'pariahs': in a number of
developing countries the colonial power set up no restrictions on
marriage: there is no longer any question of precarious legal
status. To use the words together is not to assert identity, but only
the presence of several associated phenomena: consciousness of
being pariahs, religiosity of pariahs, mythology of the absurd
world.

Karl Marx tried of course to demonstrate that the working class
is aware of being pariahs—it was not by chance that he minimized
the significance of legal guarantees, human and civil rights, which

he dismissed as abstract. The European proletariat however (despite a class-based system of justice) was neither deprived of rights nor endogamous.

According to these criteria of mine, the definition is based on the group-aspect, essential for the characteristic of endogamy. The definition excludes slaves for instance, except where they are organised as a public group (in distinction to domestic slave-groups: temple slaves, slaves of the community, e.g. in Athens: the North American Negro slaves are also identified as pariahs). The definition subsumes as pariahs both peoples and occupational castes.

To arrive at an operational definition, we have to decide to what proportion of marriages which defy the ban on endogamy (as distinct from sexual coupling) we shall continue to apply the concept. With reference to this characteristic, pariah-groups come at the lower end of the scale of social systems, stratified according to the degree of hypergamy or hypogamy in each particular case (castes, estates, classes). Weber's use of the term 'precarious legal situation' ('in a legally precarious situation' W.G., p. 536) is more precise than Mühlmann's 'diminished legal position': it marks off pariah-castes clearly from 'lower' classes. The reference is not in general to the absence of individual rights, nor to an all-round diminution of rights, but to the gradual removal of legal protection until it is completely abolished. Thus for example the Jews in Germany in the Middle Ages enjoyed special royal or episcopally granted rights, which were not granted to non-Jewish citizens or only indirectly through the Jews. But the king's protection was only granted in an opportunist way, and could be revoked at any time. Jews came under laws relating to aliens, not under the protection of the common law, which was, however, valid for the lower class of under-privileged citizens. As an indicator of the precarious legal situation we can use the inability to bear witness in court of law (and particularly to swear oaths).

It is now our task to formulate and make examinable the hypotheses entailed in the ideal type, about correlations with the two pariah characteristics. First I should like to point out a connection between 'connubium' and 'precarious legal rights'. The denial of 'connubium' means the lack of a very important subjective right. If there are no relations of affinity between majority and minority groups, the minority fails to acquire potential protectors. If a fraction of the majority wants to outlaw a minority, one of the most significant measures is the forbidding of mixed marriages—the postulate of purity of blood is not only a value *per se*, but it is also instrumental. Here is a significant difference between serfs and pariahs. Among the Mandari, a race in the south Sudan, serfs had in principle no rights. But since marriage was banned only with regard to the chief's nearest relatives, but not his whole lineage, the land-owners soon had a circle of relatives who were interested in their legal rights, even against any encroachment on the part of the chief. As a consequence of mixed marriages, the status of serfdom changed after several generations to settler-status with equal privileges. An extreme form of outlawry is the refusal of the dominant group to recognize any pairing among outcasts as legitimate marriages.

In the case of agamy between majority and minority groups only the norms of the pariah-group are internalized in the process of socialization; there is less chance of assimilation.

I will now turn to vocational specialization in pariah-groups and to a criticism of the trend previously apostrophized—the cultural–historical school. I refer in my following remarks to Danckert's book *Unehrliche Leute—die verfemten Berufe* (Berne and Munich, 1963).

Danckert's fundamental thesis is that in Europe in the Middle Ages certain occupations, such as hangman, knacker, bath-attendant, weaver, miller, were outlawed because of the church's oppression of so-called 'primitive' cults. Danckert seeks to explain the selection of certain occupational groups by reference to Bachofen's theories: those occupations were outlawed that were specially closely related to chthonic–telluric elements and so provided cult-functions. Danckert extends his exposition by following Bachofen's equation of earth and water. One has to ask, however, which trades are *not* connected in some way with earth and water. Danckert himself concedes that smiths in medieval Europe formed a contrary case (p. 172). He does not think of the most obvious objection, i.e. that if the hypothesis is valid, all farmers would have been the first to count as 'unworthy'—and yet Danckert says that the 'violent deflowering and seeding of Mother Earth' inseparable from agriculture, 'is a crime' (p. 192).

In any case Danckert proceeds from an unfounded hypothesis, the sacred unanimity of the Germanic cults before Christianization. One would first have to investigate whether the same ambivalent attitude obtains against experts in Germanic ritual which I have proved in the case of experts in segmented societies.

Danckert's argument about the non-privileged status of messengers etc. in medieval times (office servants, municipal messengers) seems to me completely unsound. He does not succeed in proving that this was due to the executioner's being outlawed. I would oppose this by the hypothesis that in the towns the use of compulsion was concentrated against the lower-ranking members of local administrative staff.

The outlawing of occupations in the Middle Ages can be explained as the result of the increasing pressure of stratification, the increase in socio-economic taxes in the medieval town. Danckert's idea that the outlawing of occupations goes back to the church's ban on heathen rites cannot explain why the patricians of the town were among those most concerned that this should be done.

From Danckert's explanations it would appear that the legalizing of the outlawed occupations was enforced against the opposition of the guilds by the central power, although weak and not committed in this instance by economic interests.

The 'intellectual–historical' argument as found, e.g. in Danckert, overlooks the fact that mythology and magic can give us only feeble explanations of social facts: in general they only lead us in vicious circles. These writers obviously do not know that transcendant complexes are based to a great extent on sociomorphic projections, in Ernst Topitsch's sense of the word.

I will now deal with the question of the ritual uncleanness of pariahs, without implying that it obtains for all pariah groupings. On the contrary, my formulation is the statistical hypothesis that pariah groups in the majority of cases are considered as virtually dangerous and unclean.

Mühlmann and Haberland have drawn attention to the fact that pariahs not only have to observe ritual taboos, to which others are not subject, but also enjoy ritual privileges. In many cases the pariah and the ruler have this particular ritual position in common. Mühlmann and Jettmar had already pointed out that ritual separation is an attribute of the role of the alien who also enjoys other special political opportunities.

As an example of the partial identity of ruler and outcast I would instance the myth of incest: the pariah-group living on the

Arabian peninsula of Sleb are considered in the eyes of the Arabs as a race begun by the incest of an Arab with his mother. The reproach of incest justifies the denial of 'connubium'. For the ruler incest is recorded not only in mythology but also in practice (Buganda, Bolia). This perverted behaviour characterizes both ruler and pariah and marks them off from the common freedmen. The evaluation of the behaviour is the same in both cases, but in one the crime is used to justify a high position, in the other to justify oppression.

In qualification of this I must warn against identifying metaphors with the social reality: the identical metaphor for pariah and ruler, like the identical ritual, can of course serve as an indicator of an identity of attitudes towards ruler and pariah. The common freedman's attitude to both is ambivalent. Both have precarious roles: ambivalent attitudes in both cases can go as far as physical annihilation, whether by ritual assassination of a king, or by pogrom.

In my essay on segmentary societies I have already drawn attention to the precarious position of ritual experts. The example mentioned therein of the Gisu, who in the case of drought rob and beat up the rainmaker, can be supplemented by observations we owe to S. R. Nadel.[1]

Among the ethnically homogeneous Tira who live in the Nuba mountains (Sudan) specific cosmological–ritual functions are ascribed to individual lineages. Among these, two are in a special situation. One of these lineages is worried about storms and insanity. The fear of going mad through touching the food of this group leads to the banning of commensality on the part of other groups. They also keep as far away as possible when working in the fields. The ritually more important rain-lineage is found as a closed colony in a marginal situation—a consequence of the way other lineages avoid them especially in the critical period of transition to the rainy season. If the rain does not come, bitter resentment is shown against every member of the rain-lineage. A victim is beaten until his blood runs into the ground—and this breaks the spell. If the beating ends in death, the killer is not subject to the usual ritual of atonement. The members of the isolated group are ritually 'as free as the birds'.

[1] S. F. Nadel, 'Caste and Government in Primitive Society', in *J. Anthrop. Soc.* (Bombay, 1954).

The marginal groups of the Tira represent only a transition to the pariah-groups of my definition. These are not endogamous, even if the opportunities of affinity for the individuals of this lineage are less favourable than for others. We see by this example that the two characteristics of the pariah-condition can appear in isolation.

The feelings of resentment, which at the ruler-less stage are directed against the ritual experts, the powerful leader, those with great possessions, and other prominent persons, are directed against the ruler and usually limit or abolish the permanent separateness of an individual. The close association, to which Haberland refers, between king and pariah in Africa is not explained by reference to those who exercise control. Instead of Haberland's mythological interpretation I suggest a sociological hypothesis: the association is a mechanism for deflecting the anti-ruler feelings of the common freedmen on to the pariahs, which results in the immunity of the ruler.

I should like to clarify this thesis by means of an example already mentioned: the Mandari. On the one hand we find here the identification of the chief with one of his confidants who belongs to the slave-class: both went through the same official initiation with anointing and change of name. During the period of office of the Mar the slave appeared as his representative, and had to carry out the chief's unpopular wishes, i.e. his commands, particularly organizing the enforcement of the law. The chief's 'shadow' thus turned against himself as intermediary those hostile feelings aroused by actions which offended the norms of equality in a society only weakly centralized. But we also know from the same ethnic group that complaints of witchcraft and theft—two 'crimes' paradoxically publicly prosecuted because of their secrecy—were made principally against slaves. Suspicion of witchcraft is often assumed as a motive for secession from the group of origin. (We know from other ethnic systems that the fear of witches can lead to permanent migration and joining a protective group, e.g. the Bwamba.) The Mandari, who according to our definition only represent a transition to a social–symbiotic link with pariah-groups illustrate the hypothesis that groups which are marginal in origin become the targets of psychomorphic projections to a greater degree than long-established groups, and at the same time are identified with the exercise of public influence. In this connection I form the tentative hypothesis that the more intensive and frequent the magical projections, the stronger the tendencies to endogamy in the marginal group. Now we know from a majority of cases that witchcraft is held to be an inherited crime. Further, that witchcraft and the charge of witchcraft is often directed against the wife or husband (the spouse or other relative is 'killed' as a 'substitute' for the one who took part in the witchcraft). Thus the groups who are not qualified in magic are not very ready to contract marriages with lineages who inherit such burdens—remember the Tira!

A modern example of the 'shifting' of anti-ruler projection on to a pariah minority is anti-Semitism in industrialized societies. For frustrated classes of people it acts as a safety-valve, carrying out a levelling action without challenging the class-system and its requisite social stability.

Prior to anti-Semitism there was close co-operation between public control (central power) and the outsider group. Hannah Arendt drew attention to the close interweaving of absolutist central power and Jewish capital as a prerequisite for identifying the Jews with negatively evaluated aspects of political life.

Peter Heintz thinks we cannot exclude the possibility that

middle-class culture in America has found in its prejudices against the Negroes a form of expression for their dislike of the lower classes and their culture, an attitude which, under the sign of the American democratic creed, they dare not express directly against the white lower classes: if this hypothesis turns out to be correct, anti-Negro prejudice, functionally considered, will appear as a certain relaxing of the relationships between the middle and upper classes on the one hand and the lower classes on the other.[1]

Vertically the shift is possible in both directions.

I have already mentioned that rulers and outsiders are often of alien stock. Comparative ethnological research, and social–psychological investigations carried out independently have led to the conclusion that aliens have a greater chance of carrying out institutional changes and of appropriating special economic and political opportunities (Simmel, Lowie, Hofstätter, Sigrist). According to Hofstätter 'the prerequisite for the functioning of

---

[1] Peter Heintz, *Soziale Vorurteile* (Cologne, 1957), p. 189.

these two mechanisms (projection on to, and identification with, the leader) is heightened level of fear on the part of the population.'[1] In leaderless societies it is primarily aliens who succeed in crossing the barrier of equality: their chance of doing so rises in proportion to external pressure.

Even if Hofstätter establishes the identity according to origin between élites and under-privileged minorities ('disadvantaged minorities are basically frustrated élites, i.e. the persons belonging to them would like to have the chance of being "admired" '),[2] it still remains unclear under what conditions aliens or alien groups come into high or low special positions. The following statement by Hofstätter cannot explain a group's loss of esteem: 'the protection of a separate group utilises the over-emphasis on its alien nature; it prevents the possibility of identification and robs those belonging to this group of the chance of becoming an élite.[3] Hofstätter has actually set up another hypothesis, formulated rather more strongly: "It seems as though positive separation cannot be stabilised without negative recognition".'[4]

To sum up, I will formulate the following statistical hypotheses about the rise of 'pariah-groups':

1 Pariah-groups can arise from the social-symbiosis (Park) of technically and or politically stronger groups with ethnically different minorities.
2 Increasing pressure from above increases the chance of the emergence of pariah-groups.
3 On the contrary the presence of a pariah-group makes the increase of pressure by the rulers (or by a particular group) more probable without lessening the belief in legality.
4 The confirmation of hypotheses 2 and 3 confirms the hypothesis I developed in 1962 that in leaderless societies orientation to norms of equality hinders the rise of a central power.

If the expression social pathology is at all appropriate, it is so particularly in regard to a sociology of the condition of pariahs. So far I have offered you the analytical aspects of this pathology. The demand for value-freedom in scientific statements does not

[1] Peter R. Hofstätter, 'Eliten und Minoritäten', in *Kölner Zeitschrift für Soziologie und Sozialpsychologie*, Year 14 (1962), p. 61.
[2] Op. cit., p. 60.
[3] Op. cit., p. 84.   [4] Op. cit., p. 59.

R

prevent my system of hypotheses from being transformed into 'technological' proposals for social action. I now ask what one can do, and what one must not do, to stop the formation of new outsider groups.

1. If hypotheses 2 and 3 are correct, a lessening of pressure by rulers and upper classes, which may be by welfare-state policies, will lessen the chance of outsider groups being formed. The lack of an established system of social security favours the rise and perpetuation of pariah groups (U.S.A.).

2. A halt to the attempts of governments in the twentieth century to force opposing states into a pariah-situation as regards human rights can raise the level of tolerance in internal politics. Applied to the Federal Republic this means that to maintain the Hallstein doctrine is to raise the chance of forming new outsider-groups within the Federal Republic. The objection that projection against an extra-territorial group must lessen hostility to the upper strata and therefore the shift away from them does not contradict this hypothesis. The black–white dichotomy is also generalized in the working out of conflicts in domestic politics. The intervention of the 'entente' powers against the Soviet Union and the consequent boycott favoured Stalin's policy of 'socialism in one country', of self-isolation as far as an extensive banning of 'connubium'.

3. A system of justice which persecutes homosexuals stimulates and legitimizes movements which persecute minorities, people who are felt to be 'different'. The relative generosity which is generally exercised by our justice against such 'offenders' does not weaken this argument. The position of tolerated homosexuals is just as precarious as that of tolerated witches, Jews, etc.

A reform of the penal code would be a kind of 'therapy'.

4. In general a therapy can be influential in overcoming complexes of magic which stimulate discrimination and persecution against marginal groups. I am not thinking only of questionable German fairytales, witch-centred to a high degree, but also of the magical elements of Christian notions of blood and sacrifice and the related liturgical practices.

By clarifying such complexes analytically the social sciences make a contribution to the disenchantment of the world. While Max Weber commented sadly on this process, it would appear to us a more healthy matter.

Max Weber and the concept of pariah-communities

WILHELM E. MUHLMANN

'Pariah' as an ethnological and ethno-sociological type-concept was first evolved by Max Weber. It is necessary to follow up further its substantial repercussions. It lay in Weber's nature to master all material which was observable for the construction of ideal types in the sociology of culture and history, and there is no doubt that if he had lived longer, he would have mastered the ethnographical material too. He had already begun to do this both in the analyses contained in the second and third volumes of the *Religionssoziologie* and in his amazing writings about the rational and sociological bases of music. These are lines for further research. Weber starts in his sociology of Hinduism from the concept of the minority group (R.S. (1923); II, pp. 11 f.). Starting from the familiar, he calls the gipsies, who are of ancient Indian origin, the rudimentary prototype. Of course it is not necessary for a minority to be without a definite area of land. But far more often the 'minorities' appear

in the less developed forms of tribes who possess a few village settlements, but trade with others in the products of their labour, or hire themselves out periodically to other places to work in the harvest, or to do odd jobs, such as repairs, or who, traditionally, monopolise the trade between villages in certain products.

Weber then correctly points out the 'numerous menial or ritually unclean' services, which the local inhabitants would not undertake, but which are undertaken by the out-castes who are outside the legal unit of the ritually correct Hindu community, and who 'live on the waste land', as Weber aptly called it, since the type of settlement reflected the social order. The pariahs live 'outside the order', they belong to the slums or ghetto-like quarter. With such minorities there is of course no connubium, or commensality; ritual limitations impose on them an ethnic *apartheid*, and so endogamy.

Weber applies the term 'pariah people' as meaning in practice the same as minority, and instances the gipsies, and the Jews in the Middle Ages. It did not escape his notice that the term 'pariah' is philologically incorrect, since the Paraya of Hindu society were indeed a relatively low caste, but by no means outcasts (R.S. (1923), II, p. 12). Yet the expression 'pariah', through the writings of the Abbé Raynal, became technical in Europe, in the sense in which Weber applies it universally. It is an ethno-sociological type-concept, and if we also consult Weber's further writings on ancient Judaism, it becomes clear that he acquired the terms 'immigrant group' (Gastvolk) and 'pariah-group' by ethno-sociological analogy. In *Wirtschaft und Gesellschaft* he says: 'The Jews are the most superb historical example' (W.G., 1956, p. 536). Here we are looking into the workshop of Weber's ideal-typological method: the ideal-type concept of the minority and the pariah-group is formed with the aid of the most complete, 'superb' historical example, but only after the less distinctive Hindu variants have been recognized.

Weber's arguments about the pariah phenomenon are interesting. He starts from the concept of the *caste* or rather the *class*, understanding 'caste' as the form of the class taken to its extreme, a form which contains a 'ritual guarantee' of class isolation, as well as conventional and legal isolation: 'in such a way that any physical contact with a member of a caste labelled "lower" constitutes for members of a "higher" caste a ritual sullying to be atoned for religiously and to some extent individual castes develop quite separate cults and deities' (W.G. (1956), p. 536).

This begins the development of the pariah concept. Pariah-peoples are

social units who have acquired specific vocational traditions of a craft or other nature, who practise the faith of their ethnic community, and now live in political entities, strictly separated from all personal contact except that which is unavoidable, in a precarious legal position, but who thanks to their economic indispensability are tolerated and often even privileged. (ibid.)

He then points out the legality specific to castes and the hierarchical structure of the whole system. Even the most despised pariah-group has, and cultivates, its own feeling of dignity, connected with its specific activities. Weber was, of course aware that in this matter there is an important difference between the Hindu and the Israelite–Jewish pariah concept: there was no caste-system, no caste order in ancient Jewry. 'Separation through promotion to a "caste", according to class, and mere "ethnic" separation differ structurally in that the former changes the horizontally disconnected position of the latter into a vertical social structure, one above the other' (ibid., cf. R.S. (1923), III, p. 47). On the other hand Weber points out in his postscript to the third volume of R.S., p. 433 f.) that the Pharisaic ritualism of cleanliness finally led to a 'linking up in castes of the old believers in Jahwe'.

Weber's assertions are of decisive importance: they stand up to our increased historical and ethnographical knowledge, in fact the heuristic value of ideal types is shown in the perspective of our increased knowledge of the facts.[1] The arguments can be increased and refined and the points of view made subtler and differentiated. I have attempted this in several works.[2]

Among others, Weber's concept of 'ethnic' separation must be altered: he himself uses inverted commas, for it is dubious and becomes even more so when we analyse the problems it contains. Here I should like merely to remark that 'ethnic' does not describe a given state of affairs, which could provide a basis for the ideological separation of two groups: it emerges during the process of separation, of 'schismogenesis', and consequently separation cannot explain it.

There are pariah-groups who have grown into regular, relatively closed settled units, as for example the smiths of the Asur in Chota Nagpur (Central India) whom Walter Ruben has described.[3] The minority situation is thus a way by which quite new ethnic units, in servitude to their stronger neighbours, can be formed by a corresponding increase in population.

It can however happen that monopolist masters of certain arts and skills can be attracted to royal courts and then are not 'underprivileged' but even particularly esteemed: more exactly, their

---

[1] The obvious misunderstanding of Weber's 'ideal type' by certain American neo-positivists like E. Nagel and C. G. Hempel has already been noted by Alfred Schutz: 'Concept and Theory Formation in the Social Sciences', *Journal of Philosophy*, 51 (April, 1954), now also in Alfred Schutz, *Collected Papers I: The Problem of Social Reality* (The Hague, 1962), pp. 48 ff. and II *Studies in Social Theory* (The Hague, 1964), passim; on the 'ideal type', cf. my article 'Geschichts- und Kultursoziologie', *Hwb. d. Sozialwiss*, IV (1964), 408–25, especially pp. 411 ff.

[2] W. E. Muhlmann and collaborators, *Chiliasmus und Nativismus* (Berlin, 1961; 2nd ed. 1964); other works now collected in *Rassen, Ethuien, Kulturen* (Neuwied, 1964), Section: *Der revolutionäre Umbruch*. Also on the phenomenon of immigrant groups ('Gastvölker') ibid., pp. 194 ff.

[3] W. Ruben, 'Dämonen und Eisenschmiede in Indien', suppl. 37, *Int. Arch. Ethnogr.* (Lieden, 1939).

Summaries of Group Discussions

art is prized and their competence in demand, but they themselves are kept at a distance, they remain alien: for the very aura of magic and mystery which clings to a stranger's ability, which is not understood, added to the ritual business of secrecy, keeps alive a mistrust of these 'royal craftsmen', and they are never completely trusted. Such Eastern 'royal craftsmen' in olden times were gold-, silver- and copper-smiths, architects, doctors and soothsayers. If highly cultured groups migrate, they often take their 'royal crafts-men' and families with them: this is probably how work in iron, and other arts, came to different parts of Africa: the ambiguous position of the smith in many African tribes must go back in history to the ambivalent attitude to the 'royal craftsmen'. Another point is that the bellows, an instrument characteristic of African smiths, originated in the Near East: thus relations within the 'caste-belt' can be demonstrated historically through this charac-teristic.

In the Sudan the smiths, and probably other castes too, are still recognized as 'royal craftsmen' in the courts. There are also many regular, hierarchically distinct, endogamous occupational castes, e.g. in the Ful, weavers and woodcarvers, silversmiths and leather-workers, ironsmiths and potters, boatmen and fishermen, bards and minstrels. In the Mande the smiths who are particularly privileged are also woodcarvers, doctors, magicians and sooth-sayers. Below them in rank are the tanners and leatherworkers, then come the bards, and ordinary minstrels, the menders of calabashes, the boatbuilder and slaves. The ethnic and racial alien nature of the smiths is specially clear among the 'white African' Tuareg in the Sahara, where the smith's art is practised by negroid migrant workers.

Weber had seen the role of the 'royal craftsmen' quite correctly, but he does not seem to have known that there are also pariah-groups among the Bedouin Arabs.

With regard to the contempt for pariah-castes one must point out the particular ambivalence which causes the products of their art to be highly prized while the mode of their origin, ritually incorrect, is despised. In this connection we must remember that the ruling castes in the East and in North Africa are partly intellectuals, like the Brahmins, partly cattle-raisers who despise physical work (Bedouin, Tuareg), that classical antiquity revered an 'anti-craftsman' attitude (Jakob Burckhardt), which for example esteemed the products of the plastic arts, but despised their creators because they stood by the fireside to work—and finally that our higher esteem of physical labour is quite recent in social history, and even today counterbalanced by opposite trends, like the familiar 'white collar' attitude: it is 'not nice' to soil one's hands. There are still quite lively traces of the ritualistic fear of contact (taboo) connected with certain tasks, especially in the nature of essential services. From this point of view rebellion from below, which is associated with the pariah-classes, and generally with a reversal of the esteem of physical labour, is particularly important in the history of culture. We were simply concerned in this excursus to throw light on the ethnographical basis for this process of reversal of values.

One last problem, but not the least important, concerns the so-called 'pariah-ethics', with which Weber has also already dealt (R.S. (1923), III, pp. 392 f. and *passim*). Without doubt the term 'pariah' has pejorative connotations: one hears in it the scorn of the rest of the world. It is self-evident that in the case of Weber's value-free observation everything that is said about the fundamental pacifism of the pariahs, their code of waiting in patience, non-resistance, etc. (Resist not evil with evil) is to be understood objectively. This means the sociologist has to hear the rest of the world's scorn of the pariah in the term, but must not share it. Besides this, the problem of evaluation here is complicated, since there is not only the self-justification of pariahs as an élite (with a special awareness of being chosen and having a mission), but also a diffusion, a universalizing of the pariah-ethos, and to a certain extent a cultural upgrading of this code of ethics from 'below' to 'above'. I have analysed these processes in detail in my book. Even here Weber acutely anticipated some decisive points. He writes:

The feeling of dignity of the positively-privileged classes is naturally relative to their integral 'being', their 'beauty and bravery' (kalokagathia). Their kingdom is 'of this world' and lives for the present, and on past greatness. The feeling of dignity of the negatively-privileged classes can naturally only relate to a future, either in this world or the next; it is to be nourished by the belief in a providential 'mission', in a specific honour before God as 'a chosen people', in the idea that 'the last shall be first.' (W.G. (1956), p. 536).

The putting into practice of the myths and ideologies of the upside-down world in the social sphere is explained by this basic relationship. But the pariah-code can also rise *culturally*, without the 'last' *socially* taking the place of the 'first', i.e. without the pariahs necessarily becoming the governing élite. This is the sociologically real background to Nietzsche's criticism of Christianity, which at heart is nothing other than a criticism of pariah values. Nietzsche does not use the expression 'pariah', but, prefers, not without reason, an Indian term related to it in meaning, 'Tschandala morality'. (For the Candals are nothing more than a pariah caste—in the technical sense.) When Nietzsche says: 'The Tschandala turn values upside-down', he himself is aiming at a restoration of aristocratic values.

Weber recognized the *revolutionary* character of pariah ethics in all its programmatic 'pacifism'. What he did not experience was the most significant manifestation of this ethical code in the history of the world: the Indian revolution of 'passive resistance' by Mahatma Gandhi.[1]

And when one realizes that Gandhi in forming the style of his revolutionary programme consciously associated Indian traditions with the teachings of the Sermon on the Mount—both stimulated by 'pariah' motives—the problem of the pariah code of ethics becomes excitingly up to date: the Indian element is not only the symbol of something alien, it is actually historically connected with those motives of the late Judaic prophets, from whom spring not only English Puritanism, which influenced Gandhi, but also in the last resort the intellectual life of the whole of Europe.

[1] W. E. Muhlmann, *Mahatma Gandhi—Der Mann, sein Werk und seine Wirkung. Eine Untersuchung zur Religionssoziologie und politischen Ethik* (Tübingen, 1950), esp. pp. 246 ff.